MW00786104

ALEXANDER McQUEEN

First published by V&A Publishing to accompany the
exhibition *Alexander McQueen: Savage Beauty* in 2015 at
the Victoria and Albert Museum, South Kensington
London SW7 2RL

With thanks to

ALEXANDER MℚUEEN

Every effort has been made to seek permission to
reproduce those images whose copyright does not reside
with the V&A, and we are grateful to the individuals and
institutions who have assisted in this task. Any omissions
are entirely unintentional, and the details should be
addressed to V&A Publishing.

Designer: Charlie Smith Design
Copy editor: Denny Hemming

Library of Congress Control Number: 2014958324

ISBN: 978-1-4197-1723-9

Printed and bound in Italy

10 9 8 7 6

Abrams books are available at special discounts when
purchased in quantity for premiums and promotions as
well as fundraising or educational use. Special editions
can also be created to specification. For details, contact
specialsales@abramsbooks.com or the address below.

ABRAMS The Art of Books
195 Broadway, New York, NY 10007
abramsbooks.com

p.6: 'Star' headpiece,
In Memory of Elizabeth How, Salem 1692,
Autumn/Winter 2007
Silver and Swarovski crystals
Shaun Leane for Alexander McQueen

p.9: 'Bird's Nest' headdress
The Widows of Culloden, Autumn/Winter 2006
Silver, Swarovski crystals and mallard's wings
Philip Treacy and Shaun Leane for Alexander McQueen

ALEXANDER McQUEEN

EDITED BY CLAIRE WILCOX

ABRAMS, NEW YORK

CONTENTS

JONATHAN AKEROYD

CEO, ALEXANDER MCQUEEN

When *Alexander McQueen: Savage Beauty* was first staged in 2011, at The Metropolitan Museum of Art in New York, its popularity took us all by surprise – it proved to be one of the most successful exhibitions in the museum's history. I am now so very proud that we have been able to help the V&A bring *Savage Beauty* to London. It really does feel like a homecoming, and I know that Lee McQueen – a true Londoner – would have loved the idea of having his work exhibited at this great museum, in the heart of the city that constantly inspired him.

As is often said, Lee was the real thing – a visionary, an artist, a man whose imagination was so inventive and original that he managed to capture the world's attention and create a lasting legacy. Under Lee's direction, the Alexander McQueen show was always the highlight of any fashion week, more a dramatic performance than a catwalk display.

We are very fortunate in having a comprehensive and largely complete archive of work that enables us to show original pieces by Lee. This is important because it is only through seeing the work that you can really understand his genius – the remarkable way he used the materials and tools available to him to create extraordinary garments, quite unlike anything that had been seen before.

Ultimately, it is the work that speaks of the unique talent of this ingenious designer. For those of us who were privileged enough to know him and experience his artistry at first hand, it is now a privilege to be able to share his brilliance and his legacy with a wider audience.

MARTIN
ROTH

DIRECTOR, VICTORIA AND ALBERT MUSEUM

———

Lee Alexander McQueen has left an indelible imprint on the fashion world as one of the most visionary designers of his generation. He pushed the boundaries of fashion with the garments he crafted and the theatrical catwalk shows that became synonymous with his name.

McQueen was born, raised and worked in London, and he saw the city as both his home and the place from which he drew inspiration. He forged a special relationship with the V&A, and from his days as a student at Central Saint Martins he regularly visited the Museum's rich textiles and fashion archives and galleries. Now his own astounding creations inspire those who follow in his footsteps. Claire Wilcox, editor of this publication, is a longstanding admirer and champion of McQueen's work. She invited him to stage two of the Museum's pioneering Fashion in Motion catwalk events in 1999 and 2001, and included his designs in the exhibition *Radical Fashion* (2001). His work has been on display in the V&A's Fashion Gallery ever since.

It gives me particular pleasure to thank our sponsors, without whom this exhibition would not have been possible. The V&A is delighted to work with Swarovski as the lead exhibition sponsor, a fitting partner given their long-standing collaboration with McQueen. The Museum is also appreciative of the support from American Express, who first began partnering with Alexander McQueen in 1997. We also gratefully acknowledge M·A·C Cosmetics and Samsung.

Many thousands of visitors were thrilled by the original staging of *Alexander McQueen: Savage Beauty* in 2011 at the Metropolitan Museum of Art, New York. The V&A is honoured to present Alexander McQueen's remarkable body of work afresh. The exhibition has come home to London thanks to the generosity and vision of many people, including Andrew Bolton, the exhibition's original curator, Thomas P. Campbell, Director of the Metropolitan Museum of Art, Jonathan Akeroyd, CEO of Alexander McQueen, Sarah Burton and her team, and Sam Gainsbury of Gainsbury and Whiting. Their vision and resolve has enabled the V&A to ensure that this exhibition pays worthy tribute to the inimitable Lee Alexander McQueen.

Opposite
Alexander McQueen, London
August 1999
Photographs by Anne Deniau

INTRODUCTION

—

IN SEARCH OF THE SUBLIME

ANDREW BOLTON

'Whereas the beautiful is limited,
the sublime is limitless'

IMMANUEL KANT, *CRITIQUE OF PURE REASON*, 1781

I was a curatorial assistant at the Victoria and Albert Museum in London when I saw my first Alexander McQueen runway presentation. It was the designer's thirteenth collection, and rallying against superstition he called it simply *No.13*. The collection was inspired by the Arts and Crafts Movement, and focused on the contrasting opposites of man and machine, craft and technology. I had been both an admirer and an advocate of McQueen's work since his first catwalk show, *Nihilism* (Spring/Summer 1994), when he sent a latex dress covered with locusts down the runway, a comment on the cyclical occurrence of famine in Africa.

People had come to expect such provocations from McQueen, even to the point of conjuring up images from their own imagination. During the presentation of his *Highland Rape* collection (Autumn/Winter 1995) in which the designer sent staggering, blood-spattered models down the runway, one journalist reported that the skirts had tampons dangling from the crotch. They were, in fact, metal watch fobs, and were actually more subversive than tampons. The chain was threaded in between the legs, from the bottom to the crotch. Isabella Blow, the famous stylist who was a close friend and mentor of McQueen, described at length the personal satisfaction the chain provided her as she walked.

Nothing prepared me, however, for the raw, emotional intensity and sublime, transcendent beauty of McQueen's *No.13* collection. The show was held in the Gatliff Warehouse in south-west London, now luxury apartments. Back in the autumn of 1998, however, the warehouse (a former bus depot) was totally neglected and rundown – almost dystopian. The set or stage that McQueen had fabricated with his production designers was equally as bleak and uninviting. It consisted of a simple rectangular platform made from rough, untreated planks of wood. Above it was suspended a light box with harsh fluorescent lighting that mirrored the dimensions of the platform.

As the show started, the light box was dimmed and out walked a model in a black frock coat and what looked like a pair of brown leather boots. When she reached the end of the runway, the light box brightened, and you recognized that the model was the Paralympic champion Aimee Mullins. What looked like leather boots were in fact a pair of hand-carved wooden prosthetic legs made from solid ash. Aimee was born without shinbones and had her legs amputated below the knee at the age of one. The legs had been designed by McQueen, and were inspired by the seventeenth-century woodcarver Grinling Gibbons (pl.197).

Leading up to the show, McQueen had been a guest editor of the magazine *Dazed & Confused* in which he art directed a shoot that featured Aimee and seven other men and women with physical disabilities (pp.280–3). Over time, I came to admire and deeply respect McQueen's depiction of beauty, which forced us to reflect upon both the prejudices and the limitations of our aesthetic judgments. Railing against normative conventions of beauty, McQueen saw the body as a site where normalcy was questioned and where marginality was embraced and celebrated.

The poetic beauty of Aimee's prosthetic limbs was echoed in many other pieces in the collection, most notably in a skirt and bodice made out of perforated plywood. The bodice fanned out at the back to form a pair of wings. When the light shone through the perforations, the wings looked like stained glass. On the runway, the bodice was worn by the statuesque model Erin O'Connor, and as she walked she looked like a gothic angel (pl.205). Because of their fragility, neither the plywood skirt nor the winged bodice survived. We had them re-made, however, for the exhibition by the maker of the originals, Simon Kenny, in the same materials and with the same design specifications. They are now housed in the permanent collection of The Costume Institute at The Metropolitan Museum of Art. Before entering the collection, the bodice was worn by the singer Björk at McQueen's Memorial Service in St Paul's Cathedral in London. She wore them on the altar as she sang 'Gloomy Sunday' (also known as the 'Hungarian Suicide Song'), a deeply melancholic song about lost love made famous by Billie Holiday.

While the start of the *No. 13* show was poignant and profound, the finale quite literally took your breath away. Onto the stage walked the model Shalom Harlow in a white dress that was belted under the arms. She stopped halfway down the runway, and took her position on a turntable. As she began to slowly rotate like a music-box doll, two industrial paint sprayers suddenly came to life on the runway and began spraying her dress with black and acid yellow paint (pl.62). At the time, critics interpreted the performance as a reference to *The Dying Swan*, but it was actually a re-enactment of an installation

Previous spread
02. Installation shot, Entrance,
Alexander McQueen: Savage Beauty
The Metropolitan Museum of Art,
New York, 2011

Opposite
03. Installation shot, Romantic Gothic,
Alexander McQueen: Savage Beauty
The Metropolitan Museum of Art,
New York, 2011

Right above
04. Installation shot, Cabinet of
Curiosities, *Alexander McQueen:
Savage Beauty*
The Metropolitan Museum of Art,
New York, 2011

Right below
05. Installation shot, The Romantic Mind,
Alexander McQueen: Savage Beauty
The Metropolitan Museum of Art,
New York, 2011

by the artist Rebecca Horn of two shotguns firing blood-red paint at each other (pl.157).

The image was astonishing – at once violent and beautiful, disturbing, and compelling. Later, I learned that this was the only runway presentation that made McQueen cry. Like many other members of the audience, I left the show in a state of shock. And it was a feeling that I would experience repeatedly after attending subsequent presentations. The runway was where McQueen's fantasies and creative impulses were given free reign. He used the runway to express the purity of his creative vision, imbuing his collections with strong conceptual narratives. Highly theatrical, his shows often suggested avant-garde installation and performance art. In a recent article, the artist Marina Abramović describes performance art as having 'life energy' and painting and sculpture as having 'still energy'. With McQueen's presentations, you were dealing with life energy. Like performance art, the power of his shows relied on the audience's emotional engagement. As a designer, he was unique in his ability to make his audience react emotionally to his presentations. McQueen himself once remarked, 'I don't want to do a cocktail party, I'd rather people left my shows and vomited.'[1]

When I began working on the exhibition, the only thing I was certain of was that I wanted visitors to experience the same powerful, visceral emotions that I experienced during my first McQueen runway presentation. It was never my intention to present a comprehensive retrospective on McQueen. Practically speaking, I did not have the time – I had exactly ten months to pull the exhibition together. So I approached the exhibition more as an essay or short story. I always saw the show as the first of many shows on McQueen.

Initially, there were some concerns about staging an exhibition on McQueen so soon after his suicide. Tom Campbell, the Director of The Metropolitan Museum of Art, thought the idea was both a little ghoulish and a little premature, feelings shared by many others. But I felt strongly in the immediacy of the exhibition. At the time of McQueen's death, no one knew what would become of his archive in London – whether his designs would be sold off or dispersed, as they had at Givenchy when the designer stepped down as creative director of the house in 2000. Similarly, no one knew what would become of his atelier. Throughout his career, McQueen surrounded himself with a loyal and close-knit team of co-workers and collaborators, and I felt strongly that any exhibition on the designer would benefit from their direct participation. I also felt that the rawness and freshness of their memories would enhance the integrity and authenticity of the exhibition. Over time, the work of every artist is subject to revisionism, but I wanted to avoid this as much as possible by tapping into recent memories of the designer.

In all my years as a curator at the Victoria and Albert Museum and The Metropolitan Museum of Art, I had never met any of McQueen's colleagues. I had only met McQueen a few times, and always in a professional capacity. The last time was when I was working on the exhibition *AngloMania: Tradition and Transgression in British Fashion*, which was staged in The Metropolitan Museum's English Period Rooms in 2005. The show included several examples of McQueen's work, and I was tasked with taking the designer through the exhibition. From the outset, I remember him being distracted by one of his dresses displayed towards the end of the exhibition – about 60 feet away from where we were standing. During the tour, McQueen kept throwing furtive glances at the dress. When we arrived at it finally, he quickly reached out his hand to smooth down a tiny knife pleat that had been displaced during installation. I was so impressed by the precision of his eye.

During his life, McQueen's colleagues had been deeply protective over him, and after his death their loyalty intensified. Very few of them gave interviews. The one person who did was one of McQueen's former boyfriends. With the money he received for the interview, he went on a vacation to South America. While he was there, he was bitten by a spider and died. McQueen's friends came to view it as cautionary tale. At the outset of the exhibition, McQueen's associates were, understandably, rather guarded (a feeling that derived, at least in part, from the fact that many people – notably journalists – wanted to 'own' the designer's life, and indeed, his death). To many of them, I was a stranger, an outsider. Surprisingly, it was his closest and longest-serving associates who were the most open, supportive and cooperative. I think the exhibition became a conduit through which they could not only grieve or mourn their friend but also celebrate and commemorate him. In a way, the show served as their eulogy.

In the planning and preparation of the exhibition, I got to know three of McQueen's most intimate and most respected colleagues – Sarah Burton, Sam Gainsbury and Trino Verkade. I came to view them as the 'Holy Trinity'. Indeed, the success of the exhibition is due largely to these impressive, confident and larger-than-life women. Through them, I got to understand McQueen. Each woman taught me different aspects about the designer. Sarah Burton, who was appointed creative director of the atelier after the designer's death, had worked directly with McQueen for fourteen years, 10 of them as head designer of his womenswear collections. Through Sarah, I learnt about McQueen's design process and working methods. We spoke at length about his inspirations, which were wide-ranging and far-reaching. For example, she told me that McQueen based part of one collection on a green sweater worn by the character Joey in the TV sitcom *Friends*. It was through my conversations with Sarah that I developed the themes of the exhibition, which were all based on McQueen's primary and recurrent inspirations.

Sam Gainsbury, who served as the creative director of the exhibition, had been the show producer on most of McQueen's runway presentations since *The Hunger* (Spring/Summer 1996). She taught me how critical the runway was to the designer's creative process. In fact, she told me that McQueen could never begin a collection until he had developed an idea or concept for his show. Most designers develop their fashions before their presentations, but McQueen was the opposite. For him, the runway was not only critical to his creative process, it was the catalyst.

Trino Verkade had been McQueen's first employee. She taught me the most about McQueen the man as opposed to McQueen the designer. Trino helped me understand his emotional intensity and complexity. Through her, I not only got to know McQueen but also to love him. It is a myth that curators treat the subjects of their exhibitions with cold-hearted objectivity. Curators cannot help but let their personal feelings and judgments creep into their exhibitions. Indeed, the exhibition was deeply and profoundly subjective, but I believe it was this subjectivity that contributed to its success. A more objective approach would certainly have generated very different reactions from the audience. In many ways, the exhibition was an unabashed and unapologetic love poem to McQueen.

It was through my conversations with Trino, Sam and Sarah, as well as Harold Koda, the Curator in Charge of The Costume Institute, that I decided to structure the exhibition around the concept of the Sublime, and McQueen's philosophical engagement with Romanticism. Before settling on this structure, however, I struggled with many false starts – from contextualizing McQueen's fashions within the world of contemporary art, to linking them with the theoretical arguments of the French anthropologist Claude Lévi-Strauss, to presenting them chronologically, which tends to be the traditional approach when presenting an exhibition devoted to the work of a single artist.

The main reason for deciding against a chronological approach was ideological. Like most designers, McQueen's creative brilliance and originality was inconsistent. In truth, he produced some rather mediocre collections, which a chronological approach would have emphasized. For me, McQueen's strength as a designer – beyond his technical virtuosity – lay in his conceptual provocations, which were most clearly revealed in the more magical, fantastical, and often non-wearable fashions that he created for the runway.

I decided to focus my attention on these more iconic pieces, which I felt best represented McQueen's originality and singularity. It proved to be a decisive factor in establishing the designer's reputation as an artist. Most fashion is not art, but there was a consensus of opinion among critics and visitors that McQueen's work was art, something the designer himself refuted. However, if you saw the totality of his creative output, which included beautifully tailored but wearable suits and dresses, I think people might have modified their assessment. One critic commented that The Metropolitan Museum of Art gave an imprimatur to McQueen's creativity. To an extent, this is true. From the point of view of artistic practice, there is something transformative about being in an art museum because your life's work is both treated and valued on a level that will allow it to endure through generations.

The works featured in the exhibition not only resonated with the audience on an artistic level, but also on an emotional level. McQueen had an almost shamanistic approach to materials. He favoured materials that had fetishistic qualities, such as hair, leather and feathers. One of the pieces that opened the exhibition was made entirely of razor-clam shells. The idea came to the designer when he was walking on a beach carpeted with

06. Installation shot, *Plato's Atlantis*,
Alexander McQueen: Savage Beauty
The Metropolitan Museum of Art,
New York, 2011

Above
07. Installation shot, Romantic Nationalism, *Alexander McQueen: Savage Beauty*
The Metropolitan Museum of Art, New York, 2011

Left
08. Installation shot, Romantic Naturalism, *Alexander McQueen: Savage Beauty*
The Metropolitan Museum of Art, New York, 2011

Overleaf
09. Dress, Autumn/Winter 2010
Silk organza printed with an image of the *Virgin of the Annunciation from the Portinari Altarpiece* by Hugo van der Goes, *c.*1475
Photograph by Sølve Sundsbø

razor-clam shells in Norfolk in England with his boyfriend – the same one who was killed by a spider. Such materials imbued McQueen's fashions with a strange affecting presence that evoked feelings of ambiguity and ambivalence.

One of my favourite pieces in the exhibition was a cuirass made of glass. To me, it seemed to capture the tragic, poetic beauty of McQueen's fashions. Usually, a cuirass is made of metal and is designed to protect the wearer. A cuirass made of glass, however, can easily shatter and puncture the body. There was a truth to McQueen's use of materials that seemed to reflect his own search for truth. No subject was off limits for the designer, no matter how personal or how painful. He once said, 'My shows aren't instead of a shrink, they're what come out of the sessions.'[2] Indeed, McQueen's shows were deeply and unapologetically autobiographical. One of the main reasons why I did not include any biographical information in the exhibition was that his life was laid bare in his work for all to see. It was this exposure of the self, this vulnerability that imbued his fashions with their dignity and humanity, and that instilled in them their potency and poignancy.

In her review of the exhibition in *The New Yorker*, Judith Thurman described McQueen's fashions as a form of confessional poetry. It was an astute observation, and one that was bolstered by the designer's own commentary on his collections, which was deeply connected to and reflective of his psychic interiority. Early on, I wanted McQueen to generate the personal narrative of the exhibition, which was distinctive yet complementary to the curatorial narrative. His 'voice', comprised of quotations culled from hundreds of interviews from his 17-year career, was present throughout the exhibition, carrying visitors on a journey that mirrored the designer's own interior journey. The experience of walking through the exhibition was like having a conversation with someone very present but not present at all.

In total, the exhibition attracted 661,509 visitors over three months. To date, it is the Museum's most popular fashion exhibition, and the Museum's eighth most popular exhibition – the most popular being *Treasures of Tutankhamun*, which drew over 1.3 million visitors. Critics often describe the exhibition as a 'blockbuster', a term I find misleading as it seems to imply some sort of Machiavellian intentionality on the part of the Museum. In truth, the show's success came as a complete surprise to everyone. You only need to look at how badly equipped we were to deal with the number of visitors as evidence of our lack of intent.

Scholars have written papers on the reasons for the show's success, naming factors such as the morbid appeal of McQueen's suicide. Undoubtedly, McQueen's death added to the pathos of the exhibition, as did the multi-sensory, immersive galleries designed by Sam Gainsbury and Joseph Bennett and sound curated by John Gosling, which channelled the drama and spirit of the designer's runway presentations. But I firmly believe that it was the sublime beauty and emotional intensity of McQueen's fashions that determined the success of the exhibition. Like his shows, his fashions elicited extreme reactions that were often destabilizing and transformative, exceeding our capacities for self-control and rational comprehension. Unlike any designer before

or after, McQueen validated powerful emotions as compelling and undeniable sources of aesthetic experience. For many visitors, McQueen conformed to our ideal of the tragic, tortured artistic genius. Indeed, he was a designer of unrivalled courage who seemed to find creative freedom through his torments. What you saw in his work was the man himself.

In life, McQueen was an enigma, and in death he became an icon. In part, the exhibition at The Metropolitan Museum of Art was instrumental in conferring this iconicity – not because of the institution and what it represents but because of what the visitors represented. People make icons, and over 660,000 people made McQueen an icon. Many stood in line for five hours to see the show. The Museum extended the exhibition for a week and made the unprecedented decision to keep the Museum open until midnight on the final weekend to accommodate the crowds. The show became a pilgrimage site for many visitors. Some created replicas of the fashions in the exhibition. One girl made a facsimile of the dress made out of razor-clam shells, using strips of toilet paper instead of razor clams. The queue took on a life of its own. One couple found love while waiting in line, while another, quite dramatically, broke up – the girlfriend left in tears while the boyfriend stayed to see the exhibition.

After the show closed, I asked Sarah, Sam and Trino if McQueen would have been happy with the exhibition. They all said the same thing – that he would have been thrilled to have his name on a huge banner outside the Museum, but furious that fewer people came to see his show than King Tut's.

I was a fully-fledged curator at The Metropolitan Museum when I saw my last Alexander McQueen runway show. It was called *The Widows of Culloden*, (Autumn/Winter 2006) and was one of the designer's most autobiographical collections. The finale was a Pepper's Ghost of Kate Moss, and it filled me with the same sublime feelings of awe and wonder as the finale to *No.13*. Of the collection, McQueen said poignantly, 'There's no way back for me now. I'm going to take you on journeys you've never dreamed were possible.'[3] It is heartbreaking to think that McQueen produced only seven more collections before his untimely death. But his comment proved prophetic, as we continue to be both inspired and astonished by his sweeping, unbridled imagination.

EDWARD SCISSORHANDS

CLAIRE WILCOX

*'Well, there are all kinds of scissors. And once
there was even a man who had scissors for hands'*

TIM BURTON, *EDWARD SCISSORHANDS*, 1990

Lee Alexander McQueen was born in London on 17 March 1969. Despite his untimely death in 2010, his life's work has much to celebrate. McQueen was a complex, creative and driven man; perhaps even a visionary. But whatever the contradictions inherent in his persona, what was indisputable was his extraordinary artistry in rendering fabric – and a diversity of other materials – in a completely original way. From the slashed and distressed fabrics of his early years, to the luxurious jacquards, delicate chiffons and fine Italian suiting of his later collections, fabric, scissors, chalk and thread were the agents of his trade.

Early in his career, McQueen found a way of investing his collections with emotion, through the subjects that he cared deeply about or was intrigued by. He created his clothes to illustrate these autobiographical narratives to the very end, and he wanted to be noticed. In typically visceral style, he said, 'my work is autobiographical, so anything I experience, I digest and then vomit back into society.'[1] After a series of brilliant shows, at the age of only 26, he became chief designer at Givenchy where he remained for nearly five years before his label became part of the Gucci Group in 2000 (now Kering). McQueen was named British Designer of the Year four times and was awarded a CBE for services to fashion in 2003, having become one of the most respected fashion designers in the world.

The early 1990s was a crucial time for British fashion. John Galliano set the bar for McQueen and his fellow students on the MA Fashion course at Central Saint Martins, while magazines such as *Visionaire* (founded 1991) and *Dazed & Confused* (founded 1992) reflected a new efflorescence in fashion and art, the 'Sensation' generation that McQueen identified with so strongly. The impact of the digital revolution created a world of new possibilities, led by photographers such as Nick Knight, who began to create hyper-real images that, like McQueen's work, questioned the boundaries and limits of fashion (pl.15).

Previous spread
10. Backstage, *The Girl Who Lived in the Tree*, Autumn/Winter 2008
Dress: silk tulle and feathers
Photograph by Anne Deniau

Above left
11. Dress, *Sarabande*,
Spring/Summer 2007
Silk with fresh flowers and silk flowers
Modelled by Tanya Dziahileva
Photograph by Pierre Verdy

Above right
12. Installation shot
Radical Fashion, Victoria and Albert Museum, 2001
Dress, *Voss*, Spring/Summer 2001
Silk with appliquéd embroidered roundels and ostrich feathers

Below right
13. Fashion in Motion
Victoria and Albert Museum, June 1999
Dress, *No.13*, Spring/Summer 1999
Hessian with silk embroidery

Opposite
14. Ensemble, Sarabande,
Spring/Summer 2007
Top and skirt: silk tulle and boning with silk flowers
Modelled by Raquel Zimmermann
Photograph by Chris Moore

McQueen's champion, Isabella Blow, described his work as 'sabotage and tradition – all the things that the '90s represented.'[2]

In 1999 the V&A established the live catwalk event, Fashion in Motion. The first designer to take part was Philip Treacy, followed by McQueen (pl.13). Even though he was by now working with Givenchy, he still exuded rawness and a genuine disregard for authority that, to the museum world, was somewhat alarming. But he could be gracious; installing a plywood skirt from *No.13* in the main entrance, he invoked the disapproval of a Museum volunteer who did not realise who he was (he never really looked like a fashion designer). He simply laughed it off and said she reminded him of his mother. Two years later he took part in another Fashion in Motion with Shaun Leane (pl.207). By then, McQueen had become renowned. The Museum was totally unprepared as 3,000 people gathered in the main entrance, a 'McQueen' effect felt to much greater extent with the extraordinary success of The Metropolitan Museum of Art's *Alexander McQueen: Savage Beauty* exhibition in New York in 2011, now restaged at the V&A, that this publication celebrates.[3]

McQueen already knew the V&A well. As a child, he and his siblings had been taken to the South Kensington museums on Sundays and as a designer he was a regular visitor to the fashion archives, saying 'The collections at the V&A never fail to intrigue and inspire me. The nation is privileged to have access to such a resource.'[4] During appointments he was knowledgeable, observant and impatient. He knew exactly what he was looking for and, once he had it, he would leave. Nick Knight recalled, 'Lee was very insightful ... I think he used to get frustrated by that. Because he could see things that other people couldn't see. And therefore he knew when he had got it or when he hadn't got it. So he'd keep on pushing when other people wanted to give up, or he'd want to stop because he knew he had it'.[5]

McQueen's interests ranged far and wide of fashion to embrace film, dance, art and, above all, nature, as the various chapters in this book demonstrate. He loved the V&A's William Morris room, for example, and had a profound respect for the Arts and Crafts Movement, identifying with its idealism, and the way it placed value on the joy of craftsmanship and the natural beauty of materials. He was intrigued by the Victorian eccentricities of the Museum's interiors, in particular the Cast Courts, saying, 'It's the sort of place I'd like to be shut in overnight'.[6] Amie Witton-Wallace, McQueen's global communications director

between 1995 and 2007, recalled: 'He loved the V&A. Lee only worked with people or places that he believed in and loved.'[7]

McQueen was one of eleven avant-garde designers, including Comme des Garçons (whom he greatly respected), represented in the V&A exhibition *Radical Fashion* in 2001 (pl.12).[8] The demands were great; the Museum found itself commissioning a vast glass box, in emulation of the scenography of his dramatic *Voss* collection of the same year. Committing to work with McQueen meant forgoing compromise, but the impact was electric. A soundscape and accompanying film reflected a new movement in fashion that did not just offer clothes to adorn the body, but asserted that this was an entirely new world for all the senses.

McQueen's singular vision was achievable because of his ability to recognize talent in others, whether jeweller, milliner, fabricator or film-maker. He invariably worked with a small, closely knit team of loyal people who understood and supported him. His stylist Katy England recalled of the early days, 'We were never paid, it was really personal. He was brave and courageous, and said, "we can do whatever we want".'[9] McQueen's charismatic leadership continued to the end of his working life. Film-maker Ruth Hogben, who worked with Nick Knight on the film for McQueen's last complete collection, *Plato's Atlantis* (Spring/Summer 2010), said, 'I don't think I have ever worked as hard as I worked for him. There was no question. Of course I am not going to sleep. Of course I am not going to leave this room until you are entirely happy. There was no question.'[10]

In a recent interview McQueen's sister, Tracy Chapman, said, 'It was such a remarkable achievement for a working-class boy.'[11] McQueen himself concurred, 'It's a good testament for people like myself who come from working-class backgrounds that it can be done, that you can do what you really want to do in life, everything is possible.'[12] McQueen spoke a lot; sometimes he was shockingly eloquent; at other times he struggled. The words 'romantic' and 'melancholy' occurred frequently. Such extracts provide his all-important voice in this book, a voice of directness and fearlessness that was anti-establishment, anti-pomposity and wanted to prick the bubble of fashion.

McQueen's style may have been subversive but it was entirely underpinned by his exceptional skill. His formal training on Savile Row gave him the technical ability to cut cloth with speed, accuracy and conviction, and it was a facility he never lost.

Opposite
15. Devon Aoki wearing silk brocade
cheongsam. *La Poupée*.
Spring/Summer 1997
Visionaire, 20, 1997
Photograph by Nick Knight

Far left
16. Backstage, *It's Only a Game*, Spring/
Summer 2005
Dress: tulle with embroidered flowers
Photograph by Anne Deniau

Left above
17. Backstage, *Sarabande*, Spring/
Summer 2007
Dress: silk tulle with silk embroidery
Silk rose bouquet headpiece, Philip
Treacy for Alexander McQueen
Photograph by Anne Deniau

Below
18. Backstage, *Voss*, Spring/Summer
2001
Photograph by Anne Deniau

19. Razor clam shells
Titchwell, Norfolk, England
Photograph by Ernie Janes

There are many stories about his prowess with scissors. The atelier staff at Givenchy took fright at the speed and confidence with which he cut their expensive fabric, while Sarah Burton, then McQueen's assistant designer and today creative director at McQueen, recalled in conversation with Tim Blanks, 'Lee could literally create a dress on the spot – embroidery here, fabric there, chop this, and he would completely have it. He would cut on the stand. He spent a lot of time with mannequins, cutting things … He came alive when he was fitting clothes. He made you feel you might as well pack your bags and go home.'[13]

McQueen's view of the body was particular; his drawings, unpublished until now, often focused on the side view, emphasizing the sinuousness of the spine's curvature, and were informed by a profound understanding of the skeletal armature of the body. The profile was also the angle at which a frock coat, a bustle, a crinoline, or an ogee line looked its best. McQueen considered every single element of a show, and it would be no coincidence that the sighting of the first, dramatic and backlit look in *Plato's Atlantis* is in silhouette (pl.64). He took the view that the body was there to be altered. This could be achieved through virtuoso tailoring, as in his signature bumsters, which elongated the torso. Or, while sitting side by side with Nick Knight at a computer screen, digitally layering and remastering images, perhaps stretching the tibia of a model to create an impossibly idealized form of fashion, rather as a fashion drawing exaggerates and takes liberties with the drawn line.

To take a profile view of the body implies another, potentially sinister side, and it is this tension between dark and light that imbued his work with a captivating and sometimes repellant power. McQueen's Gothic sensibility was a recurring theme in his collections. His was always a romantic, Victorian kind of Gothic, filmic, in the spirit of Edgar Allan Poe's works and Tim Burton's films, with a touch of Miss Havisham. McQueen enjoyed the theatricality of 'Victoriana', whether creating nipped-in jackets inspired by Isabella Blow's dressing-up box or employing the drama of that most Victorian of optical illusions, 'Pepper's Ghost', which resulted in Kate Moss's appearance as a spectral apparition (pp.243–5). Nearly every collection contained a reference to nineteenth-century dress, even *Plato's Atlantis*, that most futuristic of shows, in which a bisected silk gown from another era crept in amongst the alien forms.

McQueen was an inspired colourist and established his early palette of black, burgundy and grey with his graduate collection. A deep blood red occurred again and again in the first collections, but by the 2000s he had moved from the chiaroscuro of an imagined Victorian interior to embrace natural tones of wood, leather and lace. He could have a light touch: soft, melancholy tones inspired by the nineteenth-century photographer Julia Margaret Cameron featured in *Sarabande* (Spring/Summer 2007) and mourning lilac recurred again and again (pls 11, 14). Fittingly, lilac roses were the chosen flower at his memorial service. An extraordinary colour palette inspired by nature paired yellow-green beads with taupe horsehair in *Eshu* (Autumn/Winter 2000; pl.104), while the saturated hues of *Plato's Atlantis* seemed to offer an entirely new language of colour in which the levels of Photoshop's colour wheel were turned up to maximum volume, followed finally by the muted, burnished medieval splendour of those last 16 garments from his unfinished Autumn/Winter 2010 collection.

McQueen was the master of polarities, pitting man and machine, nature and technology, water and fire, earth and air against each other. It was as if these elemental oppositions gave him energy. He also demanded energy from his army of models. For the duration of the show, they were under his aesthetic control and, once on the catwalk, he often demanded of them a performativity asked by no other designer. This engendered discomfort, and even provoked accusations of misogyny, particularly following his *La Poupée* collection (Spring/Summer 1997). In his defence McQueen said, 'It's always about pushing to the extreme, the human body, human nature. A lot of people got confused, thinking it was more to do with misogyny. It was never about misogyny, to me it was more to do with art, because the chalices, the cages, were based on Hans Bellmer, the contortion of the body. As a designer you're always working with cutting up the body to different proportions, different shapes. This is what a designer's job is, to transcend what fashion is and what it could be.'[14]

However, McQueen clearly used his mesmerizing collections as a vehicle for the metathesis of his feelings about women, whether consciously or not. Psychoanalyst Adam Phillips has commented: 'Everybody is terrorized by their own misogyny and they have to be. What you do is aestheticize it and that's one way of keeping something troubling in circulation that mustn't be forgotten about.'[15] The women McQueen created were powerful, even terrifying. Ruth Hogben observed of model Debra Shaw's manacled walk through water, towards the audience (pl.227): 'You can't stop her! She moves beautifully with the hands, the shoulders, she moves how she can. She is in control of it. Who is she? She is locked up, but she is fucking powerful.' The models' own accounts of modelling McQueen also suggest that the overwhelming experience was one of empowerment. Either way, McQueen was never afraid of controversy.

But for all the theatrics, McQueen wasn't impractical and as he matured he became more sanguine about the realities of fashion; the clothes had to sell and he enjoyed his success. Tom Ford observed, 'He's a real poet … poet and commerce united, because he's very practical, he's very real … he understands (because he wants to be successful) that you can express whatever you want on the runway but you have to have something beautiful on the hanger to sell to a store.'[16] As McQueen explained, 'my mind is constantly working overtime to come up with a concise and directional collection that is fundamentally sellable, but is also on a higher plane, on an artistic level. For myself, it's no longer about shock tactics, it's more about purely the aesthetics of a collection.'[17]

This book offers a series of extended essays intercepted by concise musings on particular aspects of McQueen's body of work. I am grateful to all the contributors for their painstaking research and insightful analysis. As historians, curators, academics and writers, their expertise does not always originate in fashion but offers prisms of knowledge through which to view those things that interested McQueen, and by which to view his legacy. Some knew him, most didn't. Almost every essay ran over length, as if the allotted word count was simply not enough to contain their subject. Several themes and objects became the subject of an almost fetishistic absorption; these overlaps have been retained, for they reflect the subject's importance.

An Encyclopedia of Collections covers every one in forensic detail, documenting and making clear the manifold references that made McQueen's collections so rich. Key images and an entire survey of show invitations provide a visual logarithm to accompany this reference text. The book includes nearly 450 illustrations, many previously unpublished, ranging from stunning editorial images to evocative backstage shots, created by the talented photographers with whom McQueen worked. Drawings and research boards show the detailed visual progress of forming a collection while illustrations of art, photography and film add context to his work. At the heart of the book lies a Cabinet of Curiosities, artefacts created and commissioned by McQueen over 20 years. Photographed by the V&A, it takes a taxonomic approach that draws out the material and tactile qualities of the objects, just as the Museum would document its own collections, for the purpose of classification and order.

Perhaps fashion attracted McQueen because of its transience, and because it offered the opportunity to make redress, again and again. In his last essay on fashion, 'Die Mode', written in 1911, sociologist Georg Simmel wrote: 'The question of fashion is not "to be or not to be" … but it always stands on the watershed between past and future'.[18] Fashion does not remain in a permanent state but dies, like the butterflies caught in the showpiece of *La Poupée* (a star-shaped cocoon), and the fresh flowers that fell from his panduriform dresses in *Sarabande*, only to wither on the catwalk (pl.11).

On a remote beach in Norfolk, there is an inlet where thousands of razor-clam shells are arranged and ordered by the departing tide in vast, sweeping ridges, stretching as far as the eye can see (pl.19). McQueen was once there, and later captured this ceaseless ebb and flow in a single, brittle, shell-encrusted dress (pl.115). It perhaps offers affirmation of his belief in the fragile but regenerative power of fashion.

No. 1

A SENSE OF PLACE

———

SU[I]TURE

TAILORING & THE FASHION METROPOLIS

CHRISTOPHER BREWARD

'An English tailor craz'd i' the brain
With the study of new fashions'

JOHN WEBSTER, *THE DUCHESS OF MALFI*, 1623

In the summer of 2002 I had the good fortune to find myself co-curating a touring exhibition on contemporary dandyism for the British Council, preparations for which included the acquisition of a suit from Alexander McQueen's new bespoke range for the Savile Row tailor Huntsman.[1] McQueen was by then at the top of his game. Since 1994 his collections had consistently achieved both notoriety and an almost hysterical level of critical acclaim that marked him out from his generation. By the late 1990s his provocations and singular vision dazzled. Yet beneath all the noise and outrage, it was clear that McQueen's startling originality drew a deeper inspiration from the quieter traditions of London's bespoke trades, their place in the long and often strange histories of the city, and their capacity for radical re-invention. In its sharp perfection, the McQueen at Huntsman suit seemed to carry all of those muffled codes and contradictions in its seams.

In line with the usual protocols of bespoke tailoring, mine was the body around which the suit was painstakingly constructed.

Over four visits between August and December I engaged with those transactions that clients of Huntsman had been enacting since 1919 at their Savile Row premises: selecting the cloth (in this case a fine merino Prince of Wales check with a graphic blue thread running through it); engaging with the cutter – who took measurements, achieved a balance, reset the baste to produce the block, and then with the tailor refined the garment through three consecutive fittings; and emerging with a unique hand-finished product that seemed, in the end, to flow over my limbs like a cooling liquid. All of this took place amongst the leather sofas, oak panelling and hunting trophies that had defined Huntsman's particularly discreet atmosphere throughout the twentieth century. The firm had earned its international reputation through the careful courting of royalty, from both the House of Windsor and Hollywood, whose tastes tended towards elegance ('piss elegance', to use a phrase that McQueen might have enjoyed). King Edward VII, Prince Albert Victor (pl.23), Edward Duke of Windsor, Lord Louis Mountbatten, Rex Harrison, Gregory Peck, Hubert

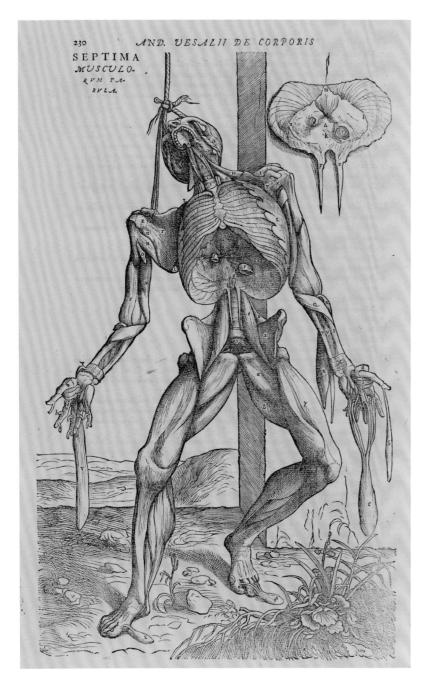

Previous spread
20. Alexander McQueen, London,
June 2002
How to Spend It magazine,
Financial Times, July 2002
Photograph by Axel Bernstorff

Above left
21. Cadaver of executed criminal
Engraving in Andreas Vesalius,
De Humani Corporis Fabrica, Italy, 1543
V&A: National Art Library

Above right
22. Agnolo Bronzino, *Portrait of
Guidobaldo II della Rovere,
Duke of Urbino*, 1531–2
Oil on panel
Galleria Palatina, Florence

Opposite
23. *Alexander Bassano, Portrait of Prince
Albert Victor, Duke of Clarence and
Avondale*, late 1880s
Photograph
National Portrait Gallery

de Givenchy, Laurence Olivier, Dirk Bogarde, Peter Ustinov and James Goldsmith were all Huntsman clients.[2] They shared a preference both for the sharp shoulders, long coat and one button cut that defined the house style, and a proclivity perhaps to a refined style of living that favoured a degree of amorality over stifling respectability. Huntsman suited McQueen's tendency towards luxurious outrage very well.

Despite the fact that menswear had made occasional appearances in McQueen's early catwalk shows, and two years later McQueen would present his first menswear collection under the aegis of the Gucci Group, the Huntsman collaboration of 2002–3 was the closest McQueen came to playing out a bespoke tailoring obsession that had needled his imagination since his formative three-year apprenticeship with Anderson & Sheppard (immediately followed by nearly two years as a junior trouser-cutter at military tailor Gieves & Hawkes). The collection constituted 12 pieces designed to form a complete wardrobe that seemed to speak more to the sybaritic rhythms of a nineteenth-century dandy's social diary than the realities of twenty-first-century life. It included everything from attenuated lounge suits, through dramatic frock and morning coats, to elaborately decorated evening dress, all engineered by Huntsman's managing director Terry Haste (whose pedigree on the Row stretched back to the glamorous years of Tommy Nutter, Haste's former business partner). Through its details and accessorization, McQueen at Huntsman spoke of luxury 'a rebours' with gold buttons, pink and yellow diamond tiepins and cufflinks, and handmade shoes of ostrich and lizard skin.

In an interview in the *Financial Times* (City high-flyers and ostentatious celebrities were the target market, able to stretch to the £1,000 premium that McQueen's name added to the standard £3,000–£4,000 Savile Row bill), Haste noted that the collection was designed to 'a totally different block … A classic Huntsman suit is cut with everything in proportion. The McQueen shaping is much narrower and more defined on the back with sleeves narrower and lapels more extreme.' McQueen amplified Haste's observation with a characteristic reference to interior human anatomy: 'A tailored jacket usually narrows into the waist. The shaping for my suits is fitted on the curvature of the spine.'[3] The final garment does indeed seem to form its centre of gravity in the small of the back, the fabric holding the shoulders firmly square as the vertical lines of the checked pattern trace the spine's curve slowly downwards and inwards to a flaring skirt, accentuating the subtle, muscular flow of the male body towards the buttocks. In its sinuous turn, McQueen's line echoes the ogee curve so evocatively described in *The Line of Beauty* (2004), Alan Hollinghurst's almost contemporaneous and celebrated novel of power, money, aesthetics and homoerotic desire in 1980s London, and underlines a queer trace that would persist in the designer's work:

The ogee curve was pure expression, decorative not structural … the snakelike flicker of an instinct, of two compulsions held in one unfolding movement. He ran his hand down Wani's back. He didn't think Hogarth had illustrated this

best example of it, the dip and swell – he had chosen harps and branches, bones rather than flesh. Really it was time for a new *Analysis of Beauty* (pl.24).[4]

Unbuttoning the jacket from the front to reveal an ice-white silk lining, edged like Victorian mourning stationery in a neat black border, produces a sensation not unlike that of a surgeon peeling muscle back from the sternum to the posterior ribs. When I place the discarded jacket over my arm I am reminded of those engravings attributed to the sixteenth-century scientist Andreas Vesalius: the cadaver presenting his flayed skin to the world (pl.21). Suit as memento mori.

The original Huntsman experiment struggled to turn a profit (though it was recently revived in made-to-measure form). As fashion journalist James Sherwood noted:

Though McQueen looked dandy posing in Huntsman's window alongside general manager Peter Smith for *l'Uomo Vogue*, the collaboration was short-lived. A couple of Gucci Group executives placed an order, and Elton John's partner David Furnish took delivery of a black frock coat embroidered with a jet bead peacock. After that [it] was quietly terminated.[5]

Short-lived though it might have been, as the Huntsman legend replayed here suggests, its tailored themes were enduring ones. The remainder of this chapter aims to record their repeated referencing through the early phases of McQueen's career and their relationship to the lifeblood of London as a creative organism in itself.

To start at the beginning: the Anderson & Sheppard story is a constant in McQueen's various biographies, in part due to the apocryphal tale of the Stratford-raised teenage cockney apprentice, blagging his way through the doors in 1984 and scrawling the equivalent of a graffiti artist's tag, 'McQueen was here', within the lining of a coat destined for the wardrobe of the current Prince of Wales.[6] In keeping with such bravado (later denied), the firm's history and clientele are at least as colourful as that boasted by Huntsman: Rudolph Valentino, Serge Diaghilev, Somerset Maugham, Sacheverell Sitwell, Marlene Dietrich, Noël Coward and Rudolph Nureyev all passed through its doors as clients.[7] But its restrained house style sits less easily with the later, distinctive development of McQueen's dramatic approach to cutting – it is softer, more inclined to drape and fit easily around the body than hold its flesh in a fierce embrace. For the teenage McQueen its traditions were in any case possibly less important than the opportunity to learn the fundamental skills from a master, any master. At Anderson & Sheppard it was coat-maker Cornelius O'Callaghan who oversaw McQueen's graduation from padding and fitting collars, through setting sleeves, placing canvas linings, putting in pockets, sewing buttonholes, pressing cloth and finally producing a 'forward' or half-completed coat for the master's approval.[8]

As he later confided to Sherwood, Savile Row held little mystique for McQueen: 'Was he ever intimidated? "No not really … Behind the façade … it's actually a bunch of working class craftsmen trained to do one job … Like plumbers."'[9] In his press

release for the launch of the Huntsman line, McQueen's tone is more respectful, if equally pragmatic. The years on the Row constituted an education in skill and a solid foundation upon which his later iconoclasm could flourish:

> The construction and architecture of the pieces employ the core techniques I learned during my four-year apprenticeship on the Row. You have to fully understand the construction of the clothes before you can begin to manipulate them. What I've done is to take these traditional techniques and inject modernity.[10]

Modernity was one thing, but McQueen's approach also owed a great debt to techniques derived from an interest in raw historicism and a dark romanticism. During his time at Gieves & Hawkes (Anderson & Sheppard had let him go on account of a certain lack of long-term commitment), the 19-year-old McQueen moonlighted as a freelance pattern-cutter and machinist. This was a peripatetic existence in line with the seemingly chaotic patterns of work that characterized the edgier fringes of London's fashion ecology in the 1980s and '90s (echoing older networks of creativity that had sustained groups of designers in 1920s bohemia, 'Swinging London' and the Punk scene).[11] As sociologist Angela McRobbie argued in her analysis of Britain's creative economy in the late 1990s, designers of McQueen's generation 'express little, if any interest in the dynamics of wealth creation and business. They work according to a different set of principles, which are about artistic integrity,

24. Plate 1, William Hogarth,
The Analysis of Beauty, London, 1753
Etching and engraving on paper
The British Museum, London

Opposite
25. Backstage, *Joan*,
Autumn/Winter 1998
Alexander McQueen fitting a model
Photograph by Anne Deniau

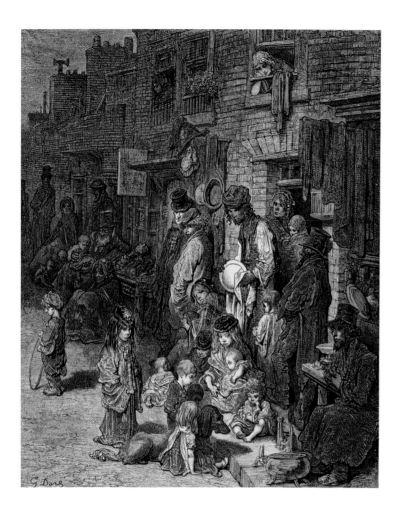

26. Gustav Doré, 'Over London by Rail'
Illustration in William Blanchard Jerrold,
London: A Pilgrimage, London, 1872
The British Library, London

creative success, recognition, approval by the art establishment and then, also, almost as an afterthought, sales.'[12] In this spirit, the hungry McQueen's seeking out of professional experience and skill (and his retrospective re-telling of this as a gritty story of auto-didacticism) makes sense. Having learned the secrets of bespoke tailoring, his attention moved to something more mysterious still, and in 1988 one of his jobbing stints entailed working for theatrical costumiers Berman's & Nathan's (Angels from 1992).[13] There his repertoire shifted from schmutter to show business, and more particularly from a study of contemporary tailoring to the practice of sartorial archaeology.

Berman's & Nathan's was a resonant choice. Founded as Nathan's in 1790, it was older than any Savile Row establishment and enjoyed an illustrious history, not only as the supplier of the West End's most spectacular productions (from Beerbohm Tree's historical and Shakespearian epics at Her Majesty's to the fantasy of Gilbert and Sullivan's operettas for D'Oyly Carte), but also as a provider of Court dress, military uniform and fancy dress. Its competitor and eventual partner, Morris Angel of Seven Dials, dealt in second-hand and 'antique' clothing, expanding to incorporate fancy-dress hire in the 1860s and the design of film costume from the 1920s. In their entirety such companies constituted a repository of historical dress greater perhaps than any museum collection and it is in this context, as a vital archive of fashion apparitions from London's past, that we might understand McQueen's passage through their workrooms.

McQueen would later disavow his period as a theatrical costumier which involved making costumes for Cameron Mackintosh's international musical hit, based on Victor Hugo's 1862 historical novel *Les Misérables*. It didn't sit well with the foul-mouthed machismo of a rougher, more 'authentic' East End queerness that formed his carefully honed public persona – and fashion and costume have always made for uneasy bedfellows. But while the fey backstage campness was quickly discarded as worthless, the careful replication of historical dressmaking techniques captured McQueen's imagination, indeed seemed to haunt him. Reference to historical pattern books was an essential part of the costumier's research method and McQueen's exposure to them while working for Berman's & Nathan's meant that an antiquarian perspective remained an integral part of his approach to design throughout his career. For example, the articulated jackets present in his Autumn/Winter 1996 *Dante* collection owe a clear debt to historic dress patterns.

And there is something more profound in this late 1980s moment, in which the unknown McQueen silently situates himself within the continuous flux of two of London's most important, deep-rooted and atmospheric clothing trades. It is almost as if he emerges organically from the rags and threads that constitute the city's sartorial past. Caroline Evans, the most perceptive of McQueen's interpreters, has written persuasively about the crucial role of London itself in the formation of complex fashion processes and narratives. Drawing on the writings of latter-day

London seers Iain Sinclair and Peter Ackroyd, she has situated the work of fashion designers such as McQueen in the city's sprawling mythology and punishing political economy, 'sketching equivalences between urban fabric and fashioned fabric'.[14] In this sense, McQueen joins a genealogy of 'cockney visionaries', creating in the same vein as Blake and Dickens, whose vision Ackroyd ascribes to London's pulsing spirit:

> All of them were preoccupied with light and darkness, in a city that is built in the shadows of money and power; all of them were entranced by the scenic and the spectacular, in a city that is continually filled with the energetic display of people and institutions. They understood the energy of London, they understood its variety, and they also understood its darkness … In this vast concourse of people they understood the pity and mystery of existence just as surely as they understood its noise and bustle.[15]

McQueen's fascination with the cruelty and darkness of London was evident from his short tenure in the studios of Ladbroke Grove based fashion brand Red or Dead, where he worked on its fetishistic leather bondage collection for Autumn/Winter 1991, to his graduating collection, which marked the culmination of his MA degree course in Fashion Design at Central Saint Martins in March 1992. In an echo of his supposed intervention in the lining of the Prince of Wales's suit at Anderson & Sheppard, 'he stitched locks of human hair under blood-red linings', a motif he would continue to use in the labels of later collections.[16] Elegiac and diaphanous sheath-like dresses were contrasted with twisted interpretations of Victorian frock coats, lined in the lavender silk of mourning and subtly pleated at the top of the sleeve to unsettle assumptions around the stiffness of masculine tailoring.[17]

On the face of it there was nothing particularly original in McQueen's referencing of this most cited of London's horrors. The tale of Jack the Ripper, deriving from the unsolved murders of poor East End women in the Whitechapel of 1888, has provided a source of morbid fascination for generations of mainly male journalists, conspiracy theorists, novelists, film-makers, psycho-geographers and local tour guides over the intervening century. As social historian Judith Walkowitz suggests in her perceptive account of the political and representational context in which this and related stories of sexual danger have been played out in London, 'the Whitechapel murders have continued to provide a common vocabulary of male violence against women, a vocabulary now more than one hundred years old.'[18] But it would be over-simplifying matters to claim, as several fashion journalists did through the 1990s, that the sickening thread of brutality that ran through McQueen's work from this moment on was just another example of banal misogyny and sadistic voyeurism.

Evans makes two important points in McQueen's defence. The first situates McQueen's bleak vision within an understanding

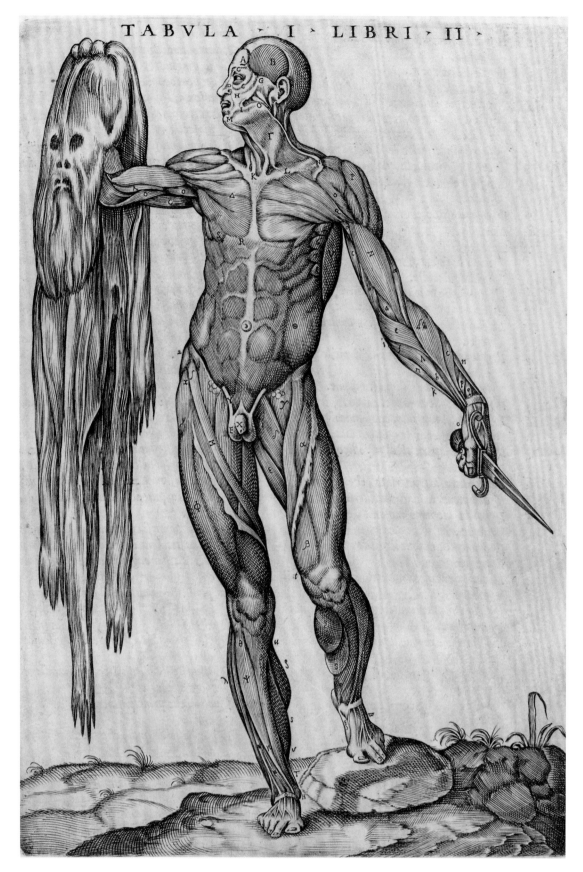

TABVLA · I · LIBRI · II ·

27. Plate 64, Juan Valverde de Amusco,
La Anatomia del Corpo Umano,
Rome, 1550
Engraving on paper
V&A: National Art Library

Opposite left
28. Arnulf Rainer, *Bauchmalerei*, 1970–3
Courtesy of Studio Arnulf Rainer

Opposite right
29. Dress, *The Hunger*,
Spring/Summer 1996

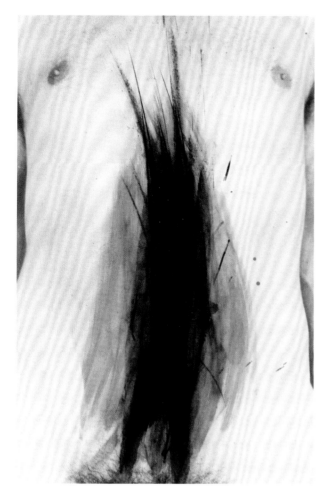

of his own queer sexuality, honestly avowed at a time when such openness was rare in the fashion world's public account of itself; and observes that rather than fetishize female victimhood, it more often referenced the 'uncompromising and aggressive sexuality' of strong lesbians.[19] The second is of even greater relevance to the consideration of the links between the craft of tailoring, London's history and McQueen's unique work in this chapter. It suggests that the 'aesthetic of cruelty' staged through the designer's striking shows was not simply a heartless theatrical flourish, but a manifestation of the very practices that informed his distinctive style of creating a garment: 'razor sharp, its seams traced the body's contours like surgical incisions, skimming it to produce pointed lapels and sharp shoulders.'[20] It was little wonder that the Ripper story formed a recurring leitmotif for McQueen with its underlying themes of butchery and evisceration (pls 28, 29). As Evans notes, it was this obsession that marked him out in the judgment of his patron, Isabella Blow, who recalled:

What attracted me to Alexander was the way he takes ideas from the past and sabotages them with his cut to make them thoroughly new and in the context of today. It is the complexity and severity of his approach to cut that makes him so modern. He is like a Peeping Tom in the way he slits and stabs at fabric to explore all the erogenous zones of the body.[21]

Perhaps the most daring exploration of the limits of tailoring in McQueen's repertoire was his re-imagining of the proportions

of the body through a radical lowering of the waist and hip. Seemingly slashed down almost to the pubic bone and coccyx, McQueen's 'bumster' trousers, first shown on the catwalk in his abrasive *Nihilism* collection (Spring/Summer 1994), reprised the ogee curve – translating its eroticism from a male to a female register (pl.33). As the designer observed in a later BBC documentary, 'that part of the body – not so much the buttocks, but the bottom of the spine – that's the most erotic part of anyone's body, man or woman.'[22] As fashion historian Judith Watt explains, the infamous trouser produced a silhouette that was half borrowed from gay pornography (the elongated torso of both the boy and the body-builder) and half from the wardrobe of the Renaissance prince (where the top of the breeches hung low on the pelvis and all focus fell on the crotch), but succeeded in presenting a new model of sexual desirability for women. The technical skill required to fabricate such an effect was considerable. In order for the bumster's waistband to sit the required five centimetres below the height of the lowest hipsters, the lining was rubberized to cling – tightly.[23]

There is perhaps an electric synergy between the fetishistic elegance of McQueen's bumsters and his brash East End sensibility. Not only do they derive from the skills learned in the tough-talking workrooms of Savile Row, but they also point to the assertive pub-and-gutter glamour of London's seamier side that McQueen found so compelling. Whether in the queer and drag bars of early 1990s Soho, or the back alleys of 1880s

32. Suit, *No.13*, Spring/Summer 1999
Silk frock coat and trousers
Photograph by Anthea Simms

Opposite

33. Ensemble, *Nihilism*,
Spring/Summer 1994
Crop top and 'bumster' trousers
Photograph by Chris Moore

Whitechapel, the siren call to outrage was always strong. There is no little irony in the fact that the introduction and rise of McQueen's bumsters coincided with a raucous craze for the display of bared stomach, pierced navel and bikini-line tattoo by working-class young women in London's nightclubs and shopping malls. He would have enjoyed the co-existence of vulgarity and naked desire that linked the mores of Oxford Street with his reinvention of couture.

The late-twentieth-century London in which McQueen learned his craft and pioneered a new vision is all but gone now. Savile Row survives, but is threatened as ever by commercial rent rises and the incursion of global luxury brands, which themselves came to dominate the later phases of McQueen's career. Soho has been sanitized and Central Saint Martins has been transplanted to King's Cross. Even Stratford has felt the gentrifying effects of the 2012 Olympics, while the rest of east London succumbs to a version of consumerist bohemianism undifferentiated from that which also blights Berlin. Steeped as he was in older traditions and a profound understanding of history, time and space, McQueen's work belongs to a time before the Shard and London's triumph as an international mega-city, yet also bridges that change – anticipating its violent transformation, its commercialized eroticism and its underlying sense of loss. It shares in its inevitable contradictions. Interviewed by Susannah Frankel for *AnOther Man* magazine in 2006, McQueen almost seemed to acknowledge it himself:

> Tailoring is just a form of construction, it's the rigour behind the design but at the end of the day you're still dealing with a single or double-breasted jacket. The narrative is what makes it interesting, plus the romance behind it and the detail … That's what makes McQueen stand out, the detail. I want the clothes to be heirlooms, like they used to be … In the end, when you go back to something, it's about how you've moved on. For me, it's all about the fact that I'm capable of doing anything as long as it comes from the heart.[24]

The McQueen at Huntsman suit still hangs in my wardrobe. I continue to wear it occasionally in Edinburgh where I now live (and where historicism generally trounces modernity). At the cuff of the left sleeve there is a small hole in the cloth, the frayed edges of wool revealing white cotton underneath. It's difficult to tell whether a cigarette, carelessly brandished in a long-forgotten South Kensington bar, or the attentions of those clothes moths that plague London houses, caused the damage. It's been there for some years. My temptation is to force a wider rend in the delusional hope that beneath the surface the familiar motto 'McQueen was here', or something more profane, will be revealed.

CLAN MACQUEEN

GHISLAINE WOOD

———

'I'm a designer with a cause. I like to challenge history'
Alexander McQueen, 2008

—

Nowhere is McQueen's extraordinary poetic imagination revealed more powerfully than in the seminal collections *Highland Rape* (Autumn/Winter 1995) and *The Widows of Culloden* (Autumn/Winter 2006). Some ten years apart, these two collections provided contrasting but cathartic narratives on specific historical events – the Highland Clearances of the eighteenth and nineteenth centuries and the Battle of Culloden in 1746 – and in many ways they reflect the complexity and drama of McQueen's vision. 'Scottishness' was for him not merely a creative wellspring but a deeply personal identification and, as for many diasporic sons of Scotland, the politics of its depiction could be problematic. McQueen acknowledged that his self-reflexive journey through these collections was beset with misunderstanding.[1] But it is also a journey that mirrors wider representations of Scottish national identity from his youthful anger for an oppressed people to the more mature romantic vision of a culture absorbed into Empire and reimagined.

The romantic construction of Highland Scotland that crystallized during the course of the nineteenth century, as the country swiftly industrialized, has provided a model for much later cultural production and with no greater impact than in the world of fashion. Tartans, tweeds, military doublets, kilts and belted plaids litter fashion's imagery providing a familiar terrain. With *Highland Rape*, though, McQueen presented an entirely different discourse. Reacting against romantic mythologizing he attempted to reveal the violence of an historical process and described the collection as 'a shout against English designers . . . doing flamboyant Scottish clothes. My father's family originates from the Isle of Skye, and I'd studied the history of the Scottish

upheavals and the Clearances. People were so unintelligent they thought this was about women being raped – yet *Highland Rape* was about England's rape of Scotland.'[2] The spare silhouettes, torn bodices, ripped fabrics and 'decimated' lace presented a metaphorical desecration that many critics misunderstood, but clearly highlighted McQueen's concern with exploring narrative. Exclusive use of his own family tartan (the MacQueen tartan) produced by the Lochcarron Mill also signalled the importance of personal biography and contrasted starkly with the more profligate use of tartan by other British fashion designers. *Highland Rape* represented a startling narrative that did much to establish McQueen's reputation (pl.34).

In 2006 *The Widows of Culloden* collection marked a return to the theme of the Highlands and in many ways presented a catharsis to the reductive, anti-romanticism of the earlier collection. McQueen later said that he saw the collection balancing *Highland Rape* by providing a positive view of Culloden and the subsequent peace for Scotland. For him, inherent in 'the fragility of the fabrics, the cut and the shape was a more positive image', directly related to his psychological state: 'I'm in a much clearer head space now than I was when I did the *Highland*.'[3] The extreme technicality of the collection was married with an extraordinary richness of imagery, much of it drawn from traditional Scottish costume (pls 35, 36). The MacQueen tartan was used not only for pieces that recall traditional dress, such as the arisaid and the Fhéilidh Mor, but also for trouser suits and jackets with military connotations.[4] The collection played with accentuated silhouettes, showing bustles, bell skirts and dresses covered in pheasant feathers presenting an altogether gentler and grander view of Scotland (pls 39, 40, 41, 118).

For McQueen, Scotland was not to be trivialized, reduced – in his words – 'to fucking haggis, fucking tartan, fucking bagpipes'.[5] Scottish history as expressed in these two collections is presented as an evolving, complex narrative bound up with his own sense of identity. Indeed, the importance with which he regarded his Scottish heritage is poignantly exemplified by the fact that he never designed a kilt for a menswear collection, but famously wore one of MacQueen tartan for The Metropolitan Museum of Art's gala benefit dinner in New York in 2006 (pl.38). A child of the Scots diaspora in the country of diaspora, there can have been no better place to express his heritage and present an ironic vision of the romantic Highlander.

Previous spread
34. Ensemble, *Highland Rape*, Autumn/Winter 1995
Dress: printed net with MacQueen tartan; knickers: MacQueen tartan
Photograph by Robert Fairer

Below left
35. Frontispiece, James Logan, *The Clans of the Scottish Highlands*, vol. 1, London, 1857
V&A: National Art Library

Below right
36. Highlander wearing the Sinclair tartan
Sketch by Robert Ronald Mclan in James Logan, *The Clans of the Scottish Highlands*, vol. 1, London, 1857
V&A: National Art Library

Below left
37. Menswear ensemble,
Autumn/Winter 2006
Robe: MacQueen tartan, silk, lace and silk
embroidery; trousers: MacQueen tartan
Photograph by Chris Moore

Right
38. Alexander McQueen and Sarah
Jessica Parker at The Metropolitan
Museum of Art gala, May 2006
Photograph by Richard Young

Below right
39. Dress, *The Widows of Culloden*,
Autumn/Winter 2006
MacQueen tartan, silk tulle and lace
Modelled by Sasha Pivovarova
Photograph by Chris Moore

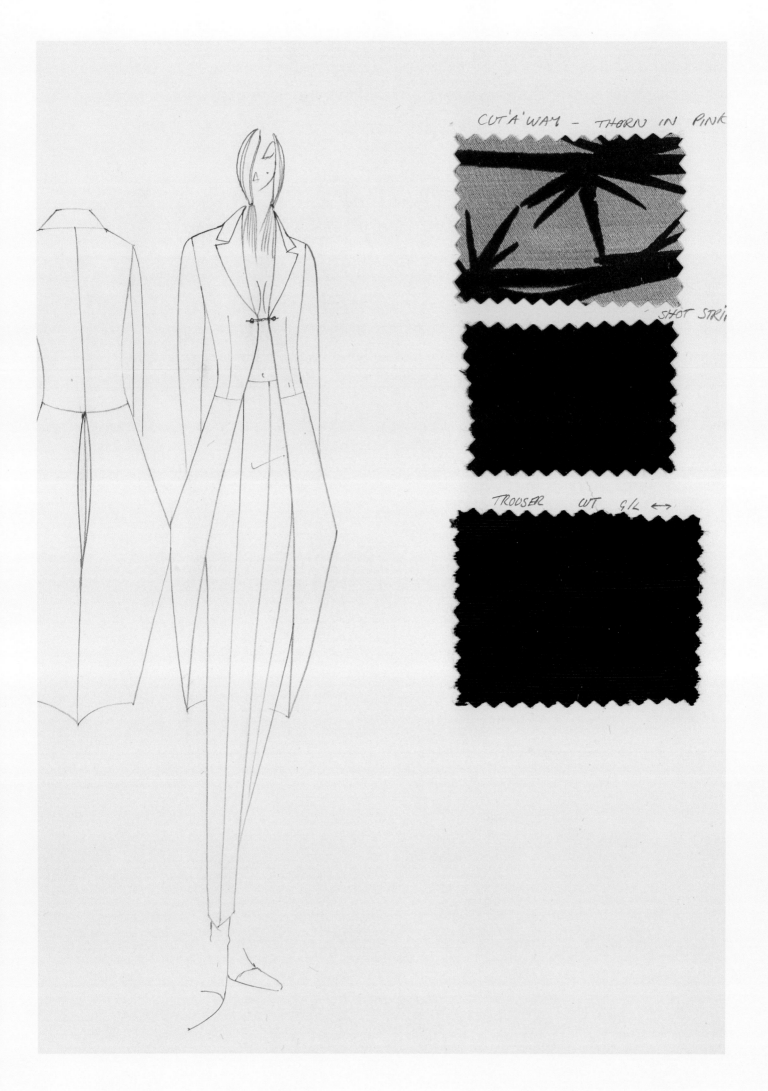

CUT'A'WAY — THORN IN PINK

SHOT STRI

TROUSER CUT S/L

CENTRAL SAINT MARTINS

LOUISE RYTTER

'... *Because I'd come from the East End, schooling wasn't*
at the top of the agenda, but my passion was fashion and
Saint Martins was the place to go'
Alexander McQueen, 2008

—

Alexander McQueen's MA graduate collection in March 1992 heralded a new era in British fashion. Showing under the name 'LEE A–McQUEEN', the young East Ender presented ten assured and individualistic looks that combined skillful tailoring with an innovative approach to manipulating fabric, traits that persisted throughout his career (pl. 44).

In 1990 McQueen was an unemployed pattern-cutter who had heard that Central Saint Martins, the prestigious college then on Charing Cross Road, had a job vacancy.[1] MA Fashion course director Bobby Hillson recalled that McQueen 'walked into my office with a bundle of clothes and asked me to give him a job. He wasn't thinking of joining the course.'[2] Hillson didn't need another pattern-cutter, but instantly recognized McQueen's raw talent and was interested in his CV, which included four years of formal training in bespoke tailoring on Savile Row, as well as working for theatrical costumier Berman's & Nathan's and avant-garde designer Koji Tatsuno, who was backed by Yohji Yamamoto. She was particularly intrigued by McQueen's work experience with Romeo Gigli in Italy, where he had absorbed Gigli's romantic sensibility. Hillson offered McQueen a place on the MA Fashion Design course after he returned the following day with drawings of his designs. McQueen's aunt agreed to cover the cost of the tuition fees, which he paid back in 1996 on his appointment as chief designer at Givenchy.

McQueen's education in fashion thus far had been through the medium of magazines such as *The Face* and *i-D*. He noted, 'I was always looking from the outside in, because it wasn't my world. I just looked at the visuals.'[3] But in November 1990 it did become his world. He now found himself studying among a group of MA and BA fashion students including Hussein Chalayan. McQueen recalled, 'It showed me there were other people out there like me ... It was an exciting period and the start of a new London thing, and it was a period that hadn't been there since Galliano left for Paris. So it was a new revolution in fashion.'[4]

The 48-week MA course was spread over five terms and students specialized in fashion design, printed textiles for fashion and knitwear. Hillson founded the MA course in 1978. One of her lasting achievements was to make the graduate show part of the official schedule during London Fashion Week; the course gained international recognition for pushing boundaries, with the students often producing eccentric and idiosyncratic work. Hillson admitted that some of the tutors found McQueen frustrating as a student, but she never doubted him: 'You can't make anyone more talented, but you can make them work more professionally.'[5] Course work was closely linked to the industry and included projects for companies such as Harvey Nichols, the Issey Miyake store and Liberty of London. Louise Wilson, who in 1992 would become course director, was visiting tutor at the time and said of her student: 'He was always interested, inquisitive really ... He used the college as it should be used, getting the most out of it.'[6]

Central Saint Martins provided McQueen with a stimulating environment. Fashion print tutor Fleet Bigwood recalls: 'Everything was very quick and immediate ... it was a chaotic mess, but that's what gave the place its energy at that point.'[7] McQueen now found himself studying in the heart of Soho, with direct access

to its haberdashers, antique bookshops, theatres and vibrant nightlife. The French patisserie Maison Bertaux was a favourite hang-out, and also Angels costumiers where McQueen would spend hours looking at the construction of theatrical garments.[8] An alchemist with textiles, McQueen devoted much of his time to the print room, burning, dying and throwing chemicals on fabrics. McQueen's lack of funds made him innovative and resourceful and he would ask the fabric shops on Berwick Street for ends of rolls. Natalie Gibson, head of fashion textile design at the time, remembers seeing McQueen 'experimenting with unusual materials' and on one occasion 'smearing red dye on fabric to simulate blood'.[9]

The course culminated in the MA Fashion show, held on 16 March 1992 in the British Fashion Council tent. McQueen's was the penultimate of 22 collections.

Titled *Jack the Ripper Stalks his Victims*, the show notes described it as a 'Day into eveningwear collection inspired by 19th century street walkers'. The narrative was embedded in his fascination with both the Victorian period and his family history.[10] The collection included fine strings of beads interwoven with grey mesh to mimic blood speeding through veins, strings of red woollen yarn imitating clotted blood, black silk riding jackets lined with red fabric to simulate human flesh, and a human hair-lined frock coat, with a hawthorn print by fellow student Simon Ungless (pls 42, 142). Despite little press recognition at the time, McQueen's collection was a sensation in the eyes of fashion editor Isabella Blow (pl.43), who bought it in its entirety. 'I just thought: this is the most beautiful thing I've ever seen. I just knew he had something really special, very modern.'[11] She recalled, '[The clothes] moved in a way I'd never seen and I wanted them'.[12]

Previous spread
42. Sketch, *Jack the Ripper Stalks his Victims*, Autumn/Winter 1992
Pencil on distressed paper with fabric swatches
Central Saint Martins MA graduate portfolio
Courtesy of Sarabande

Opposite
43. Isabella Blow wearing frock coat by Alexander McQueen and hat by Philip Treacy, Hilles, 1992
British *Vogue*, November 1992
Photograph by Oberto Gili

44. Ensemble, *Jack the Ripper Stalks his Victims*, Autumn/Winter 1992
Top: synthetic mesh and beads
Bird claw neckpiece by Simon Costin
Photograph by Niall McInerney

DRAWING A LINE

ABRAHAM THOMAS

━━━━━━━

*'I was literally three years old when I started drawing. I did it all my life
... I always, always wanted to be a designer. I read books on fashion
from the age of twelve ... I knew Giorgio Armani was a window-dresser,
Emanuel Ungaro was a tailor'*
Alexander McQueen, 2003

—

Alexander McQueen's drawings provoke a particularly intriguing set of questions, given that the designer was so well known for his skill at working directly with materials. How does one interpret the distilled qualities of a flat drawing when considered alongside the textural and sculptural possibilities of fabrics?

Very few of these drawings, whether from his student days or from his professional career, have been published or researched before. Therefore, they offer a rare glimpse into McQueen's design process. Acting both as private musings and as tools of communication within the studio, the drawings performed a number of functions. They indicated McQueen's initial thoughts; facilitated conversations between members of the design team; and at the outset established the tone, atmosphere and creative direction of a particular collection. Sarah Burton, who joined McQueen in 1996, recalled how incredibly fast McQueen was able to sketch, and described how she would run after him desperately trying to make notes on the drawings as he went along. Indeed many of the annotations on the drawings are in Burton's hand rather than McQueen's, reflecting their close collaborative relationship during these early design stages. Selected sketches were also copied and transmitted to the studio's textile partners in Italy in order to convey vital instructions for fabrication, as confirmed by the scattering of annotated faxes that exist amongst original drawings.

McQueen's drawings provide an important opportunity to understand how ideas were expressed at a stage prior to any cutting or tailoring using fabric on a mannequin. Highly accomplished and supremely confident, the boldness of these sketches creates a sense of equivalence to the bravery that was evident in his method of working with textiles and three-dimensional forms.

The drawings that relate to his Central Saint Martins MA graduation portfolio are especially interesting in that they seem to provide a direct line of evolution from his early career as an apprenticed tailor on Savile Row. Many exude a refined, almost clinical, quality (pl.42). Others demonstrate how his drawing skills were able to adapt to a variety of contexts and scales with a deftness and clarity of approach.

A fellow student, print designer Simon Ungless, recalls seeing McQueen's drawings in those early days:

> I remember the drawings. I just thought, they are so chicken-feet scratchy. Chicken-claws turning into ink. Really scratchy, feathery, girls with really pointy noses, bald heads, turtlenecks that covered their faces. A really different vibe to all the other students ... A not very cool kind of thing. He really stood out to me. Here is someone with a point of view.[1]

In many design disciplines, sketch drawings often acquire a quasi-sacred status due to their representations of the initial moments of conception. Although it is true that early drawings can play a crucial role in articulating future design thoughts, such a simplistic analysis runs the risk of belying the true situation. For example, within architecture, designers often choose to explore initial design ideas through more physical material processes such as model-making, describing spatial concepts that later will be expressed more explicitly through formal drawings. One of McQueen's drawings for his *Scanners* collection (Autumn/Winter 2003) exhibits a particularly architectural aesthetic, with the fabric articulated as a series of interconnected flat planes, and the inclusion of notes indicating a 'fully embroidered fabric ... all engineered, no flat parts' (pl.46). This interest in the volumetric qualities of a drawing might be compared to McQueen's deep engagement with textile fabrics, and his preference for directly manipulating tactile materials so as to express ideas in a way that might have been frustratingly difficult if relying exclusively on the mediated process of drawing on a flat page. Indeed, from some accounts it appears that McQueen drew less and less towards the end of his career, deciding instead to focus on working directly with fabrics, which offered him an outlet for creative expression that drawing never did.

However, in an interview with the photographer, Nick Knight, McQueen revealed that his earliest memory of wanting to design clothes expressed itself through the process of drawing. At the age of three, at a time when his family was living in a council house, he recalled outlining a sketch for a dress on an area of bare wall that had become exposed through the gradual peeling of wallpaper.[2]

This sense of immediacy and gestural flourish permeates a number of McQueen's design drawings. Some are compelling for their minimalism and reduction, as exemplified in one example (pl.49) that provides the subtlest indication of an outlined silhouette. Others are memorable for suggesting an approach towards abstraction (pl.51), where the drawing seems to exist

Previous spread
45. Sketch, *Irere*, Spring/Summer 2003
Pencil on paper, London 2002
Courtesy of Alexander McQueen

46. Sketch, *Scanners*,
Autumn/Winter 2003
Pencil on paper, London 2003
Courtesy of Alexander McQueen

Opposite left
47. Sketch, *Scanners*,
Autumn/Winter 2003
Pencil on paper, London 2003
Courtesy of Alexander McQueen

Opposite right
48. Sketch, *Scanners*,
Autumn/Winter 2003
Pencil on paper, London 2003
Courtesy of Alexander McQueen

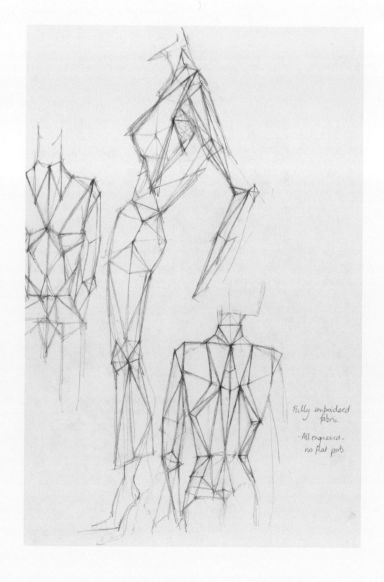

simply as a statement of pure materiality. Throughout all the sketches, though, there is a deft use of the medium to describe the various qualities of different fabrics. Subtle shifts in texture and weight are articulated through the delicate and precise application of smudging techniques (pls 50, 53). Laborious contour lines and cross-hatching are employed to indicate the quality of workmanship required for detailed embellishments and other surface details, for example, becoming intently focused on the details of a frock coat (pl.45). Perhaps most impressive is the way in which McQueen manages to suggest a sense of movement within the fabric, giving the gentlest hint as to how these textiles would behave once they were on a human body – breathing life into what might have been a rather more static image in anyone else's hands (pl.48).

Much of this was possible due to McQueen's profound sense of instinct when it came to working with fabric, and his ability to faithfully communicate his designs through his drawing techniques. He clearly strived to ensure that the emotional content of his designs would never be lost through the explicit articulation of the drawn line. These unique drawings are invaluable as records of a creative vision, capturing as they do a series of conceptual thoughts at a particular moment in time. They are also crucial to an understanding of McQueen's creative process because of their ability to maintain a sense of poignant inference and poetic ambiguity.

Opposite
49. Sketch, *Pantheon ad Lucem*,
Autumn/Winter 2004
Pencil on paper, London 2004
Courtesy of Alexander McQueen

Above
50. Sketch, *Pantheon ad Lucem*,
Autumn/Winter 2004
Pencil on paper, London 2004
Courtesy of Alexander McQueen

Below
51. Sketch, *Pantheon ad Lucem*,
Autumn/Winter 2004
Pencil on paper, London 2004
Courtesy of Alexander McQueen

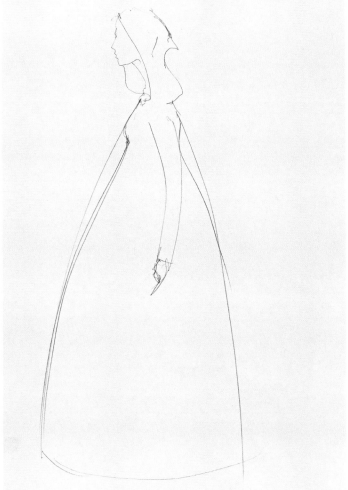

Opposite left
52. Sketch, *The Girl Who Lived in the Tree*,
Autumn/Winter 2008
Pencil on paper, London 2008
Courtesy of Alexander McQueen

Opposite right
53. Sketch, *The Girl Who Lived in the Tree*,
Autumn/Winter 2008
Pencil on paper, London 2008
Courtesy of Alexander McQueen

Above left
54. Sketch, *Irere*, Spring/Summer 2003
Pencil on paper, London 2002
Courtesy of Alexander McQueen

Above right
55. Sketch, *Irere*, Spring/Summer 2003
Pencil on paper, London 2002
Courtesy of Alexander McQueen

THE EARLY YEARS

SUSANNAH FRANKEL

'The time was the beginning of the morning,
And up the sun was mounting with those stars
That with him were, what time the Love Divine
At first in motion set those beauteous things'

DANTE ALIGHIERI, *THE DIVINE COMEDY, CANTO I: INFERNO*, c.1308–21

When Alexander McQueen graduated from Central Saint Martins in 1992, Britain was still in the throes of a recession that marked the early years of the decade, accompanied by unemployment and social discontent. It is well documented that for an early portrait by Richard Burbridge the young designer's face was covered with black gaffer tape as he was claiming social security benefits and did not want to be recognized (pl.210). That was also the reason, according to McQueen, that he used his middle name, Alexander, as opposed to his first name, Lee, when he started up his own label that same year.[1]

The fashion industry then was nothing like the corporate giant it is today. The voracious buying spree for fashion brands, acquired for the luxury market, which was spear-headed by LVMH (Moët Hennessy Louis Vuitton) with the Gucci Group[2] hot on its heels, had yet to take hold. With British designers such as John Galliano and Vivienne Westwood now showing in Paris, London was ripe for an injection of new blood. And McQueen, at the forefront of

a generation of young, hopeful, independent names, gave the fashion industry everything it could possibly have wished for – and more.

Aesthetically, McQueen's work exemplified little, if anything, that chimed with the prevailing mood. Prada had launched its women's ready-to-wear in Milan in the late 1980s, upholding a minimal point-of-view rooted in uniformity. In Paris, Helmut Lang's equally pared down, androgynous look was the most sought after (and copied) style of the era. By contrast, McQueen's first collection, *Taxi Driver* (Autumn/Winter 1993), shown in a suite at The Ritz hotel as part of what was then known as the London Collections, was remarkable for its fusion of history and craftsmanship with sheer anarchy. It showcased many of the signature traits with which McQueen would make his name.

Darkly romantic, uncompromisingly sharp-edged tailoring embellished with period ornamentation dominated 'a collection

A SENSE OF PLACE — THE EARLY YEARS

Previous spread
56. Ensemble, *The Birds*,
Spring/Summer 1995
Jacket and knickers with tyre tread print
Photograph by Neville Marriner

57. Alexander McQueen and his team,
London studio, 2000
Back row L-R: Jake Chapman, Dinos
Chapman, Kim Sion, Deepika Patel,
Jefferson Hack, Catherine Brickhill,
Leslie Johnson, Daniel Landin, Sidonie
Barton, Trino Verkade, Sarah Burton
(née Heard), Jenne Osterhoudt, David
Cooper, Isabella Blow. Centre row L-R:
Sam Taylor-Johnson (née Taylor-Wood),
Amie Witton-Wallace (née Witton),
Liberty Ross, Annabelle Neilson, Guido
Palau, Elsa-Mia Elphick, Sam Gainsbury,
John Gosling, Sarah Harmarnee, Anne
Deniau. Seated front L-R: Shaun Leane,
Val Garland, Andrew Heather. Pictured
with Alexander McQueen (far right), his
two dogs Juice and Minter
American *Vogue*, September 2000
Photograph by Annie Leibovitz

Above
58. Backstage, *The Birds*,
Spring/Summer 1995
Photograph by Gary Wallis

Left
59. Backstage, *Banshee*,
Autumn/Winter 1994
Photograph by Gary Wallis

designed solely around the female form [which], by the use of proportion, accentuated parts of the woman's anatomy to create a new shape,'[3] according to the accompanying press release. A black capelet was paired with an elongated gun-metal grey waistcoat and an exaggerated skater skirt, adorned with Victorian jet embroideries. The collar of a 'Scarlet Pimpernel' frock coat was encrusted with jewels. And there was a narrative, too, right from the start. The title, *Taxi Driver*, was a deliberate and typical curveball, referencing Martin Scorsese's film of the same name and (inevitably) the designer's own background, specifically the occupation of his father.

McQueen was living in a council flat in Tooting, with print and textile designer Simon Ungless, when he designed *Taxi Driver*. He had met and worked with Ungless at Central Saint Martins, and the latter was responsible for the print of Scorsese's anti-hero Travis Bickle, taken from a film still, that appeared on some of the clothes. 'Lee would work on the collection all day,' Ungless remembered. 'And I'd come home in the evening, take the kitchen door off its hinges, and turn it into a print table.'[4] Clothes were made out of everything – and anything – McQueen could get his hands on, including the flameproof lining of curtains, or latex bought from a local builders' supplier. Ungless often spent the weekend with his parents in the countryside where he grew up, and he would pluck the feathers from recently shot partridge and pheasant, and bring them back for McQueen – who applied them to neck- and hemlines. 'We didn't have any money,' Ungless continued. 'I came from a very similar background to Lee. I was freelancing to pay the rent, so we had to be resourceful with fabric. But I think we would have done that anyway. We wanted to do our own thing.'

None of this collection remains. It is nothing if not testimony to the free-spirited and iconoclastic beginnings of McQueen's career that, having packed the designs for *Taxi Driver* into black bin bags in order to show them to the fêted fashion editor Michael Roberts, the pair went out for a drink to celebrate and left the bags outside a bar in Soho – McQueen preferred not to pay to check them into the cloakroom. 'And then it [the collection] was lost,' said Ungless. But McQueen didn't care. He was already thinking about his next collection, *Nihilism* (Spring/Summer 1994). This was also made in Tooting and marked another signature development in McQueen's fashion career. A black glitter bodice, featured in that collection, was in fact the result of 'a happy accident'. Latex, which had been mistakenly kicked over, had fallen into a storm drain. When it was peeled off, it was found to have moulded itself to its receptacle. 'It made a beautiful shape.' And so the McQueen corset was born.

By this point, the designer had established a silhouette that was blatantly provocative and sexually charged, focusing on a cut-away coat or jacket and the 'bumster' trouser, which left the torso – from breast- to hip-bone – exposed.[5] A quarter of a century later, that line still resonates. Harnessing, too, made its entrance, as did softer fabrics and a more gentle, 'Josephine' line (pl.59). The character of McQueen's woman was emerging: she was, like her creator, at once fragile and fierce, ethereal and street-wise. And she wore clothes to match.

Janet Fischgrund was running the press office at Browns, the designer fashion store in South Molton Street, when she met McQueen in 1993. She was to work for him unofficially from that point onwards until she formally became his director of communications in 1997. Her employer, Joan Burstein, had her eye on the fledgling designer and instructed Fischgrund to seek him out. 'Mrs B had seen his degree show and she loved it,' Fischgrund said.[6] 'She wanted to put some of his work into the windows and asked me to "find that boy". And so I did, and from that moment he just assumed that I was doing his PR for him.' Like everyone who came across him in those early years, Fischgrund found it impossible to say 'no' to McQueen. 'You knew when you were working with him that you were witnessing magic,' she said. 'He was so engaging, so inspiring and so childlike in a way. He just pulled you in.' She was paid in clothes – everybody was. 'He gave me a green plastic dress because I helped him. It was so tight I couldn't walk in it. Or sit down. I just had to stand up the whole time. But so many people commented on that dress. It was amazing.'

The story of how McQueen met Katy England (pl.60), who was to become his most important collaborator, is the stuff of fashion folklore. McQueen had seen the *London Evening Standard* fashion editor at shows and liked the way she looked. In particular, a nurse's coat – strict to the point of severe – had captured his attention. Though extremely shy, it says something of the designer's ambition to succeed that he had the tenacity to approach the stylist nonetheless. That was in 1994. 'It was the outfits I wore that attracted him,' England said.[7] 'He knew my name from *ES Magazine*. He came up to me in the street one day and said, "Are you Katy England?" And I said, "Yes". And he said, "Will you style my show?" It was definitely an instinct.'

The first McQueen show England worked on was *The Birds* (Spring/Summer 1995). 'I didn't know how to style a show. I didn't know what it meant. Lee said, "Oh, it will be fine, we'll be fine, don't worry."' And so began a relationship that would deepen over a period of almost 15 years. 'We bought fabric from Berwick Street market and Brick Lane,' England continued. 'I'd go and see Lee and Jimmy Jumble [also known as Andrew Groves], and Lee would be there at the sewing machine. I remember having to feed them a bit, bring them a sandwich. Lee also did most of the fittings on me.' McQueen told the press that the subject of *The Birds* was road kill, hence the tyre print that marked the collection (pl.56). Made by rolling a spare car tyre in Indian ink, it was used initially as a screen print that was stamped over the clothes (courtesy of Ungless), and then, immediately prior to the show, it was used as a pattern across the models' bodies. The shoes were acquired at Oxfam, their uppers then removed and the soles bound to models' feet with Sellotape. The highly restrictive, pencil silhouette that characterized *The Birds* was inspired by actress Tippi Hedren's wardrobe in the Hitchcock film of the same name: her character's polished exterior, which barely masked an extreme vulnerability, was fascinating to McQueen.

The furore surrounding his next show, *Highland Rape* (Autumn/Winter 1995), made Alexander McQueen a household name.

60. Katy England, 1999
Photograph by Anne Deniau

Opposite
61. Backstage, *No.13*,
Spring/Summer 1999
Alexander McQueen and Shalom Harlow
Photograph by Anne Deniau

His business, however, remained very small. Yet he found the money to move into a basement in Hoxton Square in London's East End (he had been locked out of his previous studio for failing to pay the rent) and had by then gathered more women around him. Trino Verkade, his long-time assistant, and Sam Gainsbury, then a video director but soon to produce his shows, had both joined the fold. Verkade began working for McQueen full-time shortly before the *Highland Rape* show (indeed, it was her car's spare tyre that was used to create the screen print for *The Birds*). Prior to that she had been Katy England's assistant. 'I was still signing on [for social security benefits] at that time. And so was Lee,'[8] she said. 'Neither of us were making any money and there were times when I had to pay for bits and pieces myself. Often it was just Lee and me. Professionally he was very, very demanding. He never wanted anyone to say "no" to him. He always wanted us at least to try. We all learned that from Lee. We learned that we always had to try.'

The hype surrounding the designer was by now unprecedented. Even so, the show that followed, *The Hunger* (Spring/Summer 1996), was realised on a budget of only £600, a fraction of the five- and even six-figure sums that are regularly spent today. Sebastian Pons, a textiles student at Central Saint Martins who was introduced to McQueen by Simon Ungless, remembered starting work for McQueen immediately after the move to the new studio. 'At that time, Hoxton Square wasn't how it is today,'[9] Pons said. 'It was pretty scary, rough.' Yet it was increasingly a destination for young artists, drawn to the area for its relatively affordable commercial and living space. 'I get there,' Pons continued. 'I go down to the basement. And there's nothing there. Nothing at all. I thought I would find mannequins, sewing machines, cutting tables. But there's nothing. Just Lee, a packet of cigarettes and a few tables in boxes he'd bought from Ikea. Our first job was to put them together, so that's what we did.'

Without exception, all those who worked with McQueen during the period from 1992 to 1999 had the strong sense that they were privileged to be involved (pl.57). 'I'd seen *Highland Rape*,' Pons recalled. 'London was boring then but with McQueen you knew you were part of something new, something very exciting. Here was this guy, who not only showed clothes but also put emotion on the catwalk, whose own soul had been shaken by life and who knew how to shake people up because of that. I remember him making an S-bend spine out of clay on the studio floor, then coating it with rubber and attaching it to the open seam in the back of a jacket. I had no idea how it would turn out. I mean how do you bind rubber to wool? But I never questioned what he was doing. None of us did. He had this way of motivating people.'

Sam Gainsbury echoed Pons' sentiments. The more McQueen inspired admiration in his increasingly close-knit and protective team, the more they wanted to please him in return. 'Right from the beginning I knew I'd found someone who was incredibly special,'[10] said Gainsbury. 'There was more pressure by this time,' according to Katy England, now McQueen's creative director. 'There came a time when there were proper dates, when a collection had to be delivered at a certain time, and the deadline was looming and looming and looming. That would become increasingly stressful for Lee, and he'd start locking himself away.'

We wouldn't see him for a few days and then he would turn up with the most beautiful drawings. And he would show them to me and we'd pin them on the board and talk about them. And he'd want me to say: "Well, I'm not sure about that," or "I think that's amazing," which is strange when you think about it. I thought everything was amazing. I never wanted to say to somebody that creative, 'Don't do it.'"

In October 1996, McQueen was appointed chief designer of womenswear at Givenchy. 'When he said he was going to Givenchy,' recollected England, 'I said to him, "What do you mean? You've got your own company here, why would you want to do that?" He was definitely way ahead of me.' Sebastian Pons was now Lee's first assistant, working both in Paris on Givenchy shows and in London for McQueen's own label. 'I want you to be clever,' McQueen told him. 'I want you to see how it works and bring the information back.' According to Gainsbury, 'Givenchy took McQueen to a whole other level: the cut, the fabrication, the embroidery and the respect it afforded the company internationally. I think that was the point when everyone suddenly came to London to see the McQueen show. Because of the

extra funding, because Lee put all his wages back into it, things changed. He used Givenchy as a vehicle to finance McQueen.'

In March 1997, three months before a Labour government was voted into power for the first time in 18 years, *Vanity Fair* ran a story entitled (somewhat hysterically) 'Cool Britannia. London Swings! Again!' The cover of the British edition of the magazine featured music's most high-profile couple, Liam Gallagher and Patsy Kensit, lying on Union Jack printed pillows and bed cover: Britpop was taking the world by storm. The Royal Academy's *Sensation* exhibition – featuring the work of young British artists, such as 1995 Turner Prize winner Damien Hirst, from the Saatchi Collection – drew unprecedented crowds that same year. McQueen's models, meanwhile, were walking on water. *La Poupée* (Spring/Summer 1997), based around Hans Bellmer's surreal, pre-pubescent dolls (pl.292) and held in the Royal Horticultural Hall in Victoria, was his biggest show to date and attendance levels at the London collections had never been so high.

Katy England recalled, 'By then Lee felt much more strongly about the shows. He was like an artist presenting a dream, a story,

62. Dress, *No.13*, Spring/Summer 1999
Spray-painted cotton with silk underskirt
Modelled by Shalom Harlow
Photographs by Chris Moore

a performance. I don't think any of us really realized it at the time.' Added Janet Fischgrund, 'The shows meant so much more to him than they represented on paper. Really, he was way over somewhere else, where no one else was. The platform the shows gave him as an artist was enormous. Almost everything else became irrelevant … the message was all-important. Even if he knew that what he wanted made no financial sense, he would do it. For Lee it was all about the show at that point. I'm not sure people understand quite how passionate he was about that. The ideas were what were important to him. The clothes were a canvas in a way.'[11]

Sarah Burton had joined the company the year before and recalled commissioning the aluminium frame worn by model Debra Shaw for the finale of *La Poupée* from a metal worker in Brick Lane (pl.227). "Nothing was precious. [Lee] would use metal, rubber, foam, tubing, in just the same way as he would snakeskin or a silk jacquard, anything that was there. Now things are very edited down but it wasn't like that then. There were so many ideas and so much going on. It was about creativity and making things.'[12] Burton, too, believes that this period of McQueen's career was focused more than ever on the staging of the show. 'Of course, he cared about silhouette, about shape and pushing boundaries,' she said. 'But it was his message – so singular and yet so broad – that was key. I think he wanted to speak to a much wider audience than the people who came to the shows. That's why he loved the wide-angle images in the papers the next day. It wasn't about a collection the way we see it now. It wasn't driven by commerce. And I don't think it felt like fashion either, in the sense in which it exists now. Instead, it was about how he was feeling at the time.'

Of all McQueen's London shows, *No.13* (Spring/Summer 1999) was his most ambitious, in terms of both staging and clothes. McQueen had been introduced to double amputee and Paralympic champion, Aimee Mullins, and had featured her on the cover of the September 1998 issue of *Dazed & Confused* that he had guest-edited (pl.289). Mullins had shared with him her ambition to walk in a fashion show. From there, *No.13* evolved to include models revolving like music-box dolls, on raw wooden discs inlaid into a square runway. They were dressed in the most feminine, liquid draped jersey; signature, ultra-sharp silver-grey tailoring; asymmetric lace dresses, layered over trousers; and metal mesh designs seemingly as delicate as a butterfly's wing. There was an orthopaedic look to both clothing and footwear. Very few members of the audience realized, therefore, that when Mullins made her entrance, she was walking not in boots but on prosthetic legs of hand-carved ash, designed especially for her by McQueen (some of those present in fact asked if they could borrow the 'boots' for their forthcoming fashion editorials; pl.197). Even by McQueen's now hugely elevated standards, this was a tremendously sensitive and thought-provoking gesture. And as if that weren't enough, for the finale former ballerina Shalom Harlow (pl.61), dressed in an overblown, white strapless gown, turned and turned and turned again on the catwalk while a pair of seriously menacing robots, borrowed from a Fiat plant, sprayed her with acid-yellow and black car paint (pl.62). It was perhaps the most spectacular finale of his entire career.

No.13 was McQueen's favourite show. 'The high that followed when it had all gone to plan was incredible,' said Sam Gainsbury, who produced it. 'I don't think Lee thought we could pull it off at that time. We were all such amateurs. The fact that Shalom turned for exactly the right amount of time, that she didn't fall, that the robots sprayed her perfectly, that the lighting was just right … With that show, in particular, there was so much danger involved. But Lee gave you the courage, he gave *me* the courage. He would convince you. I will always remember running backstage afterwards, and everyone being there and saying: "Do you believe that? That was insane." Honestly, none of us could believe we'd actually done it.'

With *No.13*, the inventiveness, raw energy and layers of emotional and intellectual complexity that had characterized McQueen's work almost from the moment he began, reached a whole new level. The impact of his collections was such that on occasion he had brought his audience to the brink of tears. That was, more often or not, the desired effect after all. However, *No.13*, he told those lucky enough to work with him, was the only show that ever made the designer himself cry.

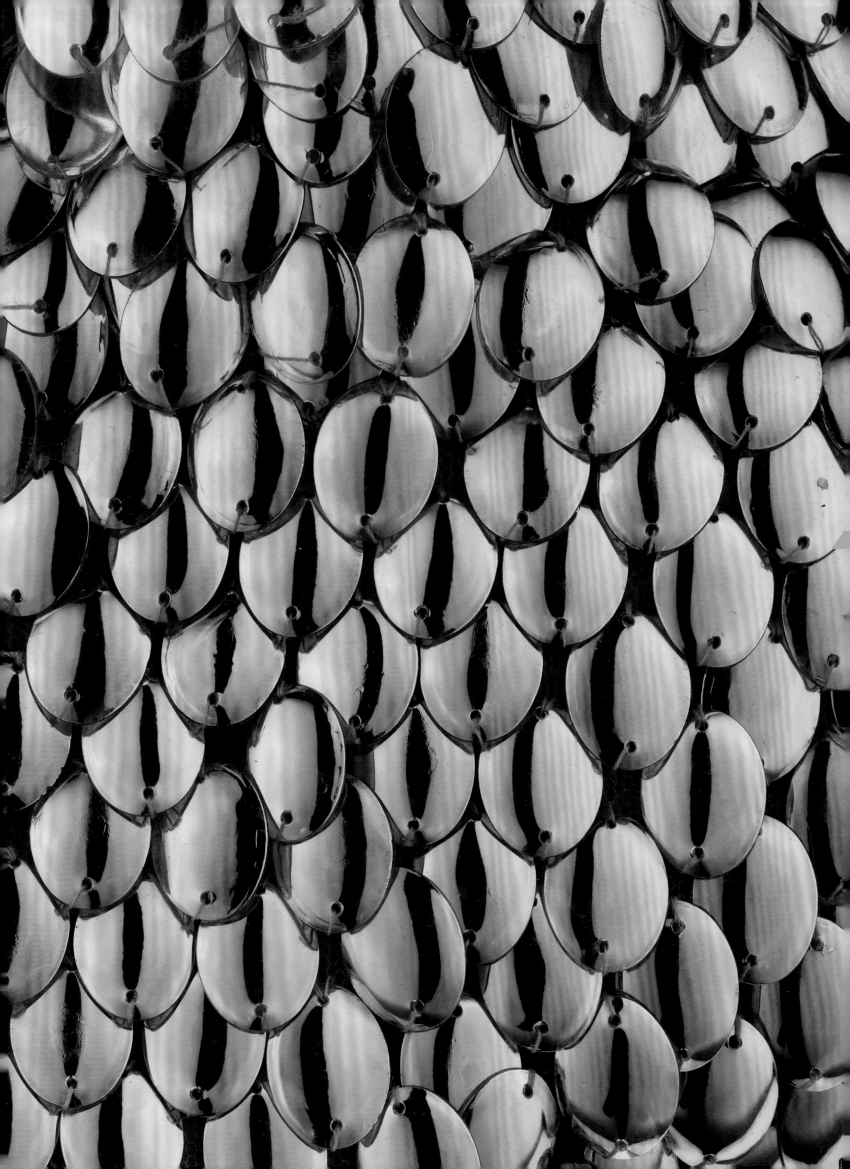

NO. 2

ARTISTRY

———

PLATO'S ATLANTIS

ANATOMY OF A COLLECTION

CLAIRE WILCOX

'Full fathom five thy father lies; / Of his bones are coral made; /
Those are pearls that were his eyes: / Nothing of him that doth fade
But doth suffer a sea change
Into something rich and strange'

WILLIAM SHAKESPEARE, *THE TEMPEST*, ACT 1 SCENE 2, 1610–11

McQueen's fascination with the elemental – earth, wind, fire and water – imbued his collections with primordial drama.[1] *Plato's Atlantis*, his last fully realized collection, was inspired by the story of the lost city of Atlantis, which according to the classical philosopher Plato was submerged following a volcanic eruption over 2,000 years ago. McQueen's Darwinian preoccupation with survival, in the face of rising seawater, offered an otherworldly narrative of adaptation on the part of the human race by reversion to an amphibian state. His exquisite digitally printed and engineered designs, corroded metallic embroidery and scale-like beading reflected this process of morphogenesis, as the garments mutated and disintegrated, finally transforming his army of replicants into a glistening new aquatic species.

Water had already featured in McQueen's collections, beginning with *La Poupée* (Spring/Summer 1997), in which models splashed through a watery catwalk. In *Untitled* (Spring/Summer 1998), Perspex rills beneath the runway were flooded with black ink,

followed by a deluge of yellow-lit rain that soaked the models to the skin, while *The Overlook* (Autumn/Winter 1999) featured frozen water in the form of ice and snow.

Water was where McQueen felt at home, from his early forays into synchronized swimming and taking part in galas at his local swimming club, Plaistow United, to later explorations, as an experienced scuba diver, of the coral reefs of the Maldives. His country home in Fairlight Cove, East Sussex, was situated moments from a shingle beach from which, on a calm day, France could be seen. McQueen said, 'I have an affinity with the sea, maybe because I'm Pisces. It's very calming'.[2] He was fascinated with fish, and avidly watched sea-life documentaries as well as visiting aquaria such as one at the Horniman Museum in south London, known for its collection of luminous pelagic jellyfish.[3] At home, he built fish tanks and adorned his chest with a tattoo of a Koi carp.[4] Isabella Blow observed of the blue-eyed McQueen, 'He was Poseidon and we were his mermaids.'[5]

Previous spread
64. 'Jellyfish' ensemble and
'Armadillo' boots, *Plato's Atlantis*,
Spring/Summer 2010
Dress and leggings: net,
sequins and paillettes
Modelled by Polina Kasina
Photograph by Anthea Simms

Opposite
65. Backstage, *Plato's Atlantis*,
Spring/Summer 2010
Jacket with enamel paillettes on
a mannequin
Photograph by Anne Deniau

66. Backstage, *Plato's Atlantis*,
Spring/Summer 2010
Models (from left) Alice Gibb, Heidi
Mount, Anya Kazakova, Kate Sommers
Photograph by Anne Deniau

Bronze (Black)
Silver
Gold.
Blue
Solar Panels
Wind Turbines

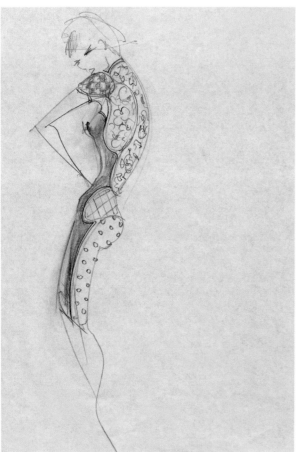

McQueen's oceanic preoccupations were also reflected through film, in both its still and moving forms. *Irere* (Spring/Summer 2003) began with an aquatic sequence directed by film-maker John Maybury. Here, a young woman plunged beneath the waves, entangled in the pale fronds of her chiffon dress, and appeared momentarily to drown before rising up again in a sea of bubbles. The scene recalled the drowning Ophelia in Shakespeare's *Hamlet*: 'Her clothes spread wide; And, mermaid-like, awhile they bore her up', before 'heavy with their drink' they pulled her under. The deathly property of water was alluded to in an advertising campaign for McQueen's Autumn/Winter 2002 collection, *Supercalifragilisticexpialidocious*, which situated a fashion model before a glass vitrine in which a lifeless body lay suspended in water, recalling Damien Hirst's formaldehyde-trapped life forms. Photographer Steven Klein captured McQueen jumping, fully clothed, into the tank following the shoot (pl.75). This watery fixation was echoed by the photographer Sølve Sundsbø's crystalline images of a mermaid-like model (pl.82), clothed in an iridescent body suit (the final look of *Plato's Atlantis*), taken for *Vogue Nippon* (2010).[6]

Plato's Atlantis was shown at the Palais Omnisports de Paris-Bercy on 6 October 2009. The show opened with a mesmerizing and discomfiting film, conceived by McQueen with Nick Knight and Ruth Hogben, which depicted a woman mutating into an aquatic creature (pl.72). It was punctuated with sweeping black fades that represented the passing of millennia, and accompanied by an unearthly sound track by John Gosling. The shoot, featuring Brazilian model Raquel Zimmermann, took place at Knight's studios at Park Royal.[7] McQueen had been determined to cast Zimmermann because of her powerful femininity yet willingness to help realise his vision. She lay prone in a sand-filled box and writhed in ecstasy as snakes slithered over her naked body although, once the filming had stopped, retched as she tried to disentangle them from her hair.[8] As if this was not enough, Zimmermann was then immersed in a water tank, filled with black eels. Throughout, digital prints from the collection were projected onto her body, transforming her into a semi-reptilian being, and culminated in the digital multiplication of first, the snakes, and then her body, in a series of fractals. The effect was that of an exquisite kaleidoscopic image, even Mandala-like, that suggested both the mechanized cogs of a machine and the birth of a hybrid species.

Setting the cold intelligence of the machine in opposition to the beauty and fragility of nature was a conceit typical of McQueen, first explored in *No.13* (Spring/Summer 1999) with the robotic defloration of Shalom Harlow's white dress. It was re-enacted in *Plato's Atlantis* through the prowling motion control cameras that tracked the models and also coldly surveyed the audience, projecting the entire spectacle onto a vast backdrop that became part of the phenomenon, just as the mirrored box in *Voss* (Spring/Summer 2001) had subverted the audience's role to become one of uncomfortable self-scrutiny. Nick Knight recalled that the cameras were programmed to swoop within inches of the models, 'like velociraptors',[9] but they had not taken into account the height of the extreme, backcombed and plaited fin-like shapes created by hair artist Guido (pl.73). Sam Gainsbury, the show producer, observed, 'Once you switched them on, they were unstoppable.'[10]

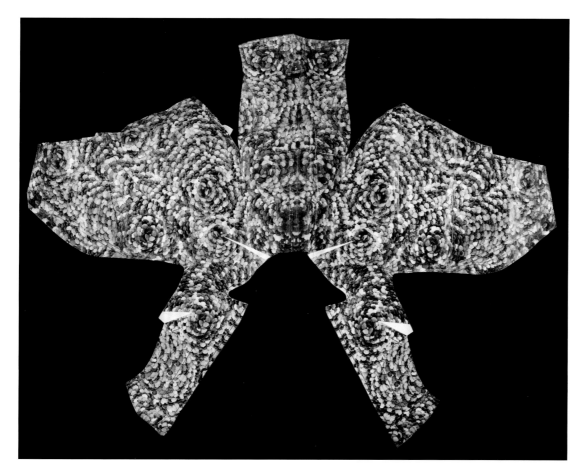

Opposite

67 and 68. Sketches, *Plato's Atlantis*,
Spring/Summer 2010
Pencil on paper, London, 2009
Courtesy of Alexander McQueen

69. Pattern, *Plato's Atlantis*,
Spring/Summer 2010
Digital print on paper, London, 2009
Courtesy of Alexander McQueen

McQueen's futuristic vision of the relationship between man, nature and machine may have drawn on science fiction films, such as *Tron* (Steven Lisberger, 1982), and the emergence of computer-generated imagery. One of the digital prints that McQueen designed was named 'Abyss' after the film of the same name directed by James Cameron (1989). Used to form the body and lining of a grey coat dress, the print emulates the watery form of the film's benevolent alien. Design practitioner Jane Harris explains that the 'computer-generated form, appearing as a nebulous, glass-like apparition from an underwater realm … its surface using very early 3D shader capability, both mimics and mirrors the characteristics of the subject that it faces … the mutating form appears as a combination of water and blown glass or mirror with a pulsing, violet blue glow'.[11] Stills from *The Abyss*, along with others of the molten-skinned cyborg in *Terminator 2, Judgment Day* (1991), accompany numerous images of reflective surfaces on the research boards with which the collection began: anamorphic figures wrapped in silvered cloth (pl.79), a mirrored mannequin, glass buildings reflecting the sky, solar panels and reflections in car wing mirrors, the resulting refractions and distortions perhaps a metaphor for McQueen's unique design eye.

The elemental spark for *Plato's Atlantis* appeared, as McQueen's ideas so often did, in a blaze of inspiration, on holiday with his friend and muse Annabelle Neilson. 'We were in Thailand when the idea came to him. Then he started drawing. He had drawn on several pages, but on four or five they were just drawings of a female form, lying there on the table … was this unbelievable drawing. It was there straight away. It was perfect. I remember thinking that show was like he had found a new canvas (pl.68).'[12] The drawing, carefully preserved in the McQueen archive, depicts an arching, humanoid figure, extenuated with a skin-tight, patterned garment. Neilson remarked later, 'Lee always knew when he had it and he had that look in his eyes. The drawing came to life on the catwalk and they [the garments] were exactly how he envisioned them on paper. It was his last collection.'[13] The photographer Anne Deniau, who documented his work for 13 years, described 'the silhouettes wandering, appearing backlit, like a visual echo to the essence, the first drawings, the lines. The "épure".'[14]

Yet McQueen had, over the years, drawn less, relying more on draping and working in the round, on a dress stand or, on his long-term Russian fit model, Polina Kasina, whose androgynous, neat physique remained his ideal (pl.77). Image after image records McQueen's painstaking work on the collection, with the ever-patient Kasina, framed by the research boards that accumulated as the collection developed, standing sometimes in the enormous hoof-like 'Armadillo' boots, at other times in incongruous high heels.[15] Deniau recalled, 'She worked for him for so long, she said she had his memory on her body.'[16]

As his head of womenswear design and long-time interlocutor, Sarah Burton would instruct the various design teams at McQueen on the themes he had in mind, and tell them what to research. 'Lee would sit here and stick Post-its in books from our studio library. For *Plato's Atlantis*, he said, "I want thousands of

70. Dress and 'Alien' shoes,
Plato's Atlantis, Spring/Summer 2010
Dress: wool and silk synthetic with
digital print; shoes: resin
Modelled by Hanne Gaby Odiele
Photograph by Chris Moore

Opposite
71. Pattern, *Plato's Atlantis*,
Spring/Summer 2010
Print and pencil on paper, London, 2009
Courtesy of Alexander McQueen

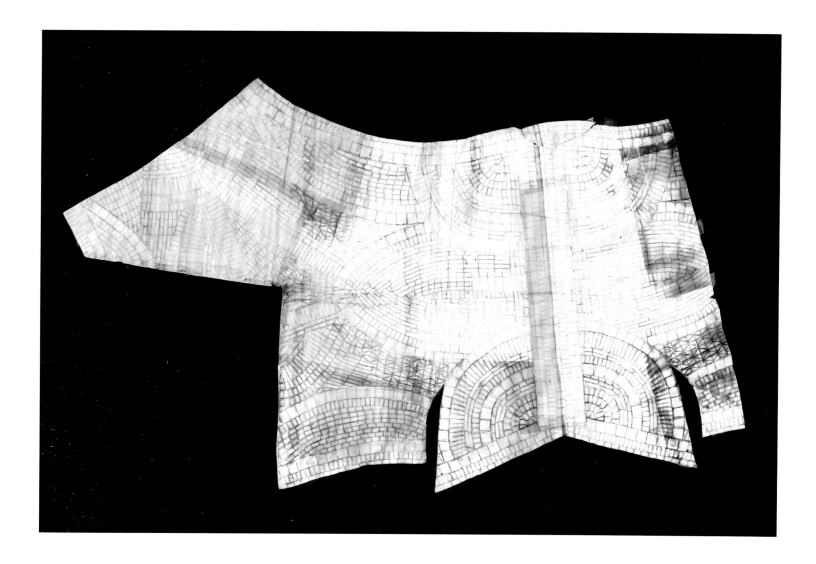

aerial views". Basically the world's surface from the sky – views of cities, oceans, mountains. I would delegate to each department, and he'd expect the results the next day. It had to be the next day because he was so immediate.'[17]

For *Plato's Atlantis*, very little fashion is evident on the boards apart from the odd Dior dress, and a Martin Margiela waistcoat. Instead, army camouflage clothing, jodhpurs and as always nineteenth-century dress, a constant presence in his collections, provided the inspiration for 'Moth' and 'Rose' camouflage prints, an all-in-one jockey suit and a silk taffeta half-dress with single 'Victorian' fringed sleeve and hip pannier. Far more prevalent were the reptiles, underwater sea creatures and tropical fish, in every hue and colour (pl.81). Even penguins featured, the curvature of their 'morning coats' an inspiration for the cut-away tailoring of the collection. Rusted, seaweed-covered shipwrecks led to verdigris neckpieces, riveted metal shoes, the 'Rusty' print used to form a skirt of fluttering chiffon ruffles (created from thousands of circles of fabric, in an age-old couture technique), which emulated aquatic movement, and McQueen's show-stopping 'Titanic' dress. Detailed, hand-drawn patterns, carefully preserved in the McQueen archive, 'map' its metallic mosaic surface, a gesture perhaps to Plato's 'gold and silver Temple of Atlantis, its walls coated with orichalcum' (pl.71).[18]

But just as McQueen eschewed drawings, he eventually abandoned the boards, too. Burton continued, 'When we were working on *Plato's Atlantis*, we turned all the research boards around so that there were just big pieces of printed fabric hanging on the wall (pl.80). Usually, his research boards consisted of an eclectic mix of images based around a specific theme. These images could reference nature, historical portraits, and the works of Old Masters and modern artists, historical fashions, and traditional and innovative fabric techniques. For *Plato's Atlantis*, he said, "I don't want to look at any shapes. I don't want to reference anything, a picture, a drawing. I want it all to be new." And he was completely right, because he then created something new, without a reference.'[19]

Although *Plato's Atlantis* was an exceptionally innovative collection it was foreshadowed by *Natural Dis-tinction Un-Natural Selection* (Spring/Summer 2009) ('Natural Selection' being the fourth chapter in Charles Darwin's *On the Origin of Species* [1859]). The collection featured short, draped dresses with boned bodices and panniered hips, constructed from intricate folds of fabric in symmetrical sepia prints, derived from raw materials such as wood-grain, granite and crystal. For *Plato's Atlantis*, however, the dresses became more complicated and the patterns emerged in a riot of colour, with mirror-image prints suggesting the thorax of a moth, the precise markings of a snake or the impressionistic depiction of a coral reef. Such vivid rendering was made possible by new graphics software, ink-jet printing and Photoshop, which offered an infinity of permutations, providing the opportunity to over-layer patterns of great complexity. As Burton explained, 'With *Plato's Atlantis*, Lee

[ever involved in every aspect of a collection] mastered how to weave, engineer, and print any digital image onto a garment so that all the pattern pieces matched up with the design on every seam.'[20]

The complexity of the garments, many created from a single length of fabric, folded and draped around the body, proved a challenge. It was also labour-intensive. Burton recalled, 'we scanned into the computer the patterns of the garments that Lee had draped. Then we would place the artwork onto these pattern pieces. It could be a print or a jacquard. Then we would print out the paper pattern in miniature with the artwork on it and stick it together to make a 3D garment. Towards the end, we'd have to make paper dolls of each outfit because his patterns were so complex to visualize. I did it so it would be easier for him to see. You had to work in a certain way with him, it was so visual.'[21]

The technical demands McQueen made on his studio were great. When the pattern changed – and hundreds of 'strike offs' were created before McQueen settled on one he liked – the artwork had to change as the print no longer matched up at the seams of the garment. This process was compounded by the varying properties of the materials used, from fragile chiffon, taffeta and organza to heavier woven jacquards, as well as the segueing together of different materials, such as jersey and mohair. *Fil coupé*, or 'cut thread' fabric, was particularly challenging. Its ability to transmute from a dense weave to a cobweb-like translucency imbued the garments with an ethereal quality and also affected the intensity of the prints, a factor that was exploited in several of the garments. Burton explained, 'For *Plato's Atlantis*, there were 36 prints altogether. They were circle-engineered to the body. By circle-engineered, I mean that the prints were based on a circle

72. Campaign image, *Plato's Atlantis*,
Spring/Summer 2010
Model: Raquel Zimmermann
Photograph by Nick Knight

shape that sat in the middle of a bolt of fabric. Not only did you have to place the print correctly, but also, for example, if a fabric went from opaque to sheer, Lee had to do that in the fitting ... His eye was so amazing he could drape an engineered print.'[22]

In addition to the exquisite, fluttering printed dresses that *Plato's Atlantis* was renowned for, the collection also included 'Stingray' jackets, skirts and leggings that resembled diving gear, rubberized jersey frock coats, and laser-cut leather detailing, all of which were demanding to render. However, the most challenging fabric of all was the expensive and fragile 'Schlaepfer' gauze,[23] from which the penultimate pieces for *Plato's Atlantis* were made in Paris at the very last minute (the entire studio would decamp to Paris in the days leading up to the show). Tops teamed with fish-scale sequin leggings, and dresses that enveloped the body in an ethereal

cloud, emulated the bioluminescent bloom of jellyfish. In order to manipulate and sculpt the gauze, McQueen's studio hand-stitched Vigilene threads onto the fabric in a flexible geometric grid that recalled the multiple views of solar panels and skyscrapers present on McQueen's research boards.[24] The final look of the collection, 'Neptune's Daughter', was created from a dress, leggings and 'Armadillo' boots covered entirely with large opalescent sequins (pl.64). The show notes described this 'hybrid' sea creature as capable of surviving 'without the use of manmade breathing apparatus'. The model was Polina Kasina.

Plato's Atlantis was widely considered to be McQueen's greatest achievement. The mixture of nature, technology and craft was a uniquely McQueen perspective, as was the showmanship, and the boldness of live-streaming the presentation on SHOWstudio for

73. Backstage, *Plato's Atlantis*,
Spring/Summer 2010
Dress: Schlaepfer fabric and plastic crin
Modelled by Yulia Lobova
Photograph by Anne Deniau

Opposite
74. Backstage, *Plato's Atlantis*,
Spring/Summer 2010
Photograph by Anne Deniau

Overleaf
75. Campaign image,
Autumn/Winter 2002
Alexander McQueen in a water tank
Photograph by Steven Klein

an audience of millions. The finale was set to the soundtrack of Lady Gaga's new single 'Bad Romance'. It was also a commercial success, justifying its production cost of close to one million pounds for a 17-minute show. The buyer for Harvey Nichols, said: 'This show was absolutely charismatic because it was so modern – every single one of those first twelve outfits that came out we are going to be buying. … it's inspiring and visionary … you leave here thinking, "I know why I'm in fashion".'[25] *Plato's Atlantis* comprised 45 outfits, as detailed in the 'look book' that was provided with every collection for buyers (pl.76). Fifteen of the more complicated, bespoke pieces were 'show only', that is, not suitable for commercial production. This also included the majority of the 'Armadillos' and the H.R. Giger-inspired, 3D-printed 'Alien' footwear. Notably, the 30 commercially produced pieces were made in Italy in the same expensive fabrics as the show collection, maintaining the sumptuous qualities of McQueen's fashion, even for ready-to-wear.

Fashion has the ability to operate on many different levels and nowhere is this more evident than in the work of Alexander McQueen. On the one hand, his collections functioned as the perfect fashion trope – new, startling and temporarily desirable. But on the other, his investment in terms of craft and his achievement in terms of a timeless kind of beauty belied the

norms of fashion. As he said, his desire was to create museum pieces of the future. But McQueen's fashion also had a mimetic quality and his collections often carried a subliminal meaning in their expression of his own, sometimes troubled, psyche. He often referred to his collections as a form of therapy.

McQueen said that *The Horn of Plenty* (Autumn/Winter 2009) – a savage satire on the fashion industry that preceded *Plato's Atlantis* – was his last collection as a young man. How strange that his first as a grown man should also be his last. An apt metaphor for McQueen's art is perhaps offered by the medium with which he so strongly identified. Water as a symbol of the unconscious, as a place of darkness, but also the source of new life, is recognized in many cultures. It is implicit in the Buddhist faith, observed to a degree by McQueen in his last years, in which fish are said to represent the freedom of the enlightened state, in that they can swim wherever they like in water, and in any direction.[26] As in *The Abyss*, where the alien imbues the film's protagonist with the power to breathe underwater and inspires his spiritual awakening, deep below the sea, McQueen experienced the dichotomy of immersion in fashion as perilous but also creatively fulfilling: 'Sometimes I feel like I am drowning but then again I've always felt peace and quiet under the ocean with me, myself and I.'[27]

Previous spread
76. Look book, *Plato's Atlantis*,
Spring/Summer 2010
Photographs by Chris Moore

77. Fittings for *Plato's Atlantis*,
Spring/Summer 2010
Clerkenwell Road studio, London, 2009
Modelled by Polina Kasina
Courtesy of Alexander McQueen

Opposite
78. Research board, *Plato's Atlantis*,
Spring/Summer 2010
Courtesy of Alexander McQueen

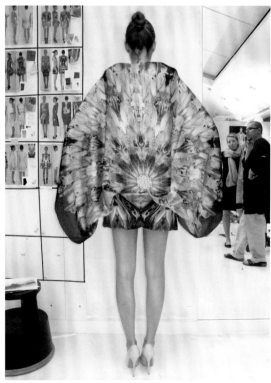

Opposite
79. Research board, *Plato's Atlantis*,
Spring/Summer 2010
Courtesy of Alexander McQueen

Above left
80. Research board with fabric samples,
Plato's Atlantis, Spring/Summer 2010
Courtesy of Alexander McQueen

Above right
81. Research board, *Plato's Atlantis*,
Spring/Summer 2010
Courtesy of Alexander McQueen

Overleaf
82. 'The Girl From Atlantis'
Vogue Nippon, May 2010
Modelled by Alla Kostromichova
Photograph by Sølve Sundsbø

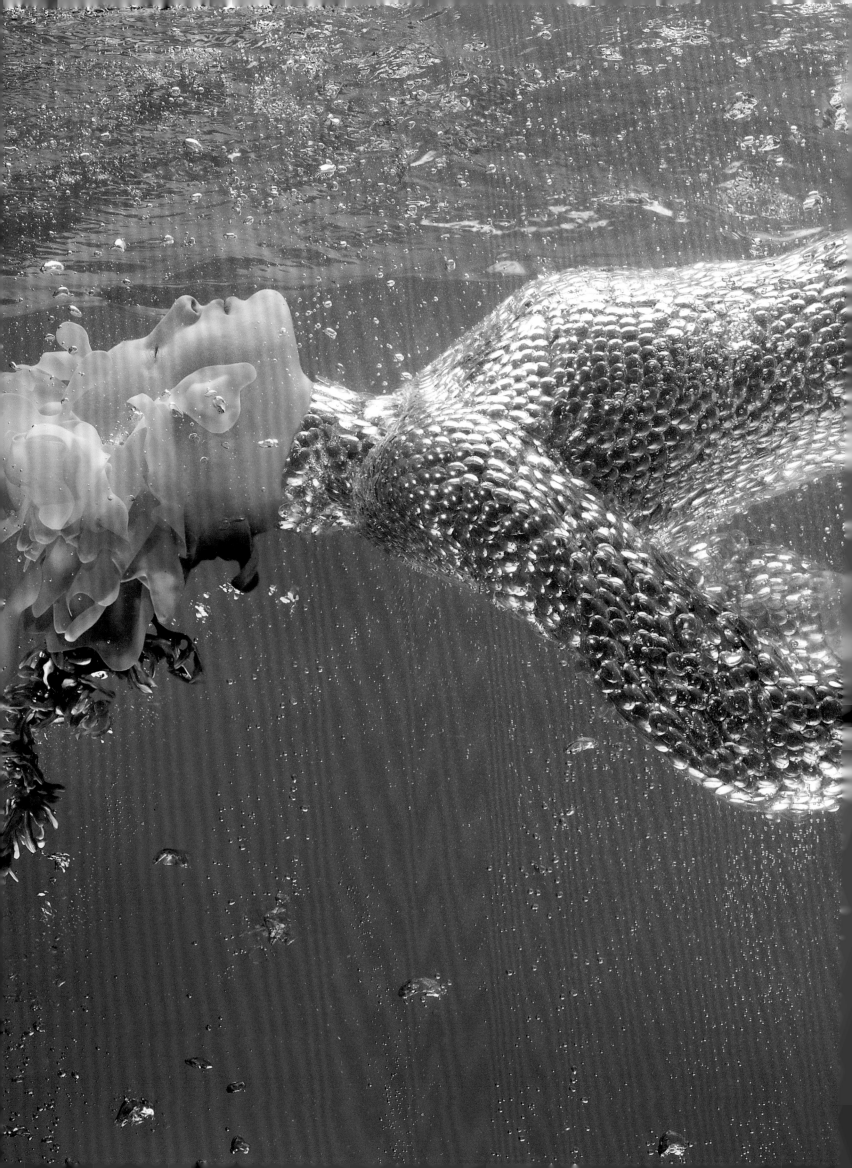

GIVENCHY

EDWINA EHRMAN

———

'Isn't a couturier a magician of sorts, who creates
illusion and perhaps beauty itself?'
Hubert de Givenchy, 1991

—

On 14 October 1996 Möet Hennessy · Louis Vuitton (LVMH) appointed Alexander McQueen as chief designer of womenswear at Givenchy following the departure of John Galliano to Dior. McQueen's truculent reputation and often morbid aesthetic were in stark contrast to Givenchy's image of polite, moneyed refinement. Yet, even before his contract was confirmed, the potential for conflict was generating the press interest that LVMH was seeking in order to attract younger customers. McQueen was not granted overall creative control, but in spite of this and other misgivings he recognized the opportunity the role offered: 'Couture is beyond beyond. It is where the dreams of your life in fashion become reality'.[1]

In his studio at Givenchy, to which the management rarely ventured, McQueen worked with a young British team. It included stylist Katy England, set designer Simon Costin and design assistants Sebastian Pons and Catherine Brickhill. Loud music and banter alternated with focused research and disciplined, demanding experimentation. McQueen talked about 'attacking the design'. 'I want people to make mistakes because something brilliant will evolve. You have to break the codes.'[2] While the design process stimulated and fulfilled him intellectually, he was also absorbed by the practice of working with garments on the body (pl.87).

McQueen's most valuable experience at Givenchy was working with the atelier. 'Working in the atelier was fundamental to my career … Because I was a tailor, I didn't totally understand softness, or lightness. I learned lightness at Givenchy. I was a tailor at Savile Row. At Givenchy I learned to soften. For me, it was an education. As a designer I could have left it behind. But working at

Givenchy helped me learn my craft'.[3] Already a highly skilled tailor, he learned to combine this knowledge with *le flou* (dressmaking). McQueen's couture collection for Spring/Summer 1998, which was dedicated to his customers and inspired by the Orient, demonstrated this fusion. Staged within the calm serenity of a Japanese garden at the Arche de la Défense, Paris, the garments combined the qualities of both '*le flou*' and '*le tailleur*' workshops in both their drapery and structure (pls 86, 88). At the show's close, the designer took his bow alongside the head tailor and chief fitter gracefully acknowledging their importance. This respect for the atelier artisans was reinforced in a later show where he listed all 115 of Givenchy's work force in the programme notes.

Givenchy's budgets also enabled McQueen to work with Paris's world-renowned craft workshops and a range of exotic materials. André Lemarié, the *plumassier* ('one who prepares feathers'), played a key role in Givenchy's *Eclect Dissect* collection (Autumn/Winter 1997). The show followed a fictional surgeon and collector, who travelled the world collecting exotic objects and women, whom he murdered, took apart and reassembled in his laboratory. The melodramatic stage set incorporated caged live crows and many garments featured bird parts and feathers. Against this macabre backdrop appeared a model dressed in a blue kimono, her head wrapped in a filmy web of quivering feather tendrils. McQueen admitted that it was difficult to know when to stop because the workrooms could make 'every dream I had a reality', but these experiments with feather, fur, skins and leather were invaluable in extending his design capability.[4] Complex designs in lace were also now made

Previous spread
83. Dress, *Eclect Dissect*, Givenchy Haute
Couture, Autumn/Winter 1997
Photograph by Chris Moore

Above
84. Ensemble, Givenchy Haute Couture,
Autumn/Winter 1998
Photograph by Chris Moore

Below
85. Show rehearsal, Givenchy Haute
Couture, Autumn/Winter 1999
Paris, 1999
Photograph by Anne Deniau

Opposite
86. *The Japanese Garden*, Givenchy
Haute Couture, Spring/Summer, 1998
Paris, 1997
Photograph by Anne Deniau

possible. At the end of Givenchy's Autumn/Winter 1998 show, McQueen, in a nod to tradition, joined the lace-clad 'bride' on the catwalk. But this was no conventional bride, rather a peacock, strutting in low slung trousers and flaunting her exquisite 'tail' of tiered lace, her neck elongated by a high-standing collar, her eyes and brow masked (pl.84).

The subjects of McQueen's shows for Givenchy were diverse. Staged as a gently mocking pantomime, the Spring/Summer 1999 show was set in an imaginary turn-of-the-century French village, watched over by Harlequin and inhabited by characters such as the Nun, the Maid, the School Mistress and the Ribbon-maker, whose ensemble featured some 1000 metres of rainbow-coloured, latticed ribbonwork that showed off the skills of the Givenchy atelier to the full.

The challenging Autumn/Winter 1999 collection was informed by Paul Delaroche's well-known painting *The Execution of Lady Jane Grey* (1833), a dramatic and emotive reconstruction of the death in 1554 of the 'nine days queen'. Its narrative – the story of a manipulated, abused young woman condemned to a brutal end by the machinations of her power hungry father-in-law – has thematic similarities with other McQueen collections that explore female martyrdom, such as *Joan* (Autumn/Winter 1998). The presentation was eerie: the clothes were displayed on fibreglass dummies with glowing heads, suggestive of the last embers of life, which rose on elevators through traps before revolving and descending into the 'hell' below the stage (pl.85).[5] An exquisite chiffon layered dress directly relates to Delaroche's painting while other designs made more general

reference to the period. McQueen explained afterwards that he had presented the collection as an art installation because 'haute couture is as close to art as fashion gets'.[6] Delaroche's masterpiece and couture share the quality of high finish. Both are painstakingly executed and demonstrate the artist's/designer's superb technique and ability to explore ideas and convey emotion.

By 2000 McQueen's maverick shows, reckless extravagance and antagonism were causing concern with the company. McQueen was equally frustrated, though his Spring/Summer 2000 collection was widely praised for its restraint and the designer's maturing signature style. He felt isolated and thwarted and asked, unsuccessfully, to be released from his contract. Eventually, following his sale of 51 per cent of his own business to the Gucci Group in December 2000, his employment with Givenchy was terminated in 2001. For McQueen things had gone wrong from the start. 'Every time I'd be doing what I was doing, they'd have a different idea instead of letting me stick to my path, [my] illusion. You have to stick to that illusion, then it becomes identifiable especially for a house that did not have an image apart from Audrey Hepburn.'[7]

While McQueen may have put Givenchy back in the limelight, albeit through headlines of a less than desirable kind, fashion journalist Suzy Menkes noted the impact of McQueen's exposure to couture on his own Spring/Summer 1999 collection, *No.13*. 'McQueen captured the raw aggression of Britpop and all the swaggering showmanship of the art scene. But the news was in his sweet, romantic side … The combination of hard/soft, salon/street and Anglo/French was a winner'.[8]

WALKING OUT

HELEN PERSSON

*'You have a curious way of arousing one's imagination, stimulating
all one's nerves, and making one's pulses beat faster ... Your ideal
is a daring courtesan of genius'*
Leopold von Sacher-Masoch, *Venus in Furs*, 1870

—

For McQueen, the allure of shoe styles from other cultures and periods of history lay in their transformative capacity. One extreme form of footwear, which informed the haute couture collection for Givenchy, *Eclect Dissect* (Autumn/Winter 1997), was the chopine. Fashionable from the late fifteenth to the early seventeenth century, especially in Venice, this pedestal-like shoe was both practical and symbolic. It protected the feet from wet streets and also signified the status of the wearer. Transformed into towering figures, Venetian noblewomen were sometimes completely destabilized by their precarious footwear. The chopine denoted wealth and privilege, but also had sexual allure. Lorenzo Lotto's painting *Susannah and the Elders* (1517) places Susannah's green chopines at the centre of the composition, further emphasizing her irresistible charm (pl.91). McQueen's versions, with their tightly fitting ankle straps, were scattered with crystals or decorated with Chinese dragons curling around their leather-covered wooden platforms, which were over 20 cm high.[1] By combining them with a concoction of traditional Mongolian hairstyles, Spanish lace, eighteenth-century-style hooped skirts and Burmese neckpieces, McQueen created a unique blend of futuristic orientalism.

Eastern traditions were clearly an inspiration for many of Alexander McQueen's footwear designs. The tall double-heeled backless shoes featured in *La Dame Bleue* (Spring/Summer 2008) derived from the geta, a form of traditional Japanese footwear. Worn by both women and men with clothing such as the kimono, one form of geta consists of a wooden base, elevated by two wooden blocks or 'teeth' and held onto the foot with a fabric thong (pl.90). The more spectacular examples were richly decorated and could reach a height of 30 cm. As with the chopine, and the equally vertiginous footwear of elite Manchu women in China's Qing dynasty (1644–1911), wearing the high geta altered the deportment and gait, slowing down movement – and allowing the viewer to take a closer look at the wearer's beauty and luxurious clothing. For *La Dame Bleue* McQueen paired his footwear designs with cheongsam-style dresses, given angular hips and pointed shoulders, while in *The Horn of Plenty* (Autumn/Winter 2009), they accompanied sharp houndstooth suits and harlequin leather outfits (pls 89, 93).

Asia not only provided inspiration for towering footwear. *The Girl Who Lived in the Tree* (Autumn/Winter 2008) featured delicate flat pumps with elongated toes, which were paired with long, crinoline-shaped skirts and regal jewellery. McQueen had earlier visited India, and influenced by its colours, shape and mood[2] he created jewel-like footwear. These were in the spirit of the French luxury shoe designer Roger Vivier's heavily embroidered and bead encrusted shoes designed for Christian Dior in the 1950s (p.319).

McQueen's most celebrated footwear creation, the 30 cm high 'Armadillo' boot from *Plato's Atlantis* (Spring/Summer 2010), combined a claw-like menace with the beauty of a ballerina's *en pointe* (pl.95). Performance pieces on the world's catwalk, in keeping with McQueen's love of theatricality, the boots appeared utterly futuristic. However, the exaggerated silhouette of the 'Armadillo' does have a historical precedent in the extraordinary form of sixteenth-century Persian riding boots which, with their rounded vamp (ending in a slight upturned toe), and inward curved heel were designed to facilitate a secure fit in the stirrup. Furthermore, Persian riding footwear was made of shagreen, the raw hide of horse or wild ass, dyed green and prepared with small indentations over the surface, which was reminiscent of one of the more reptilian versions of the 'Armadillo'. Others were wrapped in a single piece of leather or python skin, embellished with rusted sequins or clad in iridescent paillettes.

Each pair of 'Armadillos' was individually made. The wooden base was first carved and then attached to the heel and the insole board construction. The lining and the upper had to be lasted individually and therefore required four zips (two for the lining and two for the upper) to allow access for the foot.[3] The exaggerated platform is not lightweight and could have been challenging to walk in. However, a 'build out', or bulge, above the toes enabled the model to lift the boot more easily when walking, as clearly annotated on McQueen's design sketch (pl.94). Three models from the catwalk line-up nevertheless refused to wear them. They were perhaps right to be cautious for the 'Armadillo', in typical McQueen fashion, had pushed the boundaries of the traditional shoe shape.[4] No longer shoes in the conventional sense, they had become an organic part of the wearer.

Previous spread
89. Rope-tie chopines, *The Horn of Plenty*,
Autumn/Winter 2009
Leather and feathers
Photograph by Anne Deniau

Opposite left
90. Japanese woman wearing geta
Hand-coloured photograph in Felice
Beato, *Views of Japan*, 1868
V&A: 357-1918

Opposite above right
91. Detail, *Susanna and the Elders*,
Lorenzo Lotto, 1517
Oil on panel
Uffizi Gallery, Florence

Opposite below right
92. Young woman wearing bath clogs,
Damascus, nineteenth century
Hand-coloured photograph in *Costumes:
Egypt, Jerusalem, Syria etc*, sold by
Varroquier A & Co.
V&A: 45.046

93. Chopine boots, *The Horn of Plenty*,
Autumn/Winter 2009
Leather with dog-tooth print

113

94. 'Armadillo' boot sketch,
Plato's Atlantis, Spring/Summer 2010
Pencil on paper, London, 2009
Courtesy of Alexander McQueen

Opposite
95. Daphne Guinness wearing
'Armadillo' boots
Italian *Vogue*, February 2010
Photograph by Steven Meisel

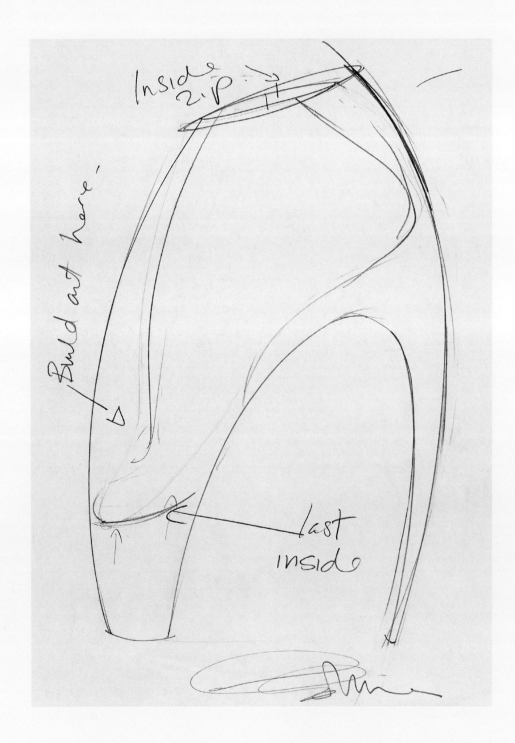

REFASHIONING JAPAN

ANNA JACKSON

———

*'Fashion can be really racist, looking at the clothes of other
cultures as costumes.... That's mundane and it's old hat.
Let's break down some barriers'*
Alexander McQueen, 2004

—

Within Alexander McQueen's mental storeroom of material culture, from which he drew such constant yet unpredictable inspiration, the fabric of Japan had a substantial presence. The country's textile history is indeed a fertile one, the main focus of artistic expression and sartorial attention being the kimono, which from the sixteenth century became the principal item of dress for both sexes and all classes.[1] Kimono are straight-seamed garments constructed with minimal cutting from a single bolt of cloth, worn wrapped around the body and secured with a waist sash called an obi. This conception and creation of clothing, which is so unlike that of the West, is born of a different notion about the relationship between dress and the body. While Western aesthetics have tended to emphasize the wearer's shape, kimono serve to lessen its presence. As a result of its standard form, the kimono is often viewed as a simple, unchanging garment, but this is not the case. In Japanese dress, the surface is the significant site of meaning and it is through colour and pattern that a wearer expresses their gender, age, wealth, status, taste and cultural sensitivities. In the sophisticated cities of the Edo period (1615–1868), a vibrant fashion culture existed within a 'floating world' of entertainment, excitement, glamour and eroticism. Courtesans were major trendsetters and woodblock prints reveal the importance of their dress and the complexity of wearing the many layers of lavishly decorated kimono with obi, high geta (shoes) and extravagant hairpins (pl.99).[2]

Textiles and dress have always played a vital role in the political and cultural encounter between Japan and Europe. After Japan was forced to open its ports to foreign powers in the mid-nineteenth century, the Western fascination for kimono became particularly pronounced. A signifier of exoticism and modernity, Japanese dress became a key ingredient of the aestheticized interior and had a radical impact on Western fashion. A century on, the influence remains strong, but can often seem mere pastiche; a frisson of the 'exotic' to add novelty to the catwalk. But in the mind and hands of McQueen something far more interesting and transformative occurred.

Japanese screens with embroidered panels were fashionable items in European homes at the turn of the last century and it was just such an object, bought by McQueen at Clignancourt flea market in Paris, which the designer utilized in a remarkable dress for the *Voss* (Spring/Summer 2001) collection (pl.96). The delicate panels, richly embroidered with flowers and birds, were removed from the screen and, without being re-shaped in any way, used flat over an underdress of polished oyster shells. The original Japanese design and craftsmanship was thus preserved yet metamorphosed into a piece of unexpected visual and tactile juxtapositions.

The subject matter, stitches and even faded colours of the panel embroidery directly inspired that used on another extraordinary ensemble in the *Voss* collection (pl.98). The elaborate construction of this piece is in direct contrast to the unfitted kimono, and the overall form bears little comparison. Yet in its rejection of natural body shape, flat expanses, elaborate sleeves, constricting wrap style and overpowering headpiece, the ensemble reveals some of the elements McQueen absorbed from his understanding of Japanese dress and how he transfigured them into something uniquely his own.

The referencing of kimono form and styles can be seen in much of McQueen's work, whether in elaborate embroidery, elongated sleeves, obi-like waist devices or v-shaped collars drawn back from the body – in the style of Edo-period courtesans – to reveal the nape of the neck, which in Japan is considered the most erogenous zone. Such features can be seen in the dramatic coat and kimono-like jackets featured in the *Scanners* collection (Autumn/Winter 2003) (pl.100); and in *It's Only a Game* (Spring/Summer 2005), which was conceived in the form of a chess match between Japan and America (pl.232). This is kimono not as exotic costume but as creative translation, which knows no barriers.

Previous spread

96. Ensemble, *Voss*,
Spring/Summer 2001
Overdress: panels from an embroidered
nineteenth-century Japanese silk screen;
underdress: oyster shells
Shoulder piece, Shaun Leane
for Alexander McQueen
Silver and Tahitian pearls
Modelled by Karen Elson
Photograph by Chris Moore

97. Ensemble, *It's Only a Game*,
Spring/Summer 2005
Dress and obi-style sash: silk; jacket:
silk and synthetic embroidered with
silk thread
'Chinese Garden' headpiece,
Philip Treacy for Alexander McQueen
Cork
Modelled by Gemma Ward

Opposite left

98. Ensemble, *Voss*,
Spring/Summer 2001
Coat: birdseye cotton embroidered
with silk thread; headpiece: birdseye
cotton embroidered with silk thread and
decorated with amaranthus
Modelled by Laura Morgan
Photograph by Victor Virgile

Opposite right

99. Keisai Eisen, Parading courtesan
in kimono and obi, Japan, 1830–40
Woodblock print
V&A: E.1904-1886

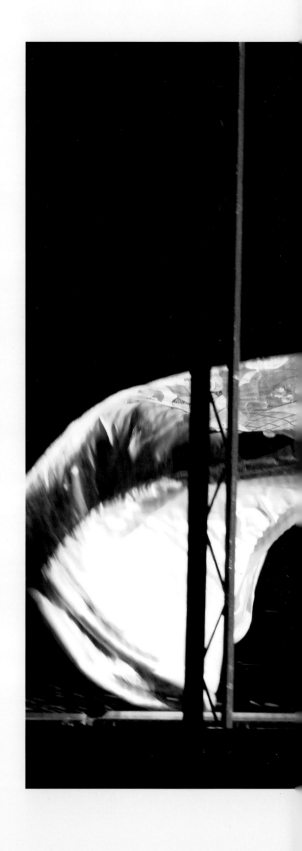

100. *Scanners*,
Autumn/Winter 2003
Kimono: embroidered silk; knickers:
cotton and synthetic; boots:
leather and synthetic
Modelled by Ai Tominaga
Photograph by Anthea Simms

NATURE BOY

JONATHAN FAIERS

'... wherever there is multiplicity, you will also find an exceptional individual, and it is with that individual that an alliance must be made in order to become–animal. There may be no such thing as a lone wolf, but there is a leader of the pack, a master of the pack...'

GILLES DELEUZE AND FÉLIX GUATTARI, *A THOUSAND PLATEAUS*, 1992

The inspiration Alexander McQueen drew from the natural world is apparent throughout his work. Whether it was the remoteness of the Scottish landscape, the depths of the ocean, the tactile frisson of bone and horsehair or the fragile complexity of a butterfly's wing, nature provided endless stimulation to his creative talents. Biographical details reveal his obsession with nature: his adolescent forays into bird watching and swimming, his later love of scuba diving, the tanks full of exotic fish that he installed in London and Paris, and his passion for the Discovery Channel and nature documentaries, such as David Attenborough's *The Blue Planet*. Nestling alongside the expected books on fashion, costume, painting and photography that still form part of McQueen's working library are collections of *National Geographic* magazine, volumes on birds and beetles, Eadweard Muybridge's explorations of animal locomotion (pl.116), Ernst Haeckel's depiction of art forms in nature (pl.114) and Peter Beard's accounts of big game hunting in Africa. A telling selection that betrays a decidedly ambivalent relationship

to the natural world, simultaneously in awe of its beauty, fascinated by its strangeness and seduced by its cruelty.

Attempts to understand this fascination have led to the construction of McQueen as a latter-day nineteenth-century enthusiast, part collector and part Romantic, communing with nature at its most sublime. This image goes some way towards explaining the extraordinary diversity of references to the natural world that characterize McQueen's work. However, when the garments themselves are considered, any finite context or account of their genesis seems inadequate, faced with their complexity and bewildering hybridity. On one level, McQueen was an artist who translated his love of the natural world into fashion; on another, his clothes can be interpreted as moments of 'becoming', becoming-animal, becoming-multiple, becoming-molecular. These concepts were originally formulated by philosopher Gilles Deleuze and psychoanalyst Félix Guattari in their work *A Thousand Plateaus* (1992). Drawing on biology and geology they proposed a revolutionary way of thinking about existence, where individuals are liberated from fixed identities and through a process of constant repositioning become nomadic. McQueen's ability to combine often startlingly different elements follows this process, so that his designs are never simple assemblages but rather a series of possibilities produced by an act of becoming-McQueen. As Deleuze and Guattari suggest, 'What is real is the becoming itself, the block of becoming, not the supposedly fixed terms through which that which becomes passes.'[1]

McQueen overtly paid tribute to nature and the natural world in *It's a Jungle Out There* (Autumn/Winter 1997), citing the African mammal, Thomson's Gazelle, as his principal inspiration. To McQueen, the gazelle was the 'food chain of Africa', and he drew an analogy between it and human life. A leather bodysuit (pl.102), featuring taxidermied baby crocodile heads nestling against the stand-up collar, appears at first to be an amalgam of reptilian and mammalian elements, evoking the predatory seductions of Africa,

the hunter and its prey, and the ever-present battle between life and violent death. But this bodysuit resists easy interpretation; the heads are obviously, almost crudely, lashed to the shoulders of the bodice, and rather than rendering the wearer part-crocodile, they act as a sign of the true process of 'becoming' that takes place elsewhere on the garment. Creeping across the back and front of the suit are vulva-like protuberances of chocolate leather, fleshy, plump and in a process of division. These suggest, at a molecular level, the armour plating that will develop on the adult crocodile, osteoderms formed of bony deposits that will act as protection. Caught midway between ossification and something more mammalian and fleshy, the swellings recede towards the lower section of the bodysuit where, instead of the expected opening at the crotch, the leather is sutured to frayed, bleached denim 'shorts' in an act of vestimentary deception. The bodysuit encapsulates a moment of becoming-crocodile, becoming-woman, becoming-denim and becoming-African, signalled in its use of an indigenous species and the reference to the globalization of distressed denim.

From the same collection, a ponyskin jacket with impala horns (pl.103) enacts a similar moment of spectacular 'becoming', masking an underlying conceptual and symbolic process, one of becoming-primitive, becoming-refined. The jacket's horns erupt violently from the shoulders, thrusting out of the body of the wearer in an evocation of the hybrid, evolving dog-becomings of John Carpenter's film *The Thing* (1982). The horns rip through the ponyskin, skin that emulates the impala's own hide, re-enacting a scene of auto-destruction. Inside, the jacket reveals a much more lasting act, that of becoming-civilized, becoming-refined. The process is signalled by the painstakingly cut and sewn silk satin lining, which belies the crudeness of the skin's assemblage and provides an interior dialogue between Western tailoring techniques and 'barbaric' outer skin. The skills McQueen learnt as an apprentice on Savile Row are here used as weaponry to coerce and constrain the unruly hide into the nipped and structured silhouette of a Victorian explorer. The multiplicities of becoming-savage, featured in *It's a Jungle Out There*, give way elsewhere in the collection, in a perfect example of McQueen's eclecticism, to a much more subtle use of the idiom of couture itself as expressive of evolution and transformation.

Couture techniques such as the imbrication of beading and hair are used to great effect for the dress featured in *Eshu* (Autumn/Winter 2000). As the yellow beaded bodice morphs into its horsehair skirt, small encrustations of beads are caught, clinging to the coarse strands of hair, like decorative head lice (pl.104). These sites of symbiotic activity are hidden from view until the skirt is set in motion by its wearer. The exquisitely beautiful yellow glass parasites exist only as a multiplicity, a pack, that has no independent existence from the host, feeding ceaselessly and transforming the carrier into a site of becoming-lice, becoming-infested. Re-examined, these parasites resemble collections of algae as might be seen on the surface of stagnant water, a primordial coalescing that perforates the horsehair like so many fertile voids. The border between solid bead and softly flowing hair is one of the many hinterlands that provide the key to McQueen's response to the natural world.

Previous spread
101. Alexander McQueen
Sam Taylor-Johnson/Alexander
McQueen collaboration for *index*
magazine/*New York Times*
September/October 2003
Photograph by Sam Taylor-Johnson

Opposite
102. Bodysuit, *It's a Jungle Out There*,
Autumn/Winter 1997
Leather, denim and crocodile heads
Photograph by Robert Fairer

103. Ensemble, *It's a Jungle Out There*,
Autumn/Winter 1997
Jacket: ponyskin with impala horns;
trousers: bleached denim
Modelled by Debra Shaw
Photograph by Robert Fairer

Below left
104. Dress, *Eshu*, Autumn/Winter 2000
Glass beads and horsehair
Modelled by Alek Wek
Photograph by Anthea Simms

Below right
105. Coat, *Eshu*, Autumn/Winter 2000
Maurizio Anzeri for Alexander McQueen
Synthetic hair
Modelled by Raquel Zimmermann
Photograph by Anthea Simms

These boundaries, where one form gives way or diffuses into another, are what imbues his designs with such power. To imitate nature perfectly would, of course, have been entirely within McQueen's capabilities, but what sets his work apart from others who use fur, feathers and other natural elements is the ability to understand these materials as part of a larger process, as possessing a liminality that speaks of further evolutions, more complex hybridities, of restlessness and potential. As Deleuze and Guattari suggest, 'all that counts is the borderline – the anomalous'.[2]

Eshu also featured one of McQueen's most terrifying demonstrations of 'becoming', a coat constructed from loops of hair, which references both Surrealism and the work of installation artist Rebecca Horn. This extraordinary garment (pl.105) becomes an amorphous meditation on the effects of time; the hair on closer observation is revealed to consist of black mixed with grey, hair that has aged giving way intermittently to reveal its webbing foundation. The coat suggests the inexorable march towards old age and death. What is hair after all but so much dead matter? Yet once worn the coat transforms the wearer into a mass of 'becomings': becoming-hair, becoming-yeti, becoming-unrecognizable. Hair, whether human or animal, is crucial to an understanding of McQueen's ability to weave together the primitive, the mythical, the mortal and the tactile, rendering the body into a site of ceaseless experimentation, in the manner of an alchemist constantly testing and transforming the body's potential.

As part of the process of becoming-McQueen, the influence of Elsa Schiaparelli cannot be underestimated. Her understanding of the ability of clothes to render the body as a site of displacement, of transformation, of 'becoming', provided McQueen with a rich lexicon from which to construct his own visions, and central to this was his use of hair, fur and feathers. As with the hair coat from *Eshu*, the black ensemble (pl.109) featured in *The Horn of Plenty* (Autumn/Winter 2009), reputed to be monkey fur but in fact made from dyed goat, can trace its couture DNA back to Schiaparelli's experiments with monkey fur in the 1930s, including monkey-fur fringed boots, which McQueen resurrected (pl.107). She also used 'angel hair', long rayon threads knotted into billowing fringes, and her 1948 collection featured sleeveless monkey-fur sweaters and tops.[3] Schiaparelli's shocking garments transformed their wearers into chic Parisian gorillas, a form of primitive 'becoming' made famous by Marlene Dietrich (incidentally one of her most loyal customers, who understood perfectly the power of clothes to effect spectacular transformations) when she enacted her striptease in Joseph von Sternberg's film *Blonde Venus* (1932), shedding her gorilla skin to emerge in platinum Afro wig, singing: 'Got voodoo, head to toes. Hot voodoo, burn my clothes …' (pl.106). *The Horn of Plenty* outfit represents McQueen's ability to combine the natural world, and its representations via film and popular culture, with references to fashion history itself. The black-fur-clad-becoming, striding down the runway, is an apparition that ricochets back and forth from Dietrich to Schiaparelli, via Dior by way of Leigh Bowery and BDSM references,[4] and onwards into a twenty-first century hybridization of twentieth-century colonialism and exoticism.

If the after-image of Schiaparelli's surreal body play was part of McQueen's personal 'becoming', so too was his awareness of his own image as a designer. An experiment in assimilation and displacement, between himself and the natural world, was acted out on the coat and dress from *Voss* (Spring/Summer 2001). The dress, made from green ostrich feathers and painted muslin, is supported by a crinoline so that the front protudes from the neck, projecting its feathery distended abdomen in the manner of a moth's body or an exotically camouflaged furry caterpillar, whose extravagant hairiness disguises its vulnerability (pl.112). But this becoming-Lepidoptera is further complicated by the coat worn over the dress, a garment of woven silk twill (made from the moth's cocoon, perhaps?). It is trimmed at the neck and cuffs with more ostrich feathers, rendering the transition from dress to coat imperceptible, a further reminder of the importance of the border, the point of transition, as well as the impeccable attention to detail in McQueen's creations.

From the front, this ensemble – with its fitted Victorian tailored 'wings' cut away to reveal the feathery swollen body – evokes another moment of seminal 'becoming': the climax to Tod Browning's film *Freaks* (1932), where the trapeze artist Cleopatra is transformed into the terrifying bird/woman. But the greatest moment of 'becoming' is reserved for the back view of the garment (p.111). Here the caterpillar has emerged from its chrysalis into the glorious McQueen species, his own eyes replacing the patterned 'eyes' of a butterfly (pl.113) in an act of human aposematism, warning potential predators (other designers?) to keep away; this butterfly cannot be consumed or commodified. The process of thermal imaging used to produce the print and the chromatic complexity of the twill weave when looked at closely forges an inevitable visual comparison with a butterfly's wing when seen under magnification, its overlapping 'scales' revealing their pattern only at a distance; seen in close proximity its secret is indecipherable. But as always with McQueen's understanding of the natural world, this outfit is not simply about the wearer looking like a butterfly or a moth; direct replication is not at stake here, but rather the process involved in moving across species. As Deleuze and Guattari concur, 'we are not interested in characteristics; what interests us are modes of expansion, propagation, occupation, contagion, peopling.'[5] The dress and coat ensemble from *Voss* is a reminder that for all of McQueen's indebtedness to the natural world and to historical references, these are always combined with innovation. New technological developments take their place alongside butterfly wings, ostrich feathers and nineteenth-century silk weaving techniques as objects of wonder and conduits for transformation.

Other experiments at different stages punctuate the tour de force of 'becoming' that is *Voss*. The dress of red and black ostrich feathers with a bodice constructed of dyed red microscope slides (pl.110) that closed the show suggests a forensic scrutiny of the art of couture, whose processes and structures are often invisible to the naked eye and need to be magnified, dissected and catalogued in order for its hidden world to be made apparent. Hence the importance of the slides as an acknowledgement of nature's internal landscapes exposed by science. Many of the set piece outfits in *Voss* act as laboratories or breeding grounds for

Above left
106. Marlene Dietrich wearing gorilla suit
Josef von Sternberg, *Blonde Venus*, 1932

Below left
107. Boots, Elsa Schiaparelli
Summer 1938
Suede and monkey fur
Philadelphia Museum of Art

Opposite
108. Jade Parfitt wearing hair coat,
Eclect Dissect, Givenchy Haute Couture,
Autumn/Winter 1997
i-D magazine, December 1997
Photograph by Donald Christie

Below left
111. Detail of coat (back), *Voss*,
Spring/Summer 2001
Silk, woven with thermal image of
Alexander McQueen's face
Photograph by Jonathan Faiers

Below right
112. Ensemble, *Voss*,
Spring/Summer 2001
Dress: dyed ostrich feathers; coat:
as above

McQueen's experiments with nature, incorporating the fascinated gaze of the botanist and zoologist with the intrepidness of H.G. Wells's Dr Moreau and the contemporary magic of gene technology.

Ostrich feathers feature prominently in *Voss* and form the skirt of another of the collection's set pieces, the dress in question suspended from and entangled in the claws of the taxidermied hawks perched on the wearer's shoulders (p.312, top). As with the crocodile heads and impala horns utilized in *It's a Jungle Out There*, this avian assemblage considers the qualities of the hawk, its piercing eyesight, its speed, its deadly accuracy; in short, what 'hawk' might become when inserted into an idea of fashion. Juxtaposed with the plumage of a very different species, the ostrich, and if, as has been suggested, inspired by Hitchcock's *The Birds*, this dress is no simple homage to bird life. As Deleuze and Guattari have proposed, 'Becoming is never imitating. When Hitchcock does birds, he does not reproduce bird calls, he produces an electronic sound like a field of intensities or a wave of vibrations, a continuous variation, like a terrible threat welling up inside us.'[6] So, too, McQueen's enthrallment here with the

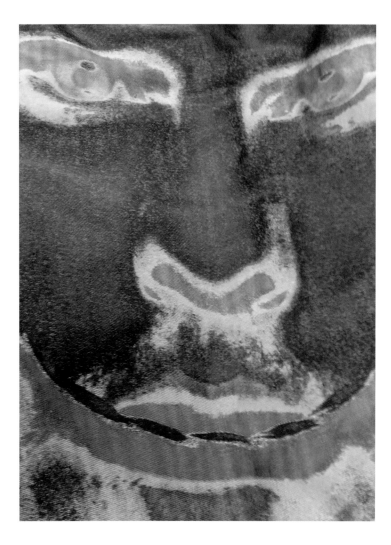

feather is less as object, more as part of the multiplicities of birds, their flocking and roosting; his aim, to understand these creatures at a molecular level, to distill 'birdliness', and marvel at their continuous variation.

Elsewhere in his work, however, feathers act as plumage, a specific understanding of feathers as multiplicities, as individual structures composed of numerous indiscernible fibres that replicate and overlap to form a constantly ruffling, shifting mass (pl.117). Becoming-weightless and airborne, these plumey congregations in turn join others and so the flock is born. The pheasant feather dress (pl.118) from *The Widows of Culloden* (Autumn/Winter 2006) and the black and white duck-feather creations from *The Horn of Plenty* evoke the flock, and all those linguistic terms used to describe groups of birds such as murmuration, pandemonium and convocation; a multitude of pheasants is described as a bouquet, and ducks in flight as a skein. Plumage also, of course, has a direct relationship to concepts of finery, decoration and adornment. These qualities rather than any straightforward bird mimicry facilitate McQueen's constant exploration of his own genetic composition as a fashion designer. Therefore, the pheasant feather

dress from *The Widows of Culloden* is more a late-Victorian, ruffle-skirted evocation of the slaughter of game birds in a Scotland that had become a sports arena for absentee English landlords, than any attempt to construct a pheasant 'costume'. Similarly, the exploration of plumage in *The Horn of Plenty* evaluates a succession of bird qualities as they hybridize into a dazzling parade of sartorial and mythical references. In a collection invoking the exaggerated shapes of 1950s couture, it is again Schiaparelli who emerges as the original host for these avian experiments. Her love of printed optical illusion is discernable in the Escher-inspired flock of bird prints, which morph from abstract pattern to individual birds, and fly free only to flock back again to their original geometry. The feather bodice topped with birdcage headdress suggests not only freedom and captivity, a bird that has had its wings clipped, but returns to Schiaparelli's famous perfumery in the Place Vendôme where customers could choose their fragrance from a giant black and gold birdcage designed by Jean-Michel Frank. Schiaparelli's love of feathers is well known, and she used them to make a series of winged headdresses (evoked in *The Widows of Culloden*) and leis, or truncated capes, that took Paris by storm in the 1930s. Feathers also constructed one of Dietrich's

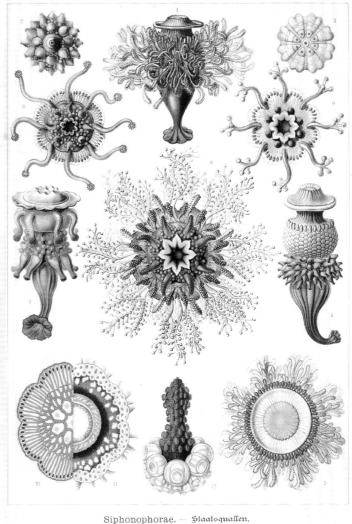

Above left
113. Detail of wing markings of an owl butterfly
Photograph by Jason Edwards

Above right
114. Plate 17, Ernst Haeckel, 'Siphonophorae',
Art Forms of Nature 1899–1904

most iconic personae, the veiled and glistening cock-feathered 'bird of paradise' in von Sternberg's *Shanghai Express* (1932).

Is it a bird, is it an exercise in feathered dysmorphia or is it a symbol of sacrifice? The black duck-feather dress in *The Horn of Plenty* is all of these and more (pl.247). On its glossy breast the feathers coalesce to form the outline of a heart; a reminder of the Christian symbolism of the pelican, which pierces its breast so as to feed its young on its own blood. The leg-of-mutton 'wings' refer to the 1890s (indeed, the pheasant feather dress from *The Widows of Culloden*, which also references this period, is deconstructed and recreated in red and black feathers in *The Horn of Plenty*). But it also evokes wimpled nuns, Dietrich's feathery campness and Schiaparelli's chic. It is as if all of these elements had been trapped in the molecular transporter from David Cronenberg's film *The Fly* (1986) and emerged as these scrambled feathered hybrids. The white duck-feathered companion to the black dress is perhaps even more remarkable, cocooning and disabling its wearer in an extended collar that renders the bird/woman, hatching inside its nest, a walking downy *matryoshka* doll, a tableau of 'becoming', hatching and rebirth.

Marine life was perhaps McQueen's greatest repository of inspiration, his use of coral, fish skins, scales and shells permeating his work with a sense of immersion, the unknown and unfathomable, the primordial and the evolutionary. It is no surprise that one of McQueen's favourite films was James Cameron's *The Abyss* (1989), where a diver encounters an alien aquatic species and experiences a spiritual awakening. The use in *Voss* of shells – mussel, oyster and razor-clam – is telling. The concept of the shoal, like the flock, is central. The vastness of oceans teaming with abundant life suggests fecundity, and yet coupled with this is a sense of the shell as a relic, carapace, something left behind that has served its purpose now that the life it contained has moved on. This shedding of skins, of feathers moulting, hair thinning, is key to an understanding of McQueen's work as being in a constant state of 'becoming' something else. The dazzling carapaces and cocoons presented in his collections evoke the wondrous new forms they helped nurture and protect in their gestation period. So while the razor-clam dress and mussel bodice and skirt from *Voss* (pls 115, 203) entrance with their subtle colour variations, their luminosity and clatter, it is as residue, as deposits, that they become most powerful. When model Erin O'Connor languorously stretches in her pearly armour, flicking off shells to left and right, so cutting her hands, and Amy Wesson kicks and hurls the mussel shells from her skirt, these actions appear representative of nature's inertia and the extinction necessary for gradual evolution. The models, like barnacled rocks, reject their ancient encrustations and continue along their evolutionary path.

A path that would eventually lead to McQueen's most complex and visionary dialogue with nature, or rather nature's possibilities, *Plato's Atlantis* (Spring/Summer 2010). For this, McQueen dived deeper than he had done before, down to the bottom of the oceans, guided by Haeckel's nineteenth-century marine fantasies, past the delicate reefs that mirrored couture's finest structures. During his subterranean journey he encountered those evolving life forms that live so deep they are as yet unnamed – primitive dolphins, pink electric knife-fish and giant black piranha – while in the deepest abyss, where no light penetrates, there exist forms without colour, their structures constantly shifting, expanding and contracting.

To bring back these visions McQueen rallied all of his technical skills, ancient and modern. Masterful cutting and tailoring merges with digital technology, to produce unique forms that offer the potential for further 'becoming'. Paillettes of bronze and blue enamel, skins of chiffon and velvet shredded together using the *fil coupé* technique, sulphurous sequins that imitate a bee's pollen baskets, and nets of perforated distressed suede with which to catch butterflies or deaths-head hawkmoths all convey a surface richness. But to be blinded by such spectacle is to fail to see the technical complexity that lies beneath. In *Plato's Atlantis* skirts are caught up, fluted, and turned inside out, a process of evagination that is seen in the movement of a jellyfish, as it throbs its way through the sea. Sequined leggings, curved to retain the shape of the limb, resemble a snake skin sloughed off from its new body. The almost imperceptible decorative skins of metamorphic printed silk that line the sequined outfits dazzle, then recede like the chromatic light show of a cuttlefish. The innovations are legion.

McQueen was enthralled by nature: its beauty, its complexity, its cruelty, its limitlessness, its decomposition, but above all by its potential. An understanding of what nature can do, what it can create, its state of constant evolution, was fundamental to his greatest work and produced a vision of what clothes can become that has not been equalled. As he himself said with characteristic simplicity: 'Everything I do is connected to nature in one way or another…'.[7]

115. Dress, *Voss*, Spring/Summer 2001
Razor clam shells
Modelled by Erin O'Connor
Photograph by Chris Moore

Above
116. Plate 769, Eadweard Muybridge,
'Bird in Flight' *Animal Locomotion*, 1887
Photograph
V&A: PH.1283-1889

Left
117. Detail of pheasant feathers
Photograph by Darlyne A. Murawski

Opposite
118. Ensemble, *The Widows of Culloden*,
Autumn/Winter 2006
Dress: pheasant feathers, ribbon and tulle
Pheasant wing headpiece, Philip Treacy
for Alexander McQueen
Modelled by Polina Kasina
Photograph by Chris Moore

NO. 03

SENSIBILITY

—

A GOTHIC MIND

CATHERINE SPOONER

McQueen's relationship with the Gothic is aptly summarized in a photograph by David LaChappelle from 1996 (pl.123). A shaven-headed McQueen, dressed in a black corset, red elbow-length gloves made of rubber and a voluminous yellow skirt, romps across a hillside with a flaming torch. His friend and muse Isabella Blow, wearing a magenta, mitre-like hat and a pale pink cheongsam with an excessively high funnel neck, trips behind him hanging on to the hem of his skirt. In the foreground is a skull; in the background a castle keep spouts fire from cross-shaped windows. LaChappelle stages McQueen as *enfant terrible* of British fashion, a rebellious Gothic heroine who has not only escaped the castle but also set fire to it. In the year he controversially took on the prestigious role of chief designer at the House of Givenchy, LaChappelle shows him literally burning down the house. The image evokes McQueen's obsession with history at the same time that it suggests his iconoclasm, his love of perversity and the macabre, and a contradictory sense of imprisonment and liberation that informs his clothes. Moreover, the theatricality of the image, its deliberate artificiality and disregard for historical authenticity, embodies the way that in Gothic texts the verisimilitude of historical setting is less important than the opportunities it provides to explore surface and performance.

The Gothic novel emerged as part of the Gothic Revival in the later eighteenth century, but unlike the broadly nostalgic view of the Middle Ages embodied in Gothic Revival architecture, it configured the past as a time of superstition, persecution and oppression. It was defined by what literary critic Chris Baldick identifies as 'a fearful sense of inheritance in time [combined] with a claustrophobic sense of enclosure in space, these two dimensions reinforcing one another to produce an impression of sickening descent into disintegration'.[1] Gothic was also from the outset a notably sartorial genre, many of its characteristic effects dependent on veils, masks and disguises. It is a genre through which bodies and their boundaries and surfaces are foregrounded and explored, in frequently excessive or unsettling ways.

Significantly, it is not a static set of conventions, but rather what might be called a discursive field, through which a recognizable set of concerns are played out in different ways at different points in history. McQueen's favoured mode of Gothic was a late-Victorian confluence of taxidermy and mourning wear, decadent sexuality and dissected bodies, but he experimented widely across the Gothic spectrum, from the medieval Gothic Revivalism of his posthumous collection (Autumn/Winter 2010) to contemporary horror and even the comic Gothic of J.K. Rowling's *Harry Potter* series. Much of his work is readily identifiable as Gothic, but even those collections with a lighter or more fantastic feel often show traces of Gothic in their conceptual framework.

McQueen once declared that 'There's something … kind of Edgar Allan Poe, kind of deep and kind of melancholic about [my] collections'.[2] Poe's 'Annabel Lee' (1849), a tale of doomed romantic love with suggestively necrophiliac overtones, was reputedly one of his favourite poems, and was read by his friend Annabelle Neilson at his memorial service. Nevertheless, it is through film that Gothic exerts most influence on his designs. McQueen's Spring/Summer 1996 collection, *The Hunger*, was named after Tony Scott's film of 1983, in which Catherine Deneuve and David Bowie play stylishly dressed vampires preying on subcultural riff-raff. There were more vampire references in his untitled menswear collection of Autumn/Winter 2006, which explicitly drew on Francis Ford Coppola's *Bram Stoker's Dracula* (1992), itself an Oscar-winner for Eiko Ishioka's Japanese-inspired costumes. Stanley Kubrick's *The Shining* (1980), an adaptation of the horror novel by Stephen King, inspired McQueen's collection *The Overlook* (Autumn/Winter 1999), while Peter Weir's *Picnic at Hanging Rock* (1975), an example of classic Australian Gothic set in 1900, influenced the Edwardiana of *It's Only a Game* (Spring/Summer 2005). Elsewhere references were more implicit: in *The Widows of Culloden* (Autumn/Winter 2006), an ivory lace dress accessorized with antlers and a torn veil suggested Charles Dickens's jilted bride (pl.40), Miss Havisham; Kate Moss's appearance as an illusory spectre evoked the spirits conjured by nineteenth-century seances (pl.248), in which ectoplasm was fashioned from white muslin soaked in luminous paint. McQueen's engagement with Gothic went further than mere citation: Gothic provided him with a distinctive idiom that he explored and refined over successive collections.

One of McQueen's most overtly Gothic collections was *Supercalifragilisticexpialidocious* (Autumn/Winter 2002), which was conceived as a tribute to film director Tim Burton, whose works are notable not only for their fantastic and stylized use of costume, but also for their portrayal of eccentric and often melancholy outsiders. The runway show was staged amongst the vaulted arches of La Conciergerie, Marie Antoinette's final prison before her execution by guillotine; the lighting was arranged by Burton, with echoes of the urban chiaroscuro of his film *Batman* (1989). Frothing ruffles and chemise tops (pl.121) recalled Marie Antoinette's scandalous depiction by Elisabeth Vigée-Lebrun in a chemise (1783), a politicized image of undress that informed the depiction of women's bodies in the early Gothic novel.[3] The collection also mixed up references to Kubrick's *A Clockwork Orange* (1971) and 1970s hard rock, with flowing black dresses and customized school uniforms that recalled Winona Ryder's

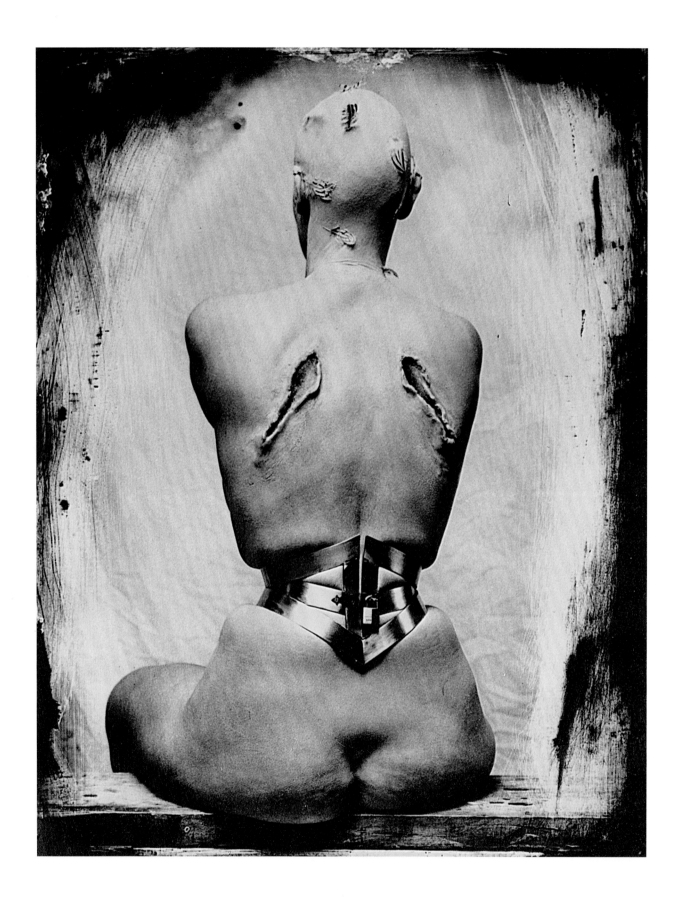

Previous spread
123. 'Burning Down the House'
Alexander McQueen and Isabella Blow,
Hedingham Castle, Essex, England, 1996
Photograph by David LaChapelle

124. Joel-Peter Witkin, *Woman Once a Bird*, 1990
Toned gelatin silver print

Opposite left
125. Félicien Rops, *Sentimental Initiation*, 1887
Pencil and watercolour on paper
Musée D'Orsay, Paris

Opposite right
126. 'Catwoman' sketch, *Pantheon ad Lucem*, Autumn/Winter 2004
Pencil on paper, London, 2004
Courtesy of Alexander McQueen

costumes in Burton's *Beetlejuice* (1988) and the masks and capes of his *Batman* films. For Burton, the superhero costume is figured Gothically as simultaneous entrapment and release,[4] properties that are crystallized in the potential of the mask. As Burton states, 'Masks in [the USA] symbolize hiding, but when I used to go to Halloween parties wearing a mask it was actually more of a doorway, a way of expressing yourself. There is something about being hidden that in some weird way helps you to be freer'.[5] If Burton Gothicizes his superheroes, McQueen takes that impulse to a fantastical extreme: in one ensemble a tricorn hat, domino mask and voluminous cape reimagined Batman in terms of the romance of the highwayman and the sinister glamour of the Venetian carnival (pl.119).

Like McQueen, Burton absorbed his knowledge of the Gothic primarily from film. James Whale's *Frankenstein* films (1931, 1935) were a formative influence, and Burton repeatedly depicts bodies that are cut up and reassembled, their artificial construction displayed through visible stitches. In *Batman Returns* (1992), Catwoman constructs her own suit from an old jacket; in *The Nightmare Before Christmas* (produced and co-written by Burton, 1993), Sally Ragdoll is continually unpicking and reassembling herself in an endlessly provisional process of self-fashioning.

Burton's specially commissioned sketches for McQueen's *Supercalifragilisticexpialidocious* show, which were reproduced on the invitation (pl.120), portray fashion models as characteristic Burton 'patchwork girls': their clothes and faces are visibly stitched together and it is unclear where dress finishes and woman begins.

Burton grasped a core tenet of McQueen's work: a radically Gothic view of the body as surface that can be made and remade. From Mary Shelley's *Frankenstein* (1818) to H.G. Wells' *The Island of Doctor Moreau* (1896), Gothic texts have been inspired by developments in nineteenth-century medicine that used dissection and vivisection to explore the limits of the human. The invitation to McQueen's *Highland Rape* (Autumn/Winter 1995) depicted a sutured wound (p.306), suggesting equivalence between skin and fabric as well as the idea of the body stitched together and remade in the wake of trauma. In a sequence of collages created for McQueen's second runway show for Givenchy haute couture, *Eclect Dissect* (Autumn/Winter 1997), set designer Simon Costin overlaid anatomical drawings with nineteenth-century fashion illustrations, so that in the tradition of the memento mori, skeleton feet are thrust into high-heeled shoes and dissected human heads are adorned with fabulous coiffures. In one image, a woman wearing an elaborately ruched 1880s bustle peels off her

flesh to reveal the musculature; flesh is constructed as one more layer of clothing. Costin's work evidently continued to inspire McQueen, as a collage in which a bisected petticoat is pinned to a flayed torso bears a striking similarity to an ensemble from *No.13* (Spring/Summer 1999), in which layers of ruched lace draped over a single leg emerge from a moulded girdle, the straps transposed from the petticoat to inferred leather 'skin' (pls 127, 129). In another variation on the same theme to appear in *No.13*, double amputee model Aimee Mullins appeared in a moulded leather corset in which the lacing ran not vertically down the back, but diagonally across the body, wittily suggesting skin cut 'on the bias'. The surgical overtones of the corset and its suggestion of suture gave it a monstrous, Frankensteinian appearance that played off against Mullins's intricately carved, wooden prosthetic legs (pl.197).

The idea of the designer as surgeon, a Dr Frankenstein or Dr Moreau piecing together bodies out of cloth, had been present in McQueen's work since his MA graduation show, inspired by suspected medic Jack the Ripper. *Eclect Dissect*, however, explicitly put forward the narrative of an 1890s surgeon who travelled the world, collecting women, costumes, textiles and animals, before returning to dissect them in his laboratory and reassemble them as exotic hybrid forms. The show constructed metamorphic female bodies reminiscent of the *femmes fatales* of *fin de siècle* Gothic literature. Model Shalom Harlow appeared in a black ballgown in the process of becoming a swan, while a black leather dress with bird-skull epaulettes was sent down the runway accessorized by a dramatic beehive, and feathery false eyelashes and eyebrows that made the model resemble a strange and exotic bird (pl.131). This metamorphic quality was one that continued to inform McQueen's work, enabling him to comment playfully on the notion of fashion as a transformational medium. Animal-women, bird-women and moth-women permeate *It's a Jungle Out There* (Autumn/Winter 1997), *Eclect Dissect* and *Voss* (Spring/Summer 2001), ultimately emerging as the aquatic hybrids of *Plato's Atlantis* (Spring/Summer 2010).

McQueen's metamorphic women are what might be called 'abhuman', a term coined by literary theorist Kelly Hurley to describe the metamorphic bodies of *fin de siècle* Gothic literature. For Hurley, 'the abhuman subject is a not-quite-human subject, characterized by its morphic variability, continually in danger of becoming not-itself, becoming other.' She argues that the abhuman in late-Victorian fiction inspires nostalgia for a 'fully human' self on the one hand, but on the other, a sort of excitement about the possibilities of a fluid human self, a 'monstrous becoming'.[6] In Richard Marsh's novel *The Beetle* (1897), the transgender monster is a human scarab; in Clemence Housman's *The Were-Wolf* (1896), a predatory woman transforms into a white wolf; at the climax of Arthur Machen's *The Great God Pan* (1890), the body of the demonic temptress Helen Vaughan dissolves from human form, through a series of bestial ones, to primordial jelly and finally to something unspeakably demonic. This morphic variability is nicely summarized in Félicien Rops' watercolour *Sentimental Initiation* (1887), in which a winged, nubile female form with skeleton head, arms and spine, carrying a bow and arrow and clothed in a gaping corset, funereal drapery and

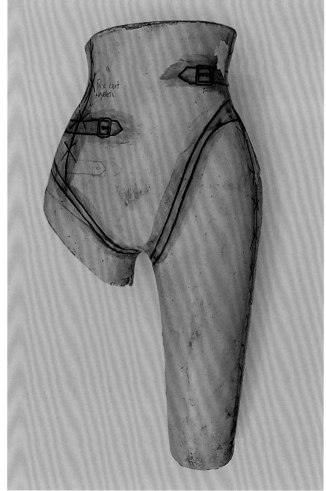

Opposite above
127. Collage, *Eclect Dissect*, Givenchy
Haute Couture, Autumn/Winter 1997
Simon Costin for Alexander McQueen
Printed paper
Courtesy of Simon Costin

Opposite below
128. Cast of model Laura Morgan,
London, 1998
Plaster of Paris and fibreglass
Kees van der Graaf for
Alexander McQueen
Courtesy of Kees van der Graaf

129. Ensemble, *No.13*,
Spring/Summer 1999
Dress: lace and tulle; hip brace:
moulded leather
Modelled by Shalom Harlow

ALEXANDER
MCQUEEN

crown of pink roses, contemplates a severed head (pl.125). Rops' painting is multiply metamorphic, an explicitly sexualized and perverse image combining the mythic figures of Cupid, Artemis and Salome; love and death; woman, skeleton and bird; and moth, bat and human pelvic bone.

Although Rops does not appear to be a direct source for McQueen, his work was a significant influence on American photographer Joel-Peter Witkin, at one time McQueen's favourite artist and an acknowledged influence on his work. Witkin's *Portrait of Joel, New Mexico* (1984) directly inspired the crucifix masks worn in *Dante* (Autumn/Winter 1996; p.307), his photographic tableaux in a more general sense influencing the celebrated glass box within a box that marked the climax of *Voss* (pl.295). Set within a psychiatric ward, the walls of the box opened to reveal fetish writer Michelle Olley as a reclining, masked nude, smothered in moths and wearing a breathing mask, so replicating Witkin's *Sanitarium* (1983). One of the images most reminiscent of McQueen, however, is *Woman Once a Bird* (1990), which evokes a sense of constriction and loss as the process of becoming 'other' is reversed. The body bears traces of its animal qualities in the

feathers stuck to its shorn scalp and the gashed skin that signifies amputated wings (pl.124). With its punitive metal corset, feathers, torn surfaces and hairless scalp, the image recalls several McQueen collections, from the appearance of corset-maker Mr Pearl in *The Birds* (Spring/Summer 1995; pl.285) and jewellery designer Shaun Leane's 'Spine' corset of *Untitled* (Spring/Summer 1998) to the ripped skin/fabrics of *Highland Rape* and the ascetic coifs of *Voss*.

The metamorphic body is also a feature of traditional fairy tale and this was another of McQueen's interests, appearing in his work in Gothicized form. The *Supercalifragilisticexpialidocious* show opened with a model in a lilac cape with an outsized hood leading two wolf-hybrid dogs. In a fashion shoot for *AnOther* magazine using clothes from this collection, directed by McQueen and shot by Sam Taylor-Johnson, McQueen described the images as 'very Grimm's fairytale (pl.134). He's Dick Whittington, she's Puss Without Her Boots'.[7] The playful sexual innuendo is reminiscent of pantomime, but the resulting photographs evoke the strangeness and horror of the tales of the Brothers Grimm as well as the degraded, disturbingly sexual bodies of Cindy Sherman's *Fairy Tales* (1985). *The Girl Who Lived in the Tree*

(Autumn/Winter 2008) offered a sweeter version of fairytale transformation, built around a story of a feral girl who lived in a 600-year-old elm tree in McQueen's Sussex garden, and descended to earth to become a princess. The ad campaign, photographed by Craig McDean, depicted a model in a red cape and white dress seated in a giant black nest beside a crow. This image obliquely recalled the scene in which a similarly attired Red Riding Hood climbs a tree and finds a bird's nest containing magical eggs in Neil Jordan's film *The Company of Wolves* (1984), an adaptation of Angela Carter's adult fairytales.

If *The Girl Who Lived in the Tree* conjured a magical transformation from feral girl to princess, elsewhere McQueen's interest in the transformational body flirted with the aesthetics of disgust. One of McQueen's most inherently Gothic garments appeared in *The Hunger*: a red silk faille skirt and elegantly cut grey jacket, matched with a moulded bodice encasing bloody worms between two layers of transparent plastic (pl.132). The worms evoked mortality and also, in their similarity to leeches, the vampires with which the collection was associated. The garment also conjured in spectacular fashion philosopher Julia Kristeva's notion of the

'abject': the feeling of disgust engendered when we encounter that which 'does not respect borders, positions, rules. The in-between, the ambiguous, the composite'.[8] The experience of the abject, Kristeva argues, most vividly expressed in waste, bodily fluids, revolting foods and above all the corpse, challenges the notion of the coherent and stable self and therefore gives rise to sensations of horror and nausea. McQueen's vampire ensemble enacts numerous disruptions of the body's boundaries. Encased in transparent 'skin', the worms are suggestively both within and without the body. The slashed sleeves, revealing a red silk faille lining, place the inside of the jacket on display, again challenging the distinction between exterior and interior. The worms, moreover, suggest a body already in decay, evoking the liminal state of the undead. The sharp silhouette of the jacket and the firm moulding of the plastic contrasts with the random pattern of the worms, structure countered with chaos, beauty with horror.

The vampire embodies the idea of the revenant past, often seen by cultural critics as the defining feature of the Gothic, whether manifested as haunting, curse, undead being or psychological neurosis. McQueen's interest in his family history is well

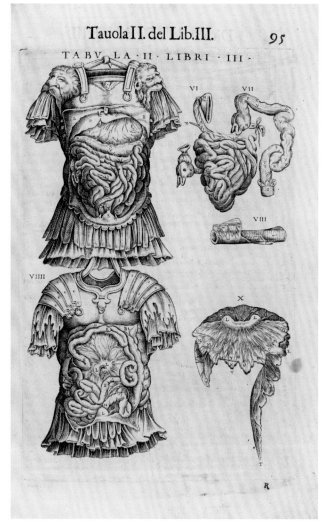

Above left
132. Ensemble, *The Hunger*,
Spring/Summer 1996
Jacket: wool, synthetic and silk; bodice:
moulded plastic and worms; skirt: silk
Moulded bodice, Kees van der Graaf for
Alexander McQueen
Silver stirrup (worn over skirt) Shaun
Leane for Alexander McQueen

Above right
133. Plate 95, Juan Valverde de Amusco,
La Anatomia del Corpo Umano, Rome,
1550
Engraving on paper
V&A: National Art Library

Opposite
134. Sam Taylor-Johnson/
Alexander McQueen collaboration
for *AnOther Magazine*
Autumn/Winter 2002
Modelled by Zora Star
Photograph by Sam Taylor-Johnson

documented; repeatedly, he constructs the past as Gothic trauma that rises and resurfaces through his work, playing itself out on the female body. In *Highland Rape*, the Scottish Clearances were evoked in slashed and distressed fabric that created the impression of women's bodies under assault. A lace dress in the green-brown tones of earth and foliage, torn at the hem, crotch and shoulder (p.306), suggested the process of decomposition, the 'descent into disintegration' that Baldick describes. In *Dante* and *Joan*, traces of historic trauma were emblazoned across jackets in the form of screen-printed photographs of the murdered Romanov children and of the Vietnam War (pl.162, no.184). *In Memory of Elizabeth How, Salem 1692* (Autumn/Winter 2007) explicitly memorialized an ancestor of McQueen's executed at the notorious Salem witch trials, although its imagery deliberately sought to re-enchant the persecuted witches, marking them not as victims of history but drawing on occult and Egyptian imagery to present them as exotic femmes fatales. The show finale of *Joan* (Autumn/Winter 1998) evoked the 19-year-old Joan of Arc's martyrdom at the stake, the masked model encircled by flame (pl.135). However, the dress made of red bugle beads resembled dripping blood, suggestively recalling the blood-drenched prom dress and burning school at the climax of Brian De Palma's film *Carrie* (1976), another tale of a persecuted teenager with supernatural powers. A baroque harpsichord soundtrack further confused the tone of the finale. Was this a woman achieving heavenly transcendence or undergoing a demonic resurrection?

In a 1998 photo shoot for *The Face* inspired by *Joan*, Nick Knight turned McQueen's Gothic imagery back on the designer by depicting him as one of his own demonic martyrs, pitted with multiple tiny wounds like a futuristic St Sebastian. The deliberate artificiality of the portrait, however, deploying computer-generated effects as well as elaborate wig, make-up and contact lenses, insisted on the image as spectacle, as performance, rather than authentic depiction of the artist's soul. Nevertheless, McQueen was repeatedly Gothicized by the press, who tended to construct him as a mercurial Jekyll and Hyde figure. This image evidently suited his purposes, allowing him to cultivate a particular brand, in which he alternately featured as East End hooligan and tortured artistic genius. In his embrace of the idea of the designer as surgeon, moreover, he gestured back towards the Romantic myth of the artist/scientist as troubled outsider, a persona that dogged his public reputation. Ultimately, perhaps, it is a 1999 portrait of McQueen by Joseph Cultice that is most telling concerning the designer's public image (pl.136). The photograph is literally divided by a light stick, and McQueen's face appears half in light and half in shadow, suggesting a divided self. Whether or not this presents an accurate picture of the man is a matter of conjecture. It is fitting tribute, however, to the rich and complex Gothic fictions that McQueen enjoyed spinning in his work.

135. Dress, *Joan*, Autumn/Winter 1998
Bugle beads
Photograph by Paul Vicente

Opposite
136. Alexander McQueen,
December 1999
Photograph by Joseph Cultice

Overleaf
137. 'McQueen's Kingdom'
W Magazine, July 2002
Photograph by Steven Klein

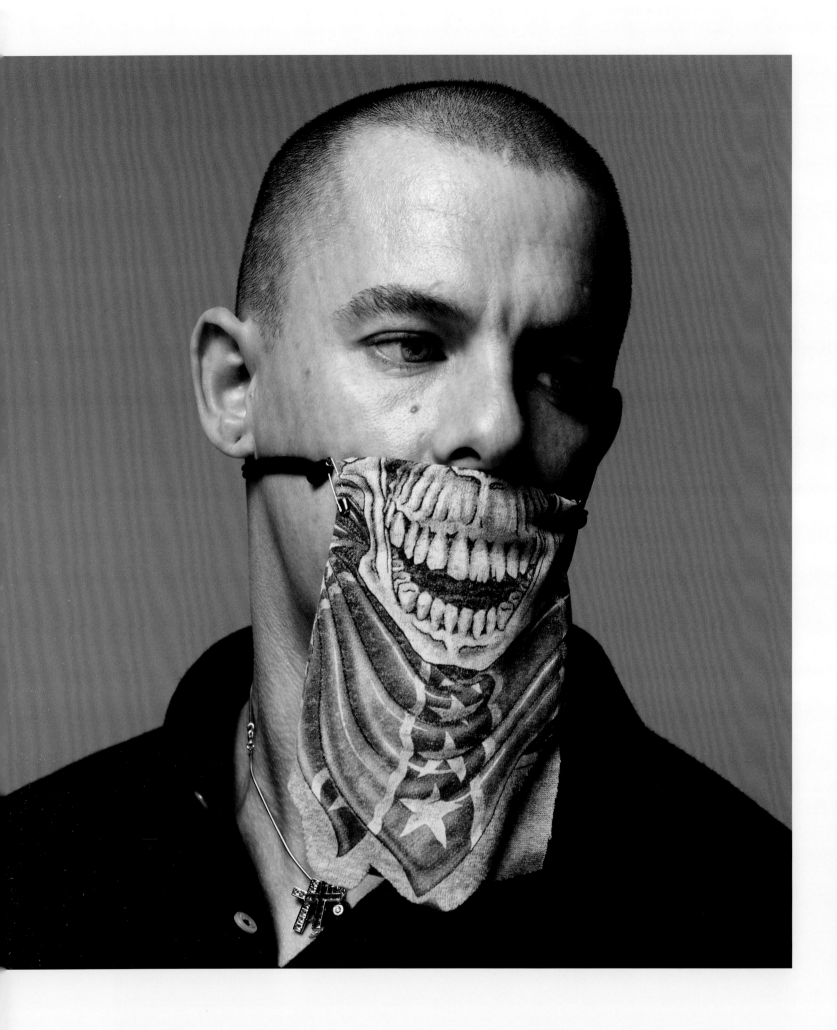

MEMENTO MORI

ELEANOR TOWNSEND

———

'Fashion: Madam Death, Madam Death!
Death: Wait until your time comes, and then I will appear
without being called by you'
Giacomo Leopardi, *Dialogue Between Fashion and Death*, 1842

—

Memento mori – images or motifs intended to remind the viewer of death – memorialize individuals but primarily memorialize death itself. In the Middle Ages, representations of the living were juxtaposed with those of the dead, making everyone's eventual fate explicit. Images of skulls and skeletons became a trope re-used consistently in subsequent centuries to jolt the onlooker into awareness of their own mortality (pl.145). McQueen's work draws directly from this rich tradition.

McQueen repeatedly set intimations of death starkly against the glamour of fashion. At the catwalk show for his early collection *Dante* (Autumn/Winter 1996), he placed a partially gilded plastic skeleton amongst the fashion editors in the front row, while one model wore an elaborate jet headdress with a skeletal hand that clutched at her face (pl.141). In *Untitled* (Spring/Summer 1998), Shaun Leane's silvered 'Jaw Bone' mouthpiece (pl.140) and exoskeletal 'Spine' corset (no.183) were overt reminders of the vulnerability of flesh, while McQueen skull jewellery directly reflected early memento mori pieces, combining the motif with precious metals and jewels.

The physical reality and mortality of the body permeated McQueen's work and thinking. A dress with a bodice covered in blood-red microscope slides from *Voss* (Spring/Summer 2001) suggested the fragility of life (pl.110). 'There's blood beneath every layer of skin',[1] McQueen once said, echoing T.S. Eliot's axiom, 'the skull beneath the skin'.[2] In the same collection, a dress of sharp razor-clam shells bloodied the model's hands.

McQueen was also aware of his own mortality: Inez van Lamsweerde and Vinoodh Matadin's striking photograph shows him swathed in a biker's scarf, the printed skeleton's mouth sitting squarely over his own in a deathly reminder of life's transience (pl.138). He chose scans of his own brain as the invitation to his Autumn/Winter 2003 show, *Scanners*, and a lenticular image morphed between his face and a skull for *Natural Distinction, Un-Natural Selection* (Spring/Summer 2009).[3] Yet McQueen also used the skull as a purely decorative device, which would ultimately become a signature motif for the McQueen brand: Kate Moss's skull dress in the American Express *Black* show (2004)[4] was echoed in the scarves that have since become ubiquitous (pl.146).

In his graduate collection, *Jack the Ripper Stalks his Victims* (1992), McQueen inserted a fine layer of human hair into the lining of several garments (pl.142). 'The inspiration behind the hair came from Victorian times when prostitutes would sell theirs for kits of hair locks, which were bought by people to give to their lovers' he explained, reflecting a strong interest in the Victorian Gothic.[5] Isabella Blow, who bought the entire collection, embraced its corporeality. She said, 'The colours were very extreme – he would do a black coat but then he would line it with human hair and it was blood red inside so it was like a body, it was like the flesh, with blood.'[6]

Early in his career McQueen used locks of his own hair, captured in transparent labels on garments. Through 'my signature label',[7] McQueen was stamping his identity firmly on collections that, since his death in 2010, have now themselves become a form of memento mori. He later returned to using locks of hair in both lockets and

Previous spread
138. Alexander McQueen
V Magazine, 2004
Photograph by Inez van Lamsweerde
& Vinoodh Matadin

139. Coatdress, *What a Merry Go Round*,
Autumn/Winter 2001
Wool and silk, styled with skeleton
Modelled by Marleen Berkova
Photograph by Anthea Simms

Opposite above
140. 'Jaw Bone' mouthpiece,
Untitled, Spring/Summer 1998
Aluminium
Shaun Leane for Alexander McQueen
Photograph by Robert Fairer

Opposite below
141. Headpiece, *Dante*,
Autumn/Winter 1996
Jet and plastic beads with skeletal hand
Simon Costin for Alexander McQueen

earrings in *Sarabande* (Spring/Summer 2007; pl.143), making direct reference to eighteenth- and nineteenth-century mourning jewellery. Jewellery incorporating a dead person's hair (pl.144) reminded the wearer of the deceased while also alluding to their own mortality.

McQueen's repeated references to death emerged from a particular strand of 1990s British culture that Caroline Evans argues reflected a fear of the unknown in a period of seismic technological change.[8] Damien Hirst, who worked in a similar context,[9] commented that, 'You can frighten people with death or an idea of their own mortality, or it can actually give them vigour'.[10] Hirst would also take the idea of setting a skull in a glamorous context to its ultimate conclusion in *For the Love of God* (2007), in which he gave a platinum skull, studded with diamonds, human teeth.[11]

In spite of his focus on physical mortality, the view of death McQueen presented was in many respects a romanticized one, swathed in a rich history of memento mori reference. 'It is important to look at death because it is a part of life', he once said. 'It is a sad thing, melancholic but romantic at the same time. It is the end of a cycle – and everything has an end. The cycle of life is positive because it gives room for new things'.[12]

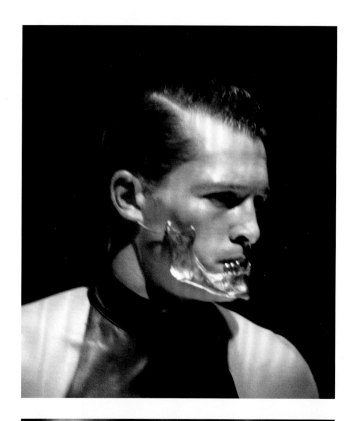

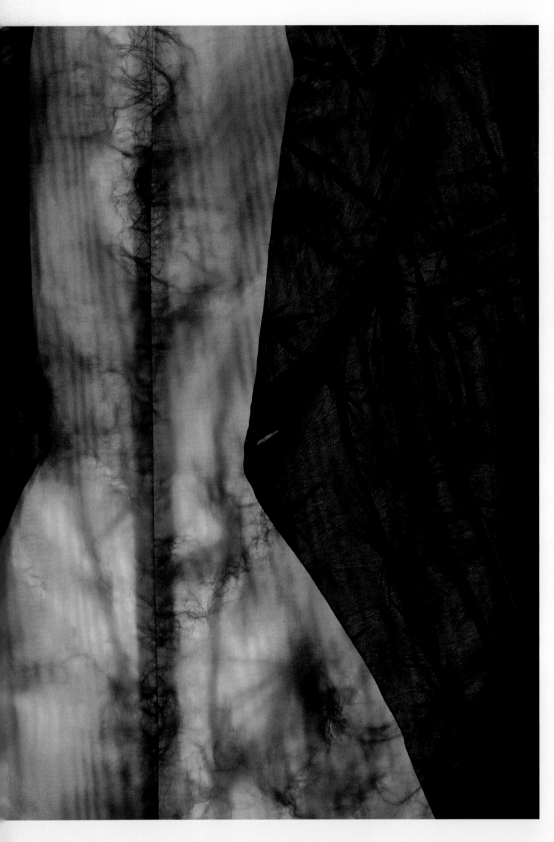

Left
142. Detail of frock coat lining,
Jack the Ripper Stalks his Victims,
Autumn/Winter 1992
Silk with human hair

Above right
143. Locket, *Sarabande*,
Spring/Summer 2007
Gold-plated metal, enamel,
hair and mother-of-pearl beads
Shaun Leane for Alexander McQueen
Modelled by Marina Peres

Below right
144. Locket, England, 1871–2
Gold, diamonds and enamel
V&A: M.11-1972

Opposite left
145. Ring, north-west Europe, 1550–75
V&A: M.280-1962

Opposite right
146. Dress, *Black* (American Express),
June 2004
Silk chiffon with skull print
Modelled by Kate Moss
Photograph by Mike Marsland

LAYERS OF MEANING

KIRSTIN KENNEDY

'My favourite art is Flemish ... [I] would love to buy a Memling,
but I don't think I could ever [afford] it'
Alexander McQueen, 2004

—

Interviewed by his mother in 2004, Alexander McQueen declared that his 'favourite part[s] of art' were the works of fifteenth-century Flemish and Dutch painters, 'because of the colours, because of the sympathetic way they approached life [...] I think they were very modern for their times'.[1] In his garments, McQueen reconfigures vivid fifteenth-century depictions of suffering and the supernatural in ways both macabre and humorous.

A coat from the Autumn/Winter 1997 collection *It's a Jungle Out There* incorporates a detail from a triptych entitled *The Last Judgement* (1467–71) by Hans Memling (pls 149, 150).[2] The detail shows St Michael using scales to determine which of the risen dead is to be saved or damned by the weight of their soul. Tall, armour-clad Michael, who led the expulsion of the rebellious angel Lucifer from heaven, contrasts with the naked, pleading man on the balance. Memling's painting shows the man to the right of his judge, a position that symbolically reflects his status among the Saved and, consequently, a figure whose fate a fifteenth-century viewer would hope to emulate. On the coat, McQueen has reversed and cropped the image so the figure of Michael looms over the cowering man, now to his left. This transmits a modern message at once protective and aggressive.

A woman's jacket from the same collection is stitched together from shaped pieces of fabric, each piece printed with a detail from a fragment of a triptych (*c*.1430) by Robert Campin (pls 151–3). The fragment depicts one of the two thieves crucified with Christ, identifiable as such because his limbs are tied, not nailed, to the cross.

The image of the thief's head and upper body span the back of the jacket, while the most prominent image on the front of the garment, emerging from the wearer's middle, are his bound feet. This anatomical disjunction may appear blackly humorous to modern viewers, but to their fifteenth-century counterparts the wounds were freighted with meaning. Campin's accurate and grisly depiction of skin stretched by fractured shinbones and distorted by tightened ropes was intended to attract the spectator's gaze and encourage feelings of horror, empathy and piety. It also reflected the Gospel narrative. The thieves' legs, faltering supports for their sagging upper bodies, were deliberately broken to hasten their deaths by asphyxiation.

McQueen's sampling of fifteenth-century religious iconography is more complex in his unfinished Autumn/Winter collection of 2010, completed by his atelier and shown after his death. Although never officially titled, it became known as *Angels and Demons*. The explicitly religious connotations are reflected in the hellish details appropriated from three different paintings by Hieronymus Bosch and woven together on a woman's evening dress (pls 147, 148). Bosch's works drew on proverbs and Scripture to encourage the viewer to reflect on the consequences of immoderate and immodest behaviour. The wailing of a red bagpipe, from the panel depicting 'Hell' in Bosch's triptych *The Garden of Earthly Delights* (*c*.1500), punishes human dancers whose ears have tempted them to sin.

Other images are from a triptych depicting the Last Judgement (*c*.1482 or later). The snakes slithering round a naked body (a detail McQueen reproduced twice) recall the Serpent that tempted Eve to sin in the Garden of Eden, and by extension the belief that snakes infest human corpses. Toads, believed to be poisonous, were bedfellows as deadly to the man wedged into a barrel as the fire-breathing dragon arched over him. On the front of the dress, the fish wrapped in robes that resemble a cardinal's attire and the naked woman who peeps from a hollow tree are both devils from Bosch's triptych *The Temptation of St Anthony* (*c*.1501 or later). This mixture of the familiar and the monstrously distorted suggests the inner turmoil that clothes can conceal. McQueen, however, is not without humour. The grotesque red bagpipe is placed at the base of the bodice, immediately above the wearer's anus.

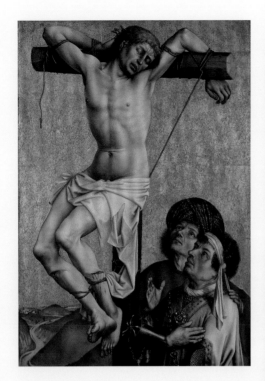

Above left
151. Robert Campin, *The Thief to the Left of Christ by the Master of Flémalle*, c.1430
Oil on panel
Städel Museum, Frankfurt

Above right and opposite
152 and 153. Jacket, *It's a Jungle Out There*, Autumn/Winter 1997
Silk and cotton, printed with a detail from Robert Campin's *The Thief to the Left of Christ by the Master of Flémalle*, c.1430
Photograph (right) by Robert Fairer

WASTELAND / WONDERLAND

ZOE WHITLEY

———

'*Denatured by transformation, things turn strange here ...*'
Andrew Graham-Dixon, *The Independent*, 1993

—

Art critic Andrew Graham-Dixon could unwittingly have written the epigraph for London's creative milieu in the 1990s with these words. In fact he was discussing Rachel Whiteread's Artangel commission *House* – a concrete cast of 193 Grove Road, in Mile End, east London, which won the 1993 Turner Prize. His description of the work, however, in terms of 'bulges', 'rounded hollows', 'chiselled incisions' and 'forms as mysterious as the hieroglyphs on Egyptian tombs,' could equally have conjured Alexander McQueen's signature details and evoked the metamorphoses at play in many contemporary artists' practices. Unrecognizable as today's fashionable enclave, the East End was then in a state of dereliction: 193 Grove Road was one of the neighbourhood's last remaining terrace houses before being razed for redevelopment. But it was a state in which resourcefulness flourished. That same year, artists Tracey Emin and Sarah Lucas set up The Shop on Bethnal Green Road, selling works both collaborative and individual, mainly using materials from Brick Lane market. 'Back then, nearly every shop on Brick Lane was boarded up – everywhere was, in fact,' noted Emin.[1] '[The Shop] was part of the Shoreditch revolution, of east London becoming somewhere to hang out,' Lucas recalled.[2]

Echoing performance-art historian RoseLee Goldberg's assertion that the dynamic environment of the New York art scene in 1960s and early '70s was fostered by then-low costs of living,[3] London's cultural ascendance in design and visual art found many artists availing themselves of affordable studio space in warehouses vacated by industry – including McQueen's Hoxton work space. Artist Jake Chapman remembered the studio he and his brother Dinos shared: 'Ours was an old warehouse in the Old Kent Road. Waste was outside our studio, next to McDonalds. It was a continuous plane of sculptural wreckage, mess and some art. Lee's [studio] was a little more organized.' This atmosphere facilitated unique opportunities for artistic exchange and collaboration. 'We gave him drawings,' said Chapman of McQueen. 'He sent clothes, which no human could physically wear. One time Lee came to the studio and saw that we had some First World War tins of prosthetic noses, and of course took them home with him.'[4]

Like McQueen, the Chapman Brothers' exacting craftsmanship fused the idyllic and the uncanny. Their arresting *Tragic Anatomies* (1996) displayed mutated child mannequins disfigured by genitalia, situated in an Edenic garden setting. Exhibited at the ICA, London, the installation was followed by McQueen's *La Poupée* collection (Spring/Summer 1997), where the designer's references to abject femininity take in Hans Bellmer's disquieting pre-war dolls of the 1930s (pl.292) as well as echo the lanky splayed limbs of Sarah Lucas's 1997 'bunny' figures, made of stuffed tights. In turn, McQueen had his assistants Sebastian Pons and Sarah Burton make a T-shirt for a six-armed Chapman Brothers' doll, where zips were incorporated into the design. '[Lee] came to the studio and we did a shot with the clothes/ sculpture,' Jake Chapman recalled. 'I have no idea what eventually happened to the collaborative piece.'

The Chapman Brothers' conflation of the innocent and profane, the enterprising anti-art sensibility of Lucas and Emin, and even the spectacle of Whiteread's monumental public sculpture were each representative of emergent practices in contemporary British art, which found a resonance in McQueen's oeuvre. Grouped together under the heading YBAs – Young British Artists – all were included in the Royal Academy's headline-grabbing *Sensation* exhibition in 1997. McQueen shared with this group an assured, singular and provocative sensibility (pl.154).

Not only did McQueen share affinities with his immediate artist contemporaries, he also referenced the complex, transformative, immersive and contemplative aspects of established international artists. A curious intellect, absorbing visual and performative elements from books, films and exhibitions, he found inspiration in the work of German artist and film-maker, Rebecca Horn (pl.157). Horn's 1994 retrospective of installations and body sculptures took place across both the Serpentine and Tate galleries. Indeed, her appendage extensions, feathered masks, fans and spectacular installations informed the construction of McQueen's garments in general and the staging of *No.13* (Spring/Summer 1999) in particular, with its finale of automated spray-paint guns (pl.62).

In 1997, the same year as *Sensation*, South London Gallery exhibited American video artist Bill Viola's watery rumination on opposing archetypes of life and death, obliteration and creation: *The Messenger* (pl.155). Originally a site-specific series of projections for Durham Cathedral, Viola's stills were appropriated by McQueen for

the credit sheet for *Untitled* (Spring/Summer 1998). They would also form a point of reference for Nick Knight and McQueen's ambitious collaboration *Angel* (2001), staged inside a Rococo chapel in Avignon to a soundtrack by Björk. The portrait comprised of delicately coloured maggots engaged in their oddly poetic life cycle (pl.156).

Indeed, *Angel* can be understood within a continuum of theatrical memento mori, following on from artists such as Damien Hirst, who had begun working with maggots and butterfly pupae a decade earlier. Hirst's notorious *A Thousand Years* (1990) featured flies breeding within a glass vitrine, which contained both their life sustenance – a severed cow's head, sugar cubes and water – and life's end, in the form of an ultraviolet-light Insect-O-cutor (pl.158). The milder installation *In and Out of Love* (1991) likewise presented hatching butterflies, living out their short existence within gallery confines.

Asked to sum up this uniquely creative period of collaboration and friendship with McQueen, Jake Chapman conceded: 'I remember it as a blur – only because the interactions between practitioners and the energy that motivated them was not objectively separable. The overlaps were the thing...'. Chapman offers, by way of a conclusion, French philosopher Georges Bataille's statement: 'The animal is in the world like water in water'. Artist and designer working in an indistinguishable flow.

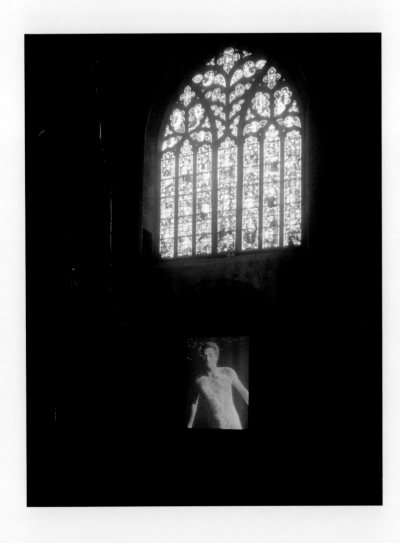

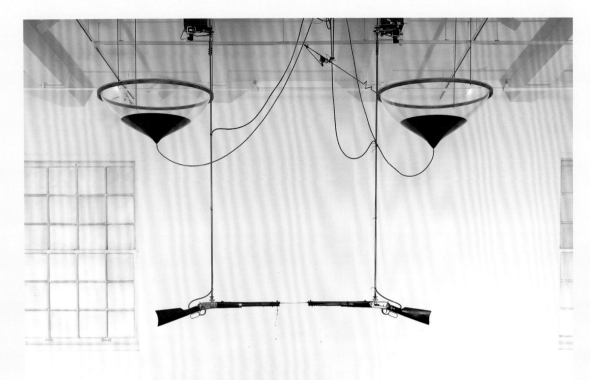

157. Rebecca Horn, *High Moon*, Marion Goodman Gallery, New York, 1991
Photograph by Jan Abbott

Opposite
158. Damien Hirst, *A Thousand Years*, 1990
Gambler, Building One, London
Photograph by Roger Wooldridge

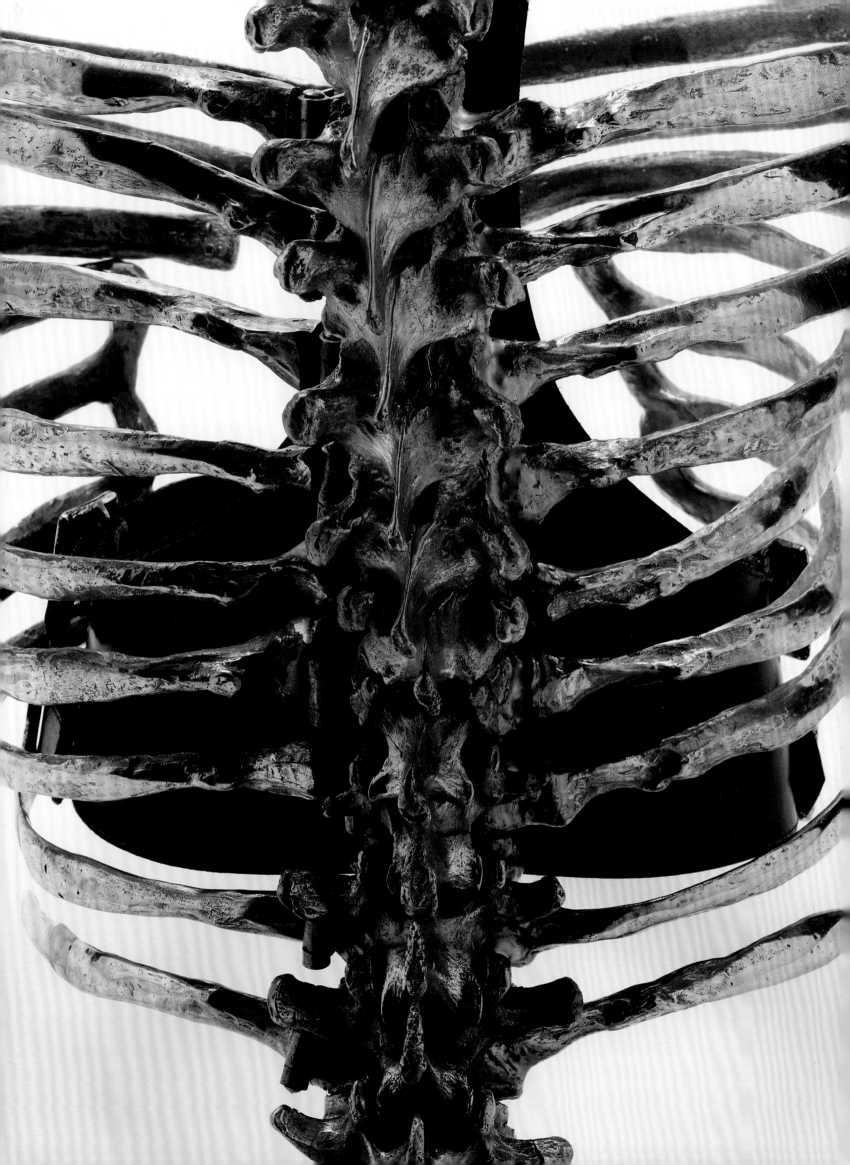

No. 4

VISCERA

———

MUSEUM OF THE MIND

LISA SKOGH

———

'It's to do with the politics of the world – the way life is
– and what is beauty'
Alexander McQueen, 2000

—

The cabinet of curiosity has long held a fascination for contemporary artists, from the 'found' objects exhibited by the Surrealists alongside their own work in the 1930s, to Damien Hirst's collections of natural history specimens of the 1990s. Today, the term 'cabinet of curiosity' may evoke haphazard collections of bizarre objects. However, the *Kunstkammer* (Cabinet of Art) or *Wunderkammer* (Cabinet of Wonders), with its roots in the sixteenth and seventeenth centuries, was far from whimsical. Its origins lay in philosophical attempts to understand nature through the act of collecting, furthered by the discovery of new continents beyond Europe, and as such it was central to the development of intellectual, political and cultural thought. Sophisticated and encyclopedic, cabinets of curiosity were systematically arranged in special rooms, which in turn became precursors of the modern public museum.

From the Renaissance onwards, cabinets were formed by natural philosophers, apothecaries and rulers, often assisted by learned advisers, with the aim of displaying the knowledge and power of the patron through collectibles that mirrored in miniature the owner's world. Unusual objects were deemed to be either crafted by the hand of God (*naturalia*) or by man (*artificialia*). The former included natural materials such as hardstones, coral and rock crystal. The latter could include nautilus shells, branches of coral, or rhinoceros horns improved by man by being set in precious mounts. Such interest in nature was implicit in a quest for knowledge of the unknown and the wondrous. Divergence from the norm was also studied with great attention and admiration; for example, the naturalist Ulisse Aldrovandi, a collector of natural specimens,

illustrated his *Monstrorum Historia* (1642) with double-headed animals, hirsute giants and deer with deformed antlers (pl.161).

Alexander McQueen was equally captivated by divergence.[1] His extensive working library reflected a wide range of interests, from the macabre to the wondrous. Amongst numerous volumes on nature, photography, art and film was Patrick Mauriès' *Cabinets of Curiosities* (2002).[2] Research boards compiled by McQueen as a source of inspiration for his collections include images taken from this book (pl.159), such as a monstrous rhinoceros cup with warthog horns and astonishing coral landscapes originating from the Imperial Habsburg *Kunstkammer* collections, some of the most significant of cabinets of curiosities.[3]

Coral, a desired rarity in cabinets of curiosities, was believed to be the frozen blood of Medusa, according to the writings of the classical author Pliny the Elder in his *Naturalis Historia* (c.AD 77–9). It was also believed to have talismanic qualities. A coral headpiece created by Philip Treacy (pl.164) for *The Girl Who Lived in the Tree* (Autumn/Winter 2008) evokes Nuremberg goldsmiths Abraham and Wenzel Jamnitzer's silver sculpture depicting Daphne, her hair transformed not into the laurel of ancient mythology but dramatically replaced by a large coral branch.[4] Minerals, too, had important properties for early collectors. In *The Overlook* (Autumn/Winter 1999), set in an imaginary frozen tundra, Kees van der Graaf was commissioned to design a spectacular quartz bodice (pl.165). It was created in the spirit of *artificialia*: both a natural hardstone rarity and a crafted object of adornment. The bodice is reminiscent of a mineral mountain constructed by the Augsburg merchant Philip Hainhofer for the cabinet given to King Gustavus Adolphus of Sweden in the early seventeenth century (pl.159).[5]

In common with many early modern collectors McQueen was fascinated by shells. *Voss* (Spring/Summer 2001) included a dress made out of hundreds of fragile razor-clam shells, a bodice covered in mussel shells and an underskirt covered in polished oyster shells (pls 96, 115, 203). Seen through a historical lens, these evoke the grotto aesthetic of princely gardens, as well as small-scale sculptures such as those in the ducal Florentine collections and illustrations of shell statuettes in Adam Olearius's *Gottorffische Kunst-Cammer* (1666; see pl.163). All these references in turn look back to the innovative composite paintings of Arcimboldo, painter to the

Habsburg court, whose portraits demonstrated the close relationship of nature and man. Continuing the marine theme, which had a particular resonance for McQueen, the jeweller Shaun Leane's silver bracelets with dangling sharks' teeth, made for *Irere* (Spring/Summer 2003), again suggest historical connotations and the notion of *artificialia*. Since the Middle Ages, serpents' tongues (in fact, fossilized sharks' teeth), which were believed to detect poison, were incorporated into lavish silver and coral table pieces for use during princely banquets.[6]

The 1655 catalogue of the Copenhagen *Kunstkammer* of Ole Worm, the Danish physician and antiquary, illustrates amongst shells, antlers and lobsters, several stuffed animals, including a polar bear and a crocodile (pl.168). Like Worm, McQueen owned his own stuffed polar bear and he was a regular client at taxidermy

Previous spread
159. Research board, *Plato's Atlantis*,
Spring/Summer 2010
Courtesy of Alexander McQueen

Opposite left
160. Backstage, *Dante*,
Autumn/Winter 1996
'Antler' headpiece, Philip Treacy
for Alexander McQueen
Modelled by Felix
Photograph by Kent Baker

Opposite right
161. Engraving of deer in Ulisse
Aldrovandi, *Monstrorum Historia*,
Bologna, 1642

Right
162. Backstage, *Dante*,
Autumn/Winter 1996
Modelled by Nikki Uberti
Photograph by Kent Baker

Below
163. Illustration of unicorn, antler
and narwhal horns in Adam Olearius,
Gottorffische Kunst-Cammer, Schleswig,
1666

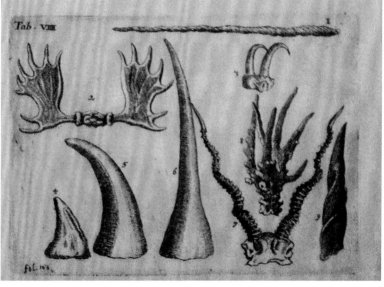

164. Headdress, *The Girl Who Lived in the Tree*, Autumn/Winter 2008
Wood and coral
Philip Treacy for Alexander McQueen
Modelled by Iris Strubegger
Photograph by Anthea Simms

Opposite
165. Bodice, *The Overlook*, Autumn/Winter 1999
Quartz
Kees van der Graaf for Alexander McQueen
Modelled by Laura Morgan
Photograph by Chris Moore

specialists, Get Stuffed, in Islington.[7] This interest in taxidermy is evidenced in the alligator heads he kept in a surgical cabinet in his bedroom, and in research boards that frequently featured dead or stuffed animals, either whole or as composites, such as winged horses and three-headed cats. In *It's a Jungle Out There* (Autumn/Winter 1997) crocodile heads highlight the shoulders of a waistcoat (pl.102), or protrude aggressively from the back of a man's jacket. In *Natural Dis-tinction, Un-Natural Selection* (Spring/Summer 2009) the catwalk was populated with stuffed giraffes, a rhinoceros, a tiger, a zebra and stags, like a re-created Garden of Eden (pl.233). The contemporary artist Polly Morgan was also an inspiration to McQueen: he owned at least two of her artworks. Having seen one of her pieces – a lifeless blue tit lying on a prayer book beneath a crystal chandelier, encased in a glass dome (pl.166) – he commissioned his own, with a robin.[8] McQueen's interest in the wildness of nature and its imaginative possibilities was equally matched by a concern for its preservation. Birds, and more specifically feathers of all kinds, repeatedly found their way into his collections in the form of dresses and headpieces, made of peacock, duck and pheasant feathers (pl.118). They also appeared as textile design sources, for example, a bird of paradise print, which featured in *Irere*. It evokes the early modern fascination with this rare bird whose feathers were brought back to Europe and, in the form of crowns and mantles, incorporated into prominent cabinet displays.[9]

McQueen was equally inspired by the spoils of hunting, repeatedly featuring antlers in his designs (pl.160).[10] Many early modern castles in Europe displayed antler trophies.[11] McQueen may well have been aware of the large collection of mutilated and deformed antlers at Moritzburg Castle, Saxony.[12] Worm's *Kunstkammer* in Copenhagen and that at Ambras Castle included not only antlers but also assorted animal crania, thought to have grown out of tree trunks. In *It's a Jungle Out There* McQueen used impala horns, which projected from the shoulders of a jacket (pl.103).[13] In *The Widows of Culloden* (Autumn/Winter 2006) antlers are partly concealed by and pierced through exquisite lace to suggest a dramatic bridal crown (pl.40). References to the medieval and early modern allure of mythical creatures, such as the one-horned unicorn and rhinoceros, can also be seen in McQueen's shows, such as *Dante* (Autumn/Winter 1996), in which a model is decorated with a horn that sprouts from her forehead (pl.162), quite possibly inspired by the German installation artist Rebecca Horn's work *Unicorn* (1970–2).[14]

McQueen was fascinated by the public collections of the Wellcome Institute, the Sir John Soane Museum, the Horniman Museum and the South Kensington museums in London,[15] and the Pitt Rivers Museum in Oxford, which encompassed the complete spectrum from medicine and art to archaeology, natural history

and ethnography. In constructing his catwalk shows, with his trusted advisers around him, McQueen acted almost like those patrons of earlier historical periods – collecting, commissioning and displaying. Whether he commissioned works privately, or as part of his official presentations, it all formed part of his created persona, most subtly revealed in portraits in which he is shown variously with a skull, crowned with an antler trophy (p.334) and posed with a hunting falcon, the epitome of princely privilege. The ephemeral displays of the runway arguably echoed the staged festivities of early modern court culture, and acted as an extension of his role as patron, tastemaker and (re)inventor.[16] As in the cabinet of curiosities painted by Johann Georg Hinz (c.1666; pl.167), in which the search for the unknown materializes in rare collectibles, McQueen's own 'museum of the mind' rendered his shows a moving tableau of curiosities. Such evocations lay at the heart of his quest to frame and understand the beauty of the unrestrained.

Left
166. Polly Morgan, *To Every Seed His Own Body*, 2006
Photograph by Tessa Angus

Below
167. Johann Georg Hinz, *Treasure Chest*, 1666
Oil on canvas
Kunsthalle, Hamburg

Opposite
168. Engraved frontispiece to Ole Worm
G. Wingendorp, *Museum Wormianum*,
Leiden, 1655
V&A: National Art Library

No. 175

'Star' headpiece
In Memory of Elizabeth How, A/W 2007
Silver and Swarovski gemstones

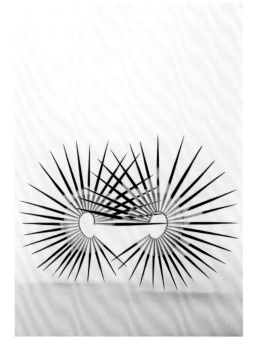

No. 176

'Alien' shoe
Plato's Atlantis, S/S 2010
3D-printed, painted resin

No. 177

Earrings
Irere, S/S 2003
Silver and porcupine quills

No. 178

Shoe
A/W 2010
Resin, leather and metallic thread

No. 179

Bust
2001
Carved and stained pinewood

No. 180

'Titanic' boot
Plato's Atlantis, S/S 2010
Leather and metal

No. 169

Prosthetic leg
No.13, S/S 1999
Carved ash wood

No. 170

Neckpiece
What a Merry Go Round, A/W 2001
Pearl and pheasant claws

No. 171

Chopine
La Dame Bleue, S/S 2008
Carved wood, leather, silver beading

No. 172

Gauntlet
A/W 2010
Kid leather with digital print

No. 173

'Armadillo' boot
Plato's Atlantis, S/S 2010
Python skin, leather and wood

No. 174

Mask
Dante, A/W 1996
Synthetic and enamelled metal

THE CABINET
OF
CURIOSITIES

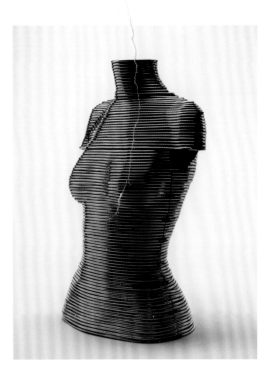

No. 187

'Coiled' corset
The Overlook, A/W 1999
Aluminium

No. 188

'Jaw Bone' mouthpiece
Untitled, S/S 1998
Aluminium

No. 189

'Bird's Nest' headdress
The Widows of Culloden, A/W 2006
Silver, Swarovski gemstones, mallard wings

No. 190

'Empire' bag
The Girl Who Lived in the Tree, A/W 2008
Enamel, gilt, leather and Swarovski crystal

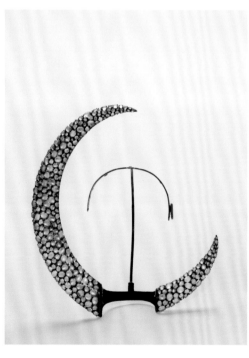

No. 191

'Crescent Moon' headpiece
In Memory of Elizabeth How, A/W 2007
Silver and Swarovski crystal

No. 192

'Bell Jar' dress
Natural Dis-tinction, S/S 2009
Swarovski crystal and stretch synthetic

No. 181
—
'Crown of Thorns' headpiece
Dante, A/W 1996
Silver

No. 182
—
'Armadillo' boot
Plato's Atlantis, S/S 2010
Paillettes, leather and wood

No. 183
—
'Spine' corset
Untitled, S/S 1998
Aluminium and leather

No. 184
—
Top
Joan, A/W 1998
Cotton and sequins with photo print

No. 185
—
Bag
In Memory of Elizabeth How, A/W 2007
Metal, leather and silver claw

No. 186
—
'Orchid' shoulder piece
Pantheon ad Lucem, A/W 2004
Silver-plated metal

No. 181

—

'Crown of Thorns' headpiece
Dante, A/W 1996
Silver

No. 182

—

'Armadillo' boot
Plato's Atlantis, S/S 2010
Paillettes, leather and wood

No. 183

—

'Spine' corset
Untitled, S/S 1998
Aluminium and leather

No. 184

—

Top
Joan, A/W 1998
Cotton and sequins with photo print

No. 185

—

Bag
In Memory of Elizabeth How, A/W 2007
Metal, leather and silver claw

No. 186

—

'Orchid' shoulder piece
Pantheon ad Lucem, A/W 2004
Silver-plated metal

MODELLING
MCQUEEN

HARD GRACE

CAROLINE EVANS

'Anything I do is based on craftsmanship. A bit of tailoring, or a bit of woodwork, or be it anything else, you know. I try to involve a lot of handcrafted things'

ALEXANDER MCQUEEN, 2000

No mean tailor himself, Alexander McQueen had a keen eye for other forms of craftsmanship, commissioning makers of all kinds to produce some of his most engaging showpieces and accessories. He was equally discerning when it came to the models he wanted to wear these clothes. They were technicians of the walk, as much as the makers were technicians of the object. This chapter explores not only the craftsmanship of the makers of the showpieces, but also the craft of the models who brought them to life on the runway. It tracks the body, beginning with the disembodied torso, from the studio in which it was made onto the runway where it was animated by the model. These two activities, making and modelling, may seem very different. Both craftsmen and fashion models, however, are engaged in a form of 'thinking through doing', and they do this through their engagement with the garment itself. This makes the garment a powerful linchpin. Especially when it is a highly crafted showpiece, it brings into dialogue the embodied knowledge of both the maker and the performer. The question, then, is what happens when the agency of the object meets the agency of the fashion model.

The Torso

Central to McQueen's aesthetic was a fascination with the torso. Perhaps it had its roots in his Savile Row training in tailoring, which teaches an awareness of the frailties of the masculine body beneath the suit. His vision of the naked female torso beneath a tailored trouser suit in *Nihilism* (Spring/Summer 1994) (pl.195) featured the infamous 'bumster' trousers that he claimed he designed in order to lengthen the torso.[1] This torso shape also determined the cut of some of his more wearable clothes in the early collections: a simple tunic, close-fitting, always with a high neck, often with short sleeves and ending at the hip. For McQueen, the female body was a one-piece, running from the chin and the upper arms down to the hips or thighs. He rarely bisected the breastbone with a décolletage, though he might leave it entirely nude instead. When he talked about designing, he explained it in terms of the spine and the torso: '[I design from the side,] that way I get the worst angle of the body. You've got all the lumps and bumps, the S-bend of the back, the bum.

Previous spread
193. Backstage, *Banshee*,
Autumn/Winter 1994
Rebecca Lowthorpe is fitted with plaster
of Paris breastplate
Photograph by Gary Wallis

194. Detail of dress, *In Memory of
Elizabeth How, Salem 1692*,
Autumn/Winter 2007
Moulded leather
Photograph by Anthea Simms

Opposite
195. Suit, *Nihilism*, Spring/Summer 1994
Wool and silk
Photograph by Anthea Simms

That way I get a cut and proportion and silhouette that
works all the way round the body'.[2]

The McQueen torso first morphed from the organic body
into a constructed bodice in *Banshee* (Autumn/Winter 1994),
where it appeared as a plaster of Paris breastplate tied on over
a diaphanous dress (pl.193). The fashion journalist Rebecca
Lowthorpe remembers that McQueen chose her to model
it because she had a particularly long neck. Quite unlike the
beautifully crafted bodices of his later collections, it was coarsely
made of chicken wire that left marks on her flesh; roughly
moulded with huge breasts, pieces of it cracked off. It was rigid to
the hips so that she could not sit down in it, and so heavy that she
had to lie down backstage before the show.[3]

In subsequent collections McQueen developed and refined the
torso into a series of hard carapaces that sheathed the body in
plastic, metal, wood, glass, crystal, shells and leather. To do so, he
enlisted the services of designers and craftsmen of all kinds, from
jewellers to props-makers. In these bodices – made of anything but
textiles – the torso came to resemble an autonomous object, distinct
from the fleshly human body. It recalled the eighteenth-century
Italian origin of the word *torso*, meaning a stalk or stump, which
referred to the trunk of a human body, or a statue without head,
arms or legs.[4]

In his later collections, McQueen was less inclined to clad the
model's body in an external corset or rigid bodice. Instead he
sculpted the body by using corsetry under the clothes. Polina
Kasina, who became his fit model[5] in 2004, recalls how much he
adored the corset and loved to accentuate the waist, losing about
five centimetres in the process. Nearly all the larger pieces had
their own corset, or waist-cincher. Their body shape varied from
collection to collection. For *The Widows of Culloden* (Autumn/
Winter 2006) he padded the bottom, suggesting the nineteenth-
century bustle, whereas in the following season's collection,
Sarabande (Spring/Summer 2007), he rounded and enlarged
the hips to create an hourglass figure. In this way McQueen
continued to develop the idea of the torso through the historical
references that typified his collections.

These later silhouettes were very different from the angular, skinny
and lithe forms of his earliest fashion shows. That body remained
only as a trace in the moulded showpieces of the middle period
of McQueen's career, between 1997 and 2007. A showpiece is
designed to attract attention on the runway and in the media.
It is never intended to be wearable off the runway. The concept
has existed since the first fashion shows in the early twentieth
century, but McQueen took it to a new level, creating enormously
scaled-up and dramatic garments in multifarious forms, from
a curiously shaped black duck-feather dress (*The Horn of Plenty*,

Autumn/Winter 2009; pl.247) to another made of oyster shells and nineteenth-century Japanese embroidery (pl.96) taken from a screen bought at a market in Paris (*Voss*, Spring/Summer 2001). Of all his showpieces, however, it is perhaps the torsos, modelled in hard materials like metal, glass, crystal, leather and wood, which have the most to say about the body beneath them. They made visible several complex contradictions, between beauty and its containment, femininity and fear, and empowerment and control. As Claire Wilcox commented, 'So often it's the face or feet or hands that draw attention, but the torso is like the engine room of the body, solid and packed with organs. It's as if McQueen was trying to remodel and beautify, but also to protect the models as if they were chrysalids'.[6]

Making

When made in rigid leather, the torso bodices invoked the organic body beneath, juxtaposing human and animal skin in ways that could be either beautiful or brutal – or both. To produce them, McQueen collaborated with a range of craftspeople and makers. For his debut Givenchy haute couture show (Spring/Summer 1997), he commissioned the designers Whitaker Malem to make two leather pieces: a white winged corset, and a gold Roman-style bodice worn by model Alek Wek in the show, and later photographed on Naomi Campbell (pl.204). The designers used construction techniques from shoe-making, first sculpting a torso

like a last onto which they drew the pattern-pieces that were then cut out, transferred to suede-lined leather, and stitched together. Finally the entire bodice was gilded with gold leaf.

Two years later, in his own-label *No.13* collection (Spring/Summer 1999), McQueen presented a series of leather bodices with a very different aesthetic. Made by prosthetists (experts at designing and fitting artificial limbs) at Queen Mary's Hospital in Roehampton, London, they were created by wet-moulding leather[7] over a plaster of Paris body cast supplied by McQueen. The result is a bodice that bears the imprint of the naked body: an indented navel, faint nipples, the angular jut of shoulder blades and slight suggestion of a ribcage. When McQueen had asked Whitaker Malem to create a 'six-pack' and a navel for the gold Givenchy bodice, the result was entirely different as it was sculpturally modelled and stitched rather than moulded from a life cast. The Givenchy bodice evokes the marble torsos of classical antiquity, in keeping with the show's theme, whereas the *No.13* pieces have medical connotations, augmented by their asymmetrical corset-lacing that resembles a suture and their high necks that recall a surgical brace.

To make the body cast from which the prosthetists worked, McQueen had enlisted Kees van der Graaf, a product designer who usually worked in Perspex. Laura Morgan was the model.

Van der Graaf recalled that 'Laura was one of Lee's favourite models. I remember how she absolutely loved it when we slapped the warm plaster onto her body! While we were stirring the buckets of Herculite and Crystacal and preparing the Modroc and jute scrim, Laura was rubbing her body with baby oil.'[8] It was a hot day, however, and the process was onerous for the model, who at one stage had to be chipped out of the cast to avoid fainting.[9]

In the course of a single day, van der Graaf and his team made several casts of Morgan's body (pl.200). Afterwards, as van der Graaf recalls:

> When I completed them [the casts], Lee asked if we could take them down to Roehampton Hospital where he had been inspired by the prosthetics workshops. I made several visits, and their highly specialist technicians blew my mind every time. … Lee talked very highly of them, and later sought out Aimee Mullins for the work that he had in mind. … The technicians at Roehampton liked my life-casts of Laura as they were solid and firm (I had taken the precaution of making them in good quality plaster and with a fibre-glass skin). Their wet-leather technique worked well on them.[10]

One cast was used to create the famous corset worn in the show by double amputee and Paralympic athlete Aimee Mullins, who walked on wooden legs of hand-carved ash (pl.197). Another, a lower-torso with a single leg (pl.128), became model Shalom Harlow's hip brace in *No.13* (pl.129); the design drawings can be seen on the cast itself. McQueen used the same wet-moulding technique for a cyborg bodice in red leather with a white prosthetic-style trim for Givenchy ready-to-wear (Autumn/ Winter 1999). He continued to use rigid leather bodices patterned with traces of the navel and ribcage in three later collections: a moulded bodice similar to the ones in *No.13*, and two leather and horsehair dresses, all three from *It's Only a Game* (Spring/Summer 2005) (pl.201); a moulded cream hand-painted leather dress in *Sarabande*; and a moulded brown leather dress from *In Memory of Elizabeth How, Salem 1692* (Autumn/Winter 2007) (pl.194).

From Morgan's body cast, van der Graaf also made several clear vac-formed torsos.[11] These were used to create a range of bodices: a mirrored bodice for McQueen's *The Overlook* (Autumn/Winter 1999); clear LED-encrusted bodices, deriving from the 1982 Disney science-fiction film *Tron*, for Givenchy's ready-to-wear collection (Autumn/Winter 1999); and a clear bodice filled with butterflies, again for Givenchy (pl.198), reminiscent of the clear plastic bodice filled with live worms from *The Hunger* (Spring/Summer 1996) (pl.132). The form was still being used as late as *Salem* in the gold breastplate of a gold paillette and peacock-feather bodysuit.

All these corsets and bodices were worn by a range of models other than Morgan, whose body cast had provided the ghostly original. In *The Overlook*, however, Morgan herself wore the coiled metal corset (pl.199) that the jeweller Shaun Leane had modelled on her body cast. Leane's brief was to transform the coiled necklace worn by Ndebele women in South Africa, and which to Western eyes resembles a neck brace, into a full body sculpture.

He thus recreated McQueen's typical torso shape in a metal body brace in shiny aluminium, with a high neck and short sleeves that restricted the model's arm movements, forced her chin up and propelled her gaze forwards. It was technically the hardest thing that Leane had done, but also the most rewarding, he claimed.[12] An accomplished goldsmith who was used to working on a small scale, Leane had to teach himself new metal skills for the demands of the runway. He made each coil one by one, and fitted them individually to the plaster of Paris torso to ensure a precise fit. The bust area was particularly difficult, relying on trial and error. Even working a 16-hour day, Leane could only make eight coils a day, and the finished corset consisted of 90 coils. It was physically demanding work, and the entire corset took six weeks to complete. It took 15 minutes to put it on the model before the show, and ten to take it off afterwards, as she had to be carefully screwed into it by means of a series of miniscule screws running down both sides of the corset. Morgan recalls the fit being so precise that her chest pushed against the metal when she breathed in.

Van der Graaf describes McQueen's ability to catalyse creativity: 'Lee appeared to be so good at persuading people but in actual fact his modus operandi was simply to provoke, prompt, arouse. People just did things because he was there. Stuff happened. There was a stimulus from being around someone as charismatic as him.'[13] Leane and jeweller Naomi Filmer both recall how McQueen recognized their craftsmanship and encouraged them to think big, producing body sculpture rather than small-scale jewellery.[14] Filmer, who made blown-glass body pieces for *The Dance of the Twisted Bull* (Spring/Summer 2002), observed:

> The scale for him was part of his vision, and frankly he was so clear about his own vision and belief that I was the right person to work on those pieces for him, that I didn't dare question the scale of the pieces. Yet he gave me complete creative freedom. … He was like a great tutor in that respect, because he could see something in others' work that would feed his project, and yet push those others towards horizons they hadn't even imagined.[15]

McQueen rarely gave explicit instructions, however. As van der Graaf recalled in an interview with Louise Rytter:

> KVDG: One day I received a box from Deyrolle, Paris. It was a wonderful surprise. Katy England had chosen some fabulous butterflies. [The model] looked so great in the resulting vac-formed bodice with the butterflies trapped inside.
>
> LR: Did you create them from first sketch to the final showpiece?
>
> KVDG: Lee and Katy (and the other stylists) were generally so manic that they didn't bother with drawings. If I got a box of butterflies in the post, I knew what to do. If Lee asked me to do a crystal bodice, I got on with it. It took him two seconds to say 'how 'bout a crystal bodice?' The next day I'd be down at the local rock wholesaler selecting quartz rock crystals. Only later I discovered that he was thinking of Swarovski crystals! As it turned out, Lee's brevity gave me room to manoeuvre (pl.165).'[16]

Above
196. Corset, *Voss*, Spring/Summer 2001
Columbia Glassworks for Alexander McQueen
Painted and etched glass
Modelled by Laura Morgan

Right
197. Ensemble, *No.13*,
Spring/Summer 1999
Corset: moulded leather; skirt: silk lace;
prosthetic legs by Bob Watts and Paul Ferguson
for Alexander McQueen: carved ash wood
Modelled by Aimee Mullins
Photograph by Mark Large

McQueen worked in many more materials with many other makers and craftspeople. The huge plywood winged bodice worn by Erin O'Connor in *No.13* was made by the specialist props-maker Simon Kenny of Souvenir (pl.205). The red glass corset worn in *Voss* by Morgan, and probably based on her body cast, was made by Columbia Glassworks in east London (pl.196). Many other showpieces, not all of them recorded, were produced in-house by the dedicated studio staff and interns who laboriously sewed red glass beads onto the bodice of a dress or drilled holes into thousands of glass microscope slides and seashells in order to hand-stitch them onto dress bodices (pl.203).

Objects with Agency

These torsos are powerful objects, even before they make it onto the runway. Polina Kasina commented that 'You can tell the mood of the collection before you try the clothes. … All the looks are powerful, but especially the last few [the showpieces].' Seen off the body as museum objects, divorced from flesh and fabric, they retain an auratic power. But, animated by the models in the shows, these hard bodices in metal, glass, quartz, leather, shells or plywood were even more evocative, strange and wonderful.

They required a certain chutzpah to wear, a particular attitude and even, sometimes, physical bravery. A model in a glass corset knows she cannot afford to fall. Laura Morgan was told jovially, just before she went on in the glass corset, 'If you trip, you're a goner!' She laughed as she recalled: 'That was the most terrifying piece to wear. … The problem with the glass corset was I got put in a really tight skirt, I just couldn't move my legs. It was petrifying because I just felt like "I'm falling! I can't move!"' Kasina remembered the extremely high shoes of *The Horn of Plenty* as 'scary – they were easy to walk in, but you never know'. The models interviewed for this chapter, however, described such experiences with amusement and admiration. They used words like 'scary' and 'terrifying' as accolades, and Erin O'Connor affirmed that modelling for McQueen 'was never fear-driven', even in the case of the most extreme showpieces.[17]

Such objects are what the French sociologist Bruno Latour has called 'objects with agency'– things that make something happen.[18] The most obvious example is a high-heeled shoe that changes the gait. Not all objects, however, have agency, argues Latour, and 'specific tricks have to be invented *to make them* [objects] *talk*, that is, to offer descriptions of themselves, to produce *scripts* of what they are making others – humans and non-humans – do'.[19] Latour lists many such catalysts, the final one being creative fiction because, he writes, 'sociologists have a lot to learn from artists'.[20] So, too, do they from fashion designers.

Following Latour, the physical restraints of the showpieces can be seen as generative design elements that produce a 'script', giving them their cue to make things happen. So, for example, the metal armature made by Shaun Leane to go underneath a gold cut-away morning coat in *La Poupée* (Spring/Summer 1997) constrained the movements of the model, forcing her to walk in a distinctive and ungainly way (pl.202). Similarly, the burgundy leather bodice from *In Memory of Elizabeth How, Salem 1692*

Opposite
198. Bodice, Givenchy Haute Couture,
Spring/Summer 1998
Moulded plastic and butterflies
Kees van der Graaf for
Alexander McQueen
Photograph by Ken Towner

Below left
199. 'Coiled' corset, *The Overlook*,
Autumn/Winter 1999
Aluminium
Shaun Leane for Alexander McQueen
Modelled by Laura Morgan
Photograph by Robert Fairer

Below right
200. Body cast of Laura Morgan,
London, 1998
Plaster of Paris and fibreglass
Kees van der Graaf for
Alexander McQueen
Courtesy of Kees van der Graaf

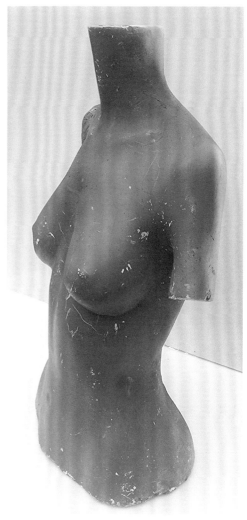

(pl.194) produced a particularly rigid, even robotic, walk. Made of rigid, wet-moulded leather, it covered the body from head to thigh which impeded the plasticity between head, neck and torso that walking requires.

This sounds like a mechanistic account, and it can be: Aimee Mullins recalled that she had practiced her model walk before the show but could not use it as the carved elm-wood legs she wore had no flexibility in the ankle. Furthermore, she had planned her route so as to avoid the revolving platforms set in the wooden floor, only to find that the corset forced her head up so that she could not see the floor as she walked, and had to trust her instincts.[21] These typically McQueen devices produce a certain hard grace: the chin impossibly high, the gaze resting on an imaginary horizon, and a rigid torso that allows no more flexion than a snaky sway, but which alters the forward thrust of each high-heeled step. This is a disciplined, uncompromising body, with nothing free-form or sloppily expressive about it. McQueen's models could sometimes look like soldiers, with their determined gait and fierce gaze. And, as O'Connor, one of his most important interpreters, observed, the job was extremely demanding physically: 'We'd sustain all sorts of minor injuries.

[Laughs.] It's like being an athlete … it has to look effortless but requires a ferocious physical discipline'. She had already learnt that discipline from her youthful training at the Royal Ballet School, which also taught 'high expectations to deliver, you're always thinking about your audience'.

Two instances of 'minor injuries', one sustained by a studio seamstress, the other by a high profile fashion model, show the physical endurance of both. Morgan, who opened *Supercalifragilisticexpialidocious* (Autumn/Winter 2002) leading two wolf-hybrid dogs on a leash, described how the hem of her mauve leather hooded cape was stained with the blood of the woman who had been frantically sewing it half an hour before Morgan went on. And O'Connor recounted that, just as she was about to go onstage in the razor-clam dress in *Voss* (pl.115), McQueen whispered in her ear, 'rip your dress off when you're out there'. Throwing herself into the role, she ran her hands through the dress lifting up and plucking off shells as she walked, cutting her hands. With hindsight she remembered:

I didn't realise that my hands were bleeding until I came off, and in classic Alexander style he was horrified and apologised,

but then [laughs] he saw the artistic moment in it, and because we were all wearing bandaged heads, he took my hands and placed them on my head. [She raises her own hands to her ears to mimic his action.] That was a real moment. That's a glimpse of the man.

Modelling

The French historian Georges Vigarello has described a range of historical phenomena, including etiquette lessons and the corset, as a kind of 'pedagogy of the body': forms of physical and moral training that produced a specific carriage and gait.[22] Something comparable might be argued for McQueen's high-necked bodices and restraining jewellery. Catherine Brickhill, who was assistant designer at McQueen and Givenchy from 1995 to 2001, has said: 'You are being worn by Lee's clothes. You are not wearing them but you are worn by the pieces'.[23] Her turn of phrase well describes the distinctive power of the clothes. The capacity of dress to act on, even to perform, the self was similarly described by Virginia Woolf in her novel *Orlando* (1928): 'There is much to support the view that it is clothes that wear us, and not we, them'.

Yet it would be a mistake to interpret Brickhill's statement simply as a deterministic or mechanical account of how clothing produces action. Laura Morgan described how the very restrictions of McQueen's designs positively enabled her performance on the runway:

I have very clear memories of putting the clothes on and automatically they made me feel proud. … You could get into character with his clothes, especially with the showpieces. They made you hold your body differently. … The hard shell gives you a strength and a rise, so the bodice is a part of *me*, it's not armour. … I just felt very proud to be a woman. … Wearing that coiled corset forced me to stand up. I couldn't turn my head, I couldn't move my arms, I couldn't move the top part of my body. So it's almost like it forces you to pay attention, forces you to be present, and be there, and be what you are. It's very commanding.

Similarly, Lily Cole has said that when she first started runway modelling she often felt like a mere clotheshorse, but when

204. Pierre et Gilles, *Diana*, 1997
Naomi Campbell wearing gold leather
dress, Givenchy Haute Couture,
The Search for the Golden Fleece,
Spring/Summer 1997
Whitaker Malem for Alexander McQueen

modelling for McQueen she felt like a performer, with a role to play.[24] Morgan agreed, and went on to say, 'Ultimately that comes from within oneself. His clothes allowed the wearer to bring out parts of themselves that you would not necessarily reveal when in a pair of jeans and a T-shirt: a confidence, a character'. And Erin O'Connor described how for each look she developed a different persona. So in *Voss* the two looks she wore (see pls 110, 115) catalysed two different performances:

> It was an asylum, I was a different character in the sense that with the shells I was in charge of my illness, that's how I interpreted it – I was breaking free. And with the red [dress], a deep sort of sensual vermillion red, it was far more whimsical, it alluded more to the fragility of a human being and a woman possessed, and my movements were different.

Naomi Campbell, too, recalled that when modelling for McQueen, 'you became another person – a character. I loved his direction. He was a director as well as a great designer. He'd explain the mood. He challenged you. It was great to be challenged.' Asked to elaborate on the nature of the challenge, she replied:

> I'm a blank canvas. The challenge was to see how Lee would invent you. He could do it in so many ways. I trusted him as a creator. I knew he'd never put me in any derogatory situation. … You had to keep your mood. It really was theatre. He'd speak to you at fittings one-on-one, not to a group. Each girl he saw in a different way. We all had our roles to play. He wasn't expecting you to become it there and then. I liked to go away and process it [before the show].[25]

Although McQueen's manipulations of the torso might be seen as Pygmalion-like, moulding women's bodies to his whim, these and other models' accounts of wearing them are always scripts of empowerment: garment and woman as one indivisible entity. Describing how much she learnt from Honor Fraser, with whom she first modelled in *Dante* (Autumn/Winter 1996), O'Connor said: 'She set the bar for me … she was an extraordinary model, she had grace, and an air, and an authority … she took ownership of the outfit and commanded with authority what she was wearing. And she wasn't the compromised victim'. Of her own experience of modelling for McQueen, O'Connor recalled:

> You were given permission, he granted you permission, to lose yourself in the moment and I've never worked with another designer who's allowed me to do that since. … So I've walked on water, I've been engulfed by flames, I was suspended in the air dressed as a geisha being struck by imaginary lightning – I mean the list is endless, but what was great for me as a woman was that I felt like I'd learned how to become a woman under his charge. … He deconstructed the idea of what a woman should look like, what a woman should possess, and for the roles that I played – whether they were dark, or mysterious, or triumphant – they were always empowered and they knew exactly who they were, and he was the enabler. I think he had a real love of women in that sense. And yes, OK, the message might have been distorted and quite extreme, but it was about

saying 'go out there and do your thing'. … The unanimous explanation among all the models who worked with him was that he actually gave you freedom of expression. That was his almighty, powerful legacy. And that's how we remember him. It's irreplaceable, we'll never experience that again. And how lucky we are that we did.

Poetry in Motion

If the showpieces were challenging to wear, they were only ever intended to be worn on the runway. This was where McQueen, the technician of materials and making, fashioned a space for the technicians of the immaterial – the models whose performance would give life to the showpiece through the walk, the pose, the gesture and the cultivated attitude.

In suggesting that the model's bodily movement is a technique, I use the term in the sense employed by Richard Sennett in his book *The Craftsman*: 'technique considered as a cultural issue rather than as a mindless procedure'.[26] If there is a technology of the body, it is not deterministic, as these examples of modelling difficult showpieces have demonstrated, but, taking its cue from the German philosopher Martin Heidegger, a technology linked to poetry: in the fashion show, a kind of poetry in motion. For Heidegger, 'the essence of technology is nothing technological'.[27] Far from being merely mechanical or instrumental, technology, he argued, was 'a way of revealing' something poetic that could be discerned, especially in the work of craftsmen or artists.[28]

Fashion modelling is not usually talked about in terms of craftsmanship, although actors often talk about their craft. The term is more generally associated with hand-making, and with expert workmanship in materials, something that McQueen was highly attuned to when he chose to work with other designers and makers. That he also had a good instinct for the right model for the job suggests he recognized their craftsmanship too. Although making and modelling are very different types of work, it is striking how similarly both designers and models have described the way he enabled them to push themselves in new directions.

Both making and modelling require a high degree of skill, commitment and judgment. But craftsmanship, Sennett argues, extends further than that: 'The craft of making physical things provides insights into the techniques of experience', and 'ways of using tools, organising bodily movements, thinking about materials' are 'viable proposals about how to conduct life with skill'.[29] Both the designer who works in materials and the fashion model who works with movement can be argued to be making this kind of proposal. It was on McQueen's runways that the craft of making the showpieces, and the craft of modelling them, came together.

McQueen's fashion shows thus staged an encounter, between the agency of the object and the agency of the model. Erin O'Connor felt that, in modelling his showpieces, 'We weren't wearing objects, they became a part of us and who we were. It was very much a performance, and I understood that. I found it really thrilling and liberating all at once. And the more daring and bold the idea – of course they [the showpieces] were all impossible and should never have happened! – the more we absolutely got stuck in and made it so.'

Her claim that the clothes actually became a part of the models is an instance of what the phenomenological philosopher Maurice Merleau-Ponty called 'being a thing'. This does not mean being objectified so much as immersing oneself, or losing oneself, in an activity so that, in Sennett's words, we are so absorbed in the craft of what we are doing that 'we have become the thing on which we are working'.[30] Like makers and designers who work with material culture, fashion models have an embodied knowledge of what they are doing, which Sennett calls 'the 'unity of head and hand'.[31] When O'Connor says, 'You know when you've nailed it. It's a feeling, and physically your body allows you to know that', she is articulating exactly this point.

The phenomenon of immersing oneself in a skilled activity produces a paradox: it involves both extreme precision, or focus, and extreme abandonment to the moment. The craftsman or craftswoman performs two contradictory activities at once: bodily control and mental surrender.[32] Reflecting on modelling for McQueen, O'Connor said:

> If you were to ask me what did I just do out there for the last few minutes, I honestly couldn't tell you, and in some ways the only uncomfortable thing … is my feeling of being uncomfortable, knowing that I've really just let myself go out there, and I didn't have much control. I've never really watched myself in a show, because I know that part of me is in there, but the other part knows that she's someone else when she goes out there. I choose not to really pay too much attention when I've come off stage, because she is who she is in the moment, and I really mean it, but it doesn't define me as a person in everyday life, otherwise I'd be a lunatic. I'd be walking down the centre aisle of a supermarket with great expectations. I would never come down from that high.

Perhaps, ultimately, the craft of modelling lies in its unscripted nature. No rehearsals, minimal walk-throughs, and the requirement to 'nail it' instantaneously mean that the model has to trust her or his instinct. Like the jazz musicians described by Sennett in his book on craftsmanship, fashion models have to anticipate, improvise and select, freely but within a certain structure.[33] So, even when O'Connor became entangled by balloon strings on a merry-go-round during a McQueen show, she was able to pose *in situ* for 20 minutes while the other models tried, imperceptibly and unsuccessfully, to disentangle her as they came and went. Unlike those craftspeople in materials who, over many weeks, meticulously and expertly craft metal, glass and leather, fashion models work with raw materials that are immaterial and immediate: intuition, improvisation, adrenalin and gut reaction.

205. Bodice, *No. 13*,
Spring/Summer 1999
Plywood
Modelled by Erin O'Connor
Photograph by Anthea Simms

ARMOURING THE BODY

CLARE PHILLIPS

———

'He opened my eyes to the world of fashion ...
and in his eyes it was one with no boundaries'
Shaun Leane, 2014

—

Jewellery was fundamental to the way Alexander McQueen presented his clothes, and from the beginning it featured prominently and provocatively in his catwalk shows. The messages it conveyed were as hard-edged as the metal from which the pieces were formed, tangible indicators of the preoccupations underlying the collection as a whole. He worked with a small number of jewellers who were kindred spirits and whose judgement he trusted.

For his graduation show in 1992 he turned to Simon Costin, a jeweller already well known for courting controversy with his use of taxidermied animal parts. His necklace 'Memento Mori' featured in the collection (pl.210). A pair of talons encircle the wearer's neck and grasp a triangular pendant encrusted with black beadwork, each corner of which is decorated with a rabbit's skull set with haematite eyes. The design was inspired by Huysmans' novel *A Rebours* (1884), in which an all-black banquet takes place. Costin imagined himself as a guest at the feast and created the necklace as a suitable adornment. Although it had been made six years previously, both aesthetically and emotionally it connected on a profound level with McQueen.

Nature was a central theme within McQueen's jewellery, usually accompanied by a preoccupation with death. It was present literally in tooth and claw (and feathers, in the case of designer Erik Halley's pieces), and more lyrically in the 'Rose' corset (pl.209) commissioned for Givenchy in 2000. Designed around the deathly fantasy of a girl with roses growing through her skin, all sinister elements were masked by the exuberant prettiness of the flowers. In contrast an earlier, starker exploration

of this theme had been made for the collection *Dante* (Autumn/Winter 1996). A trailing rose briar with savage thorns twines up the wearer's arm to her shoulder and then curls into her ear (pls 211, 213). Its further progress is shown by a line of thorns protruding from the forehead and cheek – a chilling yet beautiful evocation of nature's power.

Shaun Leane, creator of both these works, made his first jewellery pieces for Alexander McQueen in 1995. Like McQueen, he had learned his skills through apprenticeship in the trade rather than an art school education. Established in the jewellery world, Leane had immense technical expertise and the contacts to be able to make or source all manner of jewellery. It was a double life – by day producing conventional fine jewellery, and out of hours using the same workshop to create pieces of a completely different scale and purpose. The collaboration gave him an exceptional context within which to create magnificent conceptual jewellery.

A sharp silhouette and a dignified evocation of female power are conveyed by Sarah Harmarnee's armour (pl.208) created for the collection *Joan* (Autumn/Winter 1998). This followed the vicious, predatory look of *It's a Jungle Out There* (Autumn/Winter 1997), in which her ferocious jewellery may be seen in the context of McQueen's comment, 'I especially like the accessory for its sadomasochistic aspect'.[1] Her power to shock prompted her description as 'an angry young silversmith with a killer instinct'.[2]

A spirit of primitivism pervades much of the jewellery featured in McQueen's collections. This can take violent expression – as in the shocking bared teeth of the snarl-inducing mouthpiece (pl.215) from *Eshu* (Autumn/Winter 2000); or be a more serene examination of tribal jewellery, such as the multiple neck rings worn in parts of Africa and Burma to lengthen a woman's neck, which inspired the coiled necklaces and ultimately the 'Coiled' corset from *The Overlook* (Autumn/Winter 1999; pls 199, 207). This extraordinary metal garment encases the model within parallel rings of aluminium, each one individually cut and shaped to follow the curves of the model's own body. Fusing garment and jewel in a single silhouette, this masterpiece of catwalk art exudes invulnerability and an untouchable remoteness, achieving a sublimity far removed from its elemental origins.

Previous spread
206. Ensemble, *The Horn of Plenty*,
Autumn/Winter 2009
Dress: digital print on silk
Yashmak: aluminium and Swarovski crystal,
Shaun Leane for Alexander McQueen
Modelled by Charlotte di Calypso

Above
207. Fashion in Motion
Victoria and Albert Museum, October 2001
'Coiled' corset, *The Overlook*,
Autumn/Winter 1999
Aluminium
Shaun Leane for Alexander McQueen
Modelled by Laura Morgan

Centre
208. Backstage, *Joan*,
Autumn/Winter 1998
Alexander McQueen and Sarah Harmarnee
fitting model Svetlana
into silver-plated body armour
Sarah Harmarnee for Alexander McQueen
Photograph by Robert Fairer

Below
209. 'Rose' corset, Givenchy Haute Couture,
Spring/Summer 2000
Silver-plated metal
Shaun Leane for Alexander McQueen
Photograph by Anne Deniau

Opposite
210. Alexander McQueen wearing 'Memento
Mori' neckpiece, London, 1993
Rabbit skulls, birds' claws and haematite
Simon Costin, 1986
Photograph by Richard Burbridge
Courtesy of Simon Costin

Left
211. 'Thorn' arm piece, *Dante*,
Autumn/Winter 1996
Silver
Shaun Leane for Alexander McQueen
Modelled by Kirsten Owen

Above right
212. 'Crown of Thorns' headpiece, *Dante*,
Autumn/Winter 1996
Silver
Shaun Leane for Alexander McQueen
Modelled by Honor Fraser
Photograph by Robert Fairer

Below right
213. Fashion in Motion
Victoria and Albert Museum,
October 2001
Fitting of 'Thorn' arm piece, *Dante*,
Autumn/Winter 1996
Silver
Shaun Leane for Alexander McQueen

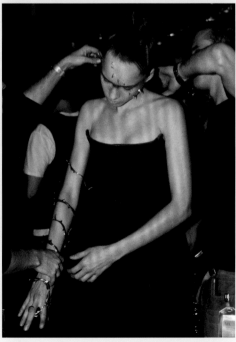

Right
214. Headpiece, *La Poupée*,
Spring/Summer 1997
Silver-plated porcupine quills
Dai Rees for Alexander McQueen
Modelled by Stella Tennant
Photograph by Anthea Simms

Below left
215. 'Tusk' mouthpiece and hoop
earrings, *Eshu*, Autumn/Winter 2000
Silver
Shaun Leane for Alexander McQueen
Photograph by Chris Moore

Below right
216. Neckpiece, *Voss*,
Spring/Summer 2001
Silver and Tahitian pearls
Shaun Leane for Alexander McQueen
Modelled by Karen Elson
Photograph by Hugo Philpott

217. 'The Dark Knight Returns'
The Face, August 1998
Alexander McQueen in armour designed
by Terry English for John Boorman's film
Excalibur, 1981
Styled by Isabella Blow
Photograph Sean Ellis

CROWNING GLORY

ORIOLE CULLEN

'With McQueen, it wasn't an option to disappoint him …
he appreciated beauty and quality, he dealt in the extraordinary.
He liked the wonderful and not every designer wants that'
Philip Treacy, 2014

—

At Paris Fashion Week in October 2007, Alexander McQueen and Philip Treacy presented *La Dame Bleue* (Spring/Summer 2008), a collaborative show commemorating their friend and mentor Isabella Blow, who had died, by suicide, five months earlier. The invitation (p.319) featured an illustration of Blow by artist Richard Gray, wearing a McQueen ensemble and a Treacy halo of black spears, commanding a winged chariot that was pulled by two horses on its ascent to heaven. McQueen quipped to Treacy that the horses in question represented the two designers themselves.[1]

The working partnership of McQueen and Treacy was originally instigated by Blow, who, frequently attired in the work of both designers, acted as an avid promoter of their respective careers. McQueen's first appearance in British *Vogue* was in 1992, in a feature on Isabella Blow 'at home'.[2] The fashion stylist was shown dressed in her own collection of McQueen ensembles, several of which were from his graduate show, combined with intricate Philip Treacy hats. As Treacy has explained, 'her devotion was inspiring for Alexander McQueen and me, because when she wanted a piece of your work, she *really* wanted it and was so grateful when she got it'.[3] Blow was insistent that the two should work together and Treacy recalled the first time they met in 1992. 'She brought him to my studio one evening. He was very complex – we were very different people in that moment, initially wary of each other, but in the end we knew each other really well because of Isabella. …We were her property and she was ours.'[4]

Blow's encouragement knew no bounds. When McQueen wanted to feature a ram's horns headpiece (pls 222, 223) for his debut haute couture show at Givenchy (Spring/

Summer 1997), Blow had one of her flock of rare Soay sheep slaughtered and the horns removed. Treacy recalls her, once back in London, triumphantly throwing the still-bloody horns onto his studio worktable.[5] Cleaned up, they were used by the milliner to act as a 'block'[6] around which he created the dramatic golden headdress worn in the show by model Naomi Campbell. For Treacy, the big difference between McQueen and other designers was 'that there was a fearlessness in him. I could make the strongest hats and it was fine, his shows could take it, that proportion, extremity, modernity…'[7]

Stylist Katy England acted as a linchpin in McQueen's collaborations with Treacy. She would visit his millinery studio about a month before a collection was due to show, laden with references and images. Her input as part of the McQueen team, and her interpretation of the designer's aesthetic, was invaluable to Treacy, who recalled how her calm approach balanced out McQueen's frenetic pace. 'They cooked it up together. … They were a brilliant combination.'[8] McQueen's appreciation of craftsmanship and Treacy's surreal and sculptural handmade creations were a good fit, yet both adopted a pragmatic approach to their work, utilizing material to hand. England would go through all Treacy's uniquely carved wooden hat blocks to see which they could reuse or adapt to form the base of a new hat or headdress, in some cases turning them around to create an entirely different shape. Such was the case with the block for a suspended, veiled hat, which was created for a Givenchy haute couture show (Autumn/Winter 1999) and later reappeared in a back-to-front construction in McQueen's *The Horn of Plenty* (Autumn/Winter 2009) collection (pl.221).

The level of mutual respect between the two designers is evident. McQueen trusted Treacy entirely to produce hats that were worthy of his collections (not for nothing was Treacy described by fashion journalist Suzy Menkes as 'the Brancusi of hat-makers').[9] He would never interfere and would not even see the hats until a couple of hours before a show. He was not effusive in his praise, but as Treacy notes: 'I knew he was happy because he'd look at the hat and say, "fuck!".'[10] However, Treacy also recalls the pressure inherent in designing for an Alexander McQueen collection. 'There was always a period of fear … when you'd wonder how you'd get it done in time. … There were never a lot of pieces but they were always strong pieces and it was never something simple; it was always tortuous'.[11]

Treacy did not visit the McQueen studio in east London that often but he remembers the last time he was there: 'There was silence in the studio – he liked silence or classical music. He was making a dress on the stand from one bolt of material and he had it all pinned. It was beautiful and I said, "Did you do that?"… He [had done] it all himself. You don't get that, those shapes, unless you know how to cut. That's why all the clothes looked like they did. He was a designer's designer, he was the top … he made new rules'.[12]

Previous spread
218. 'Butterfly' headdress, *La Dame Bleue*, Spring/Summer 2008
Hand-painted turkey feathers
Philip Treacy for Alexander McQueen
Modelled by Alana Zimmer
Photograph by Anthea Simms

Opposite left
219. Headpiece, *Eshu*,
Autumn/Winter 2000
Sparterie and horsehair
Philip Treacy for Alexander McQueen
Photograph by Chris Moore

Opposite right
220. 'Chinese Wedding' hat, *La Dame Bleue*, Spring/Summer 2008
Tin
Philip Treacy for Alexander McQueen
Modelled by Daiane Conterato
Photograph by Chris Moore

Above
221. Headpiece, *The Horn of Plenty*,
Autumn/Winter 2009
Banana fibre net and silk
Philip Treacy for Alexander McQueen
Modelled by Georgina Stojilkovic

2.

3 ram's
Horns.

Opposite

222. Sketch of ram's horns headpiece,
The Search for the Golden Fleece,
Givenchy Haute Couture,
Spring/Summer 1997
Pencil and ink on paper, London 1996
Philip Treacy for Alexander McQueen
Courtesy of Catherine Brickhill

Above

223. Ensemble with ram's horns
headpiece, *The Search for the Golden
Fleece*, Givenchy Haute Couture,
Spring/Summer 1997
Painted ram's horns and lamb's wool
Philip Treacy for Alexander McQueen

Below

224. Headpiece, *La Dame Bleue*,
Spring/Summer 2008
Straw and silk
Philip Treacy for Alexander McQueen
Modelled by Hye-rim Park

Opposite
225. Isabella Blow wearing
Alexander McQueen coat and
Philip Treacy headpiece
New Yorker, March 2001
Photograph by François-Marie Banier

226. Alexander McQueen and Philip
Treacy backstage, *La Dame Bleue*,
Spring/Summer 2008
Photograph by Anne Deniau

No. 5

SPECTACLE

—

SHOW, AND TELL

ALEXANDER FURY

'All the world's a stage, and all the men and women merely players'

WILLIAM SHAKESPEARE, *AS YOU LIKE IT*, 1600

'I'm not an aggressive person, but I do want to change attitudes,' said Lee Alexander McQueen in 1996. 'If that means I shock people, that's their problem.'[1] McQueen's comments came after his fashion show *Dante* (Autumn/Winter 1996), where models stalked a cruciform catwalk amongst the pews of Christ Church, Spitalfields. Even the devoutly secular press corps of fashion paused for thought.

That was precisely McQueen's intention. 'The show is meant to provoke an emotional response,' he said. 'It's my 30 minutes to do whatever I want.'[2] And he did, again and again. Nowhere was the extremity of McQueen's vision more clearly expressed, nor his audience more effectively provoked, than in the staging of his fashion shows. From his very earliest collections in London, McQueen heightened the impact of his clothing through their presentation. He approached fashion with the dynamic flair of a showman, pulling elements from performance art, cinema, dance and the circus and fusing them into ephemeral, one-night-only showcases that invariably lived up to the notion of the spectacular.

'A tent was never going to do his clothes justice,' said Sam Gainsbury, who began working with McQueen as casting director on *The Birds* (Spring/Summer 1995) and as show producer from *The Hunger* (Spring/Summer 1996) onwards. 'It was the whole package for Lee; the show was as important to him, I truly believe, as the clothes.'[3]

The word most frequently used to describe McQueen's *Sturm und Drang* approach to showing his work is 'theatrical'. The designer himself, however, professed a loathing for theatre. 'I've never thought of myself as an elitist designer,'[4] he once declared, whilst in a television interview in 1997 he dismissed outright the idea of finding inspiration in high culture, instead citing the dynamic London club scene as a source of his ideas.[5]

As a nascent designer in that metropolis during the 1980s and early '90s McQueen was nurtured on a visual diet of Soho nightlife, film and the music video landscape of MTV. All tended

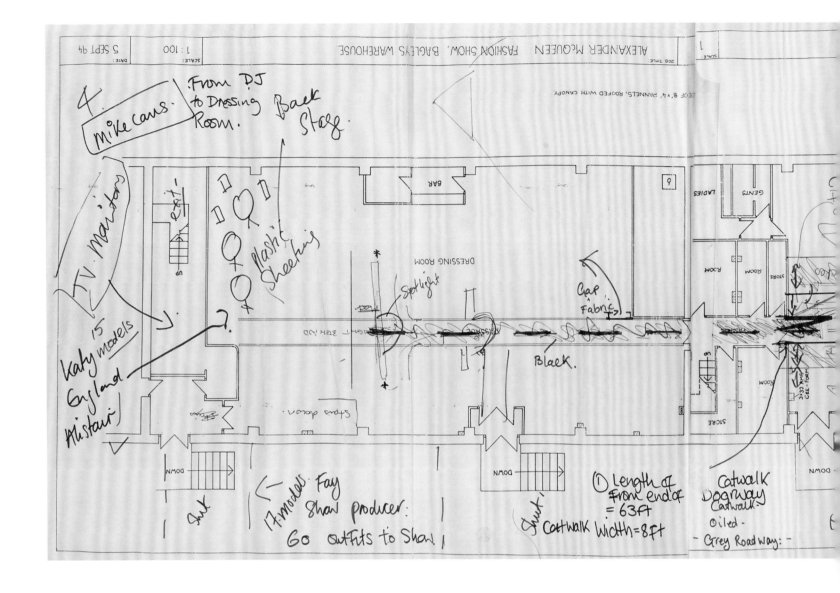

The following annotations appear on the architectural plan (some text is rotated/upside-down):

Mike cans. From DJ to Dressing Room. Back Stage.

T.V. monitor

15 Katy models England Alistair)

Plastic Sheeting

BAR

DRESSING ROOM

Spotlight

Gap Fabric?

Black.

LADIES   GENTS

STORE ROOM   ROOM   STORE

STORE

UP

DOWN   DOWN   DOWN

← 17 models Fay Show producer: 60 outfits to Show !

① Length of from end of = 63ft Catwalk Width = 8ft

Catwalk Doorway Catwalk ~ Oiled - Grey Road Way: -

---

towards spectacle, and all find reflections in his work. The neon-splashed promos of bands like The Prodigy (whose MC and vocalist Maxim modelled in McQueen's Autumn/Winter 1997 show)[6] fused with the tense, visually compelling thrillers of directors like Stanley Kubrick and Alfred Hitchcock in McQueen's shows. 'Usually communication is done through entertainment media like film and music,' commented McQueen in 2009. 'But fashion is part of that … If I like it or not, my shows are a form of entertainment.'[7] Sometimes, film itself was involved in creating backdrops to the action. For *Irere* (Spring/Summer 2003) director John Maybury devised a cinematic panorama of submarine life, eerie woods and finally thermal imaging; for *Plato's Atlantis* (Spring/Summer 2010) Nick Knight created a video of writhing snakes that blanketed the catwalk.

In considering the theatrical element in McQueen's shows, the idea of the court masque rears its head repeatedly. Not drama insomuch as the dialogue and text was a small part of the action, the masque was a form of Tudor and Jacobean entertainment that consisted largely of music, dancing, pageantry and spectacular scenic effects.[8] The period was one McQueen loved,[9] and the similarity of the masque with the wordless pageantry of a fashion show is more than coincidental. Nevertheless, both the masque

and the fashion show – at least, the fashion show in the hands of McQueen – were striving towards the same aim: to say something, without speaking a word.

Masques were also frequently ephemeral, devised for specific occasions and rarely performed more than once.[10] Again, they find a natural counterpart in the temporal nature of the fashion show. 'A week to build, a month's preparation, two weeks shop time, a fifteen-minute show and three hours later it's chopped up and in the bin,'[11] were the words of McQueen collaborator Simon Kenny when discussing the lifespan of the catwalk installation of *La Dame Bleue*, McQueen's Spring/Summer 2008 collection dedicated to Isabella Blow. Kenny installed a giant backdrop of steel and almost 400 programmable LED verger tubes that flashed in sequence to create imagery inspired by the fusion of an eagle and butterfly wings (pl.234). As with a butterfly, its lifespan is brief. 'It will be taken down, carted to London and sent to a scrapheap,' stated Kenny bluntly, of the final resting place for the piece.[12]

Regardless of their lifespan, McQueen pumped a remarkable amount of time, energy and money into the spectacular staging of his collections.[13] In 2000, McQueen sold a 51 per cent stake in his business to the Gucci Group, which eased some of the financial

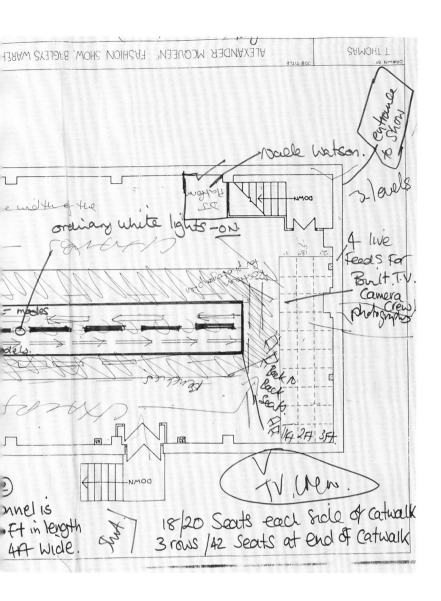

The following handwritten annotations appear on the blueprint:

ALEXANDER MCQUEEN, FASHION SHOW, BAGLEYS WAREH

DRAWN BY T THOMAS

JOB TITLE

entrance to show

Dale Watson.

2 levels

ordinary white lights – ON.

4 live feeds for Built T.V. Camera Crew photographs

models

back to back seats.

TV. Crew.

18/20 Seats each side of catwalk
3 rows/42 Seats at end of catwalk

nnel is Ft in length 4Ft wide.

Previous spread

227. Ensemble, *La Poupée*,
Spring/Summer 1997
Dress: bugle beads
Metal frame
Modelled by Debra Shaw

228. Blueprint of catwalk, *The Birds*,
Spring/Summer 1995
Simon Costin for Alexander McQueen,
London 1994
Pencil and ink on paper
V&A: National Art Library

pressures that had limited the reach of earlier presentations. Nevertheless, from the very start, McQueen approached his shows on an ambitious scale. 'There wasn't any money, but anything is possible,' Sarah Burton stated of McQueen's approach back then. 'Just don't give him no for an answer. That was how it worked.'[14] The spectacle had started early: McQueen's Spring/Summer 1997 show, *La Poupée*, was staged to make his models appear to be walking on water, via a catwalk constructed as a shallow tank and Perspex wedge shoes. Spectacle on a shoe-string.

McQueen gathered a disparate group of collaborators to help achieve the spectacular and unconventional effects he desired. 'I'd worked in music videos and Lee thought that was quite exciting,' recalled Sam Gainsbury. 'He liked the idea that there were lots of components to making a film and that it should be that complicated and that complex to make a show.' 'We used film references, so often it was the impact that film imagery has,' agreed art director Simon Costin, who worked on a clutch of early McQueen shows and recalled cinematic references peppering the designer's research boards.[15]

Other collaborators drawn from outside the fashion sphere included art directors Joseph Bennett and Michael Howells,[16]

lighting director Daniel Landin, music producer John Gosling, choreographers Les Child and Michael Clark and scenic artist Simon Kenny, alongside the retinue of hair and make-up specialists intrinsic to any catwalk show. 'He was a composer, Lee,' commented the jewellery designer Shaun Leane, who worked with McQueen from 1995 until his death. 'He knew how to get the best out of all of us.'[17] The orchestration of these presentations had more in common with Hollywood blockbusters than conventional catwalks, eventually involving nearly 200 people.[18] 'I'd say 98 per cent of [fashion designers] say, "Oh, make it a nice background,"' recalled Joseph Bennett. 'But Lee very much saw it as an integrated thing. I suspect for most fashion designers it's well outside their comfort zone, to get involved in that.'[19] Like a director manning his crew, McQueen was always in total control. 'He'd meet every single person that was the head of department that had to deliver something for him,' recalled Sam Gainsbury. 'If there were shows that involved complicated choreography, he would always come to rehearsals, he was 100 per cent hands on.'

McQueen's shows made plenty of references to spectacular events of history, from Victorian apparitions to dance marathons. However, he was undoubtedly a product of the time in which he was raised. McQueen's were decidedly a modern spectacle, staged with an eye on the screen – of cinema, television and, later, the World Wide Web. Hence the reason McQueen often disconnected his models from their audience. Both *The Overlook* (Autumn/Winter 1999)[20] and *Voss* (Spring/Summer 2001) trapped the catwalk inside a construction, preventing the audience from directly engaging with them in any way. Highlighting the importance for him of the two-way mirror that was a feature of the latter show, in a 2003 interview McQueen stated, 'There always must be some sort of interaction with the audience to get the message across that's going through your mind.'[21] Later shows in Paris were frequently staged on a central dais, what Gainsbury referred to as the 'McQueen square', which could be argued to be a horizontal manifestation of the rectilinear screen. In all cases, the action unfolded at a remove. Isolated within a world of McQueen's own creation, the models were transformed into a spectacle to be witnessed rather than a fantasy to be experienced. The audience didn't want to become the woman inside McQueen's clothing; rather, they wanted to know what would happen to her next.

As with any director searching for the perfect embodiment of his heroines, McQueen frequently presented explicit and specific demands when finding models for his catwalks. Casting director Jess Hallett, who worked with McQueen from 2003, stated that, 'It was always a very specific idea of what he wanted … it was how he wanted the story to be told.' She recalled how specific that could be from her experience working on McQueen's Spring/Summer 2004 *Deliverance* show, her second: 'There was a girl that he found in the street for that show, who was very "of the time" – she had a very 1930s face. It had to be real, it had to be believable, all of it. There was always a story.'[22]

Hallett pinpointed the primary purpose of the spectacle of McQueen's shows: the urge to elevate a fashion show from the mere mechanical act of 'showing' fashion, into a narrative medium. 'Storytelling is what we loved as kids, and this is what [a show] is about,'[23] stated McQueen in 2009, while Sarah Burton reflected his viewpoint: 'It was not really about showing clothes to the press, it was actually telling a story or painting a picture.' That is frequently a central component of British fashion – McQueen was influenced by Vivienne Westwood and John Galliano,[24] both of whom used their clothes and shows as a narrative conceit, to explore a particular idea.

The major difference? McQueen came of age as a designer in the 1990s, whereas both Westwood and Galliano began showing their clothes in the '80s. Indeed, McQueen's shows encompassed culture as a whole, expressing ideas brewed in the social and economic crucible in which he was working. They were a testament to their time, and indeed to his, expressing as they always did a link to McQueen's own life. 'Not so much the collections, but the shows are kind of autobiographical,'[25] he stated in 2003. 'I think he wanted to make a statement,' said Sarah Burton of McQueen's shows. 'About how he felt at the time and how he felt society felt.'

That alludes to the bigger picture behind McQueen shows – that the designer used them to make a pointed comment on the

world outside his workrooms on Clerkenwell Road. Nowhere was this more evident than *The Horn of Plenty* (Autumn/Winter 2009), a show about fashion shows, and indeed about the ever-increasing consumption of the industry as a whole. Staged around a mountain of former McQueen show props – a dumping-ground for the vestiges of past triumphs – the collection was a dystopian statement about waste and destruction. Inspired by the notion of recycling, the clothes used silhouettes from Dior and Balenciaga, while models were adorned with the detritus of contemporary society – drinks-cans, umbrellas, bubble-wrap recreated in silk.

It was an acerbic comment on the fashion industry, on the endemic practice of designers rehashing the work of others and presenting it as their own, as well as the moral turpitude of its intrinsic obsolescence, condemning garments to the scrap heap long before they outlived their usefulness. However, *The Horn of Plenty* also chimed with the larger picture – the global economic crisis affecting luxury fashion, as well as the everyman. In her Style.com review of the collection, Sarah Mower closed with a thought on 'a collapsed economy that doesn't know how to move forward.'[26] It is impossible to extricate the apocalyptic staging of this show from the fact that, as it was presented, world markets had begun to crash and the financial backlash was reverberating across the globe. The story that informed a McQueen spectacle often had a resonance beyond fashion.

The notion of the spectacle is multi-faceted. In the mind of French philosopher Guy Debord, spectacle was applicable to the whole of modern society, summarized as a 'relationship between people that is mediated by images.'[27] That of course finds reflection in the idea of the fashion show, the imagery spun out around these singular events that serves as a potent publicity tool for the designer. *Plato's Atlantis* is the obvious example – live streamed, with the cameras directed by Nick Knight a central decorative motif of the show as well as a technical tool – but *The Horn of Plenty* also featured an intriguing dress of houndstooth fringe that flicked out as the models walked, giving the impression of an image pixellating and falling back into focus: reality pretending to be image. With their cinematic lighting and elaborate backdrops, still photographs of McQueen shows also blur perception, reminiscent of film stills rather than conventional catwalk images. However, what first surprised his audiences then became anticipated, and finally expected. In his autobiography, Christian Dior relayed a toast by Christian Bérard, following the presentation of his triumphant debut known as the New Look and concluding with the prophetic words: 'Tomorrow begins the anguish of living up to, and if possible, surpassing yourself.'[28] McQueen perhaps felt a similar pressure. 'If we did a simple one, people felt cheated,' recalled Sam Gainsbury. In a sense, *The Horn of Plenty* harked back to that idea, its very name evoking overflowing abundance of ideas, the trashing of McQueen shows past indicative of fashion's voracious appetite for the new.

Although the show, rather than the clothes, was 'the dream', as stylist and McQueen collaborator Katy England stated, it must be emphasized, unequivocally, that McQueen was able to stage such presentations in large because his clothes invariably held up to the scrutiny. The drama inherent in his designs lent themselves to the

229. Catwalk set, *Pantheon ad Lucem*,
Autumn/Winter 2004
Grande Halle de la Villette, Paris
Photograph by Anne Deniau

225

shows – indeed, the increasing spectacle of the latter seemed to spur McQueen on creatively, to invent and experiment and push fashion forwards season after season. Many would have used the extravagance of the show to mask the cracks in their collection, but that was never the case with McQueen. If anything, the more elaborate the show, the better the collection. 'Balance is the main thing,' said McQueen. 'The show shouldn't overshadow the clothes, and vice versa.'[29]

Indeed, Alexander McQueen's spectacular visions could as readily be expressed through the bodies of his models as through the set pieces that surrounded them. *Pantheon ad Lucem* (Autumn/Winter 2004), translated as 'Towards the Light', dressed models in garments inset with LEDs, paraded in a faux-Roman coliseum; *Natural Dis-tinction, Un-Natural Selection* (Spring/Summer 2009) set

McQueen's first exploration of evolution through clothing against a taxidermy menagerie. The set for his Spring/Summer 2005 collection was stripped entirely bare: it was only when the models assembled in their entirety and a chequerboard of light demarcated the catwalk that the show's title made sense: *It's Only a Game*, an intricately choreographed life-size chess-match played out with the models' bodies. 'One of the references was Vanessa Beecroft,' stated Joseph Bennett, the show recalling her installation and performance art. 'That was Lee's idea 100 per cent,' stated Sam Gainsbury. 'He said, "I want to do a chess show and I want to go from the pawns right the way through to the King and I'm designing everybody's clothes based on that."' The models themselves – their assemblage, their movements, and their clothing – created one of McQueen's most memorable catwalk spectaculars.

Each season, the clothes were the heart and soul of Lee Alexander McQueen's story, but the shows were the spectacular means by which McQueen told that story to the world at large. Invariably, with McQueen, that story was sometimes confrontational, always provocative. 'If he could butt the system then he would,' remembered Simon Costin. And that was the root of his genius. McQueen knew how – and when – to go too far. The seasonal spectaculars McQueen staged – under the mundane and entirely unsuitable epithet of 'fashion show' – were the best expression of that. They were the distilled essence of his aesthetic, his unadulterated message without constraint. They were extreme. 'The thing about Lee was the pure, pure vision,' said Sarah Burton. 'He wanted to move people. Whether you liked it or hated it, he really wanted you to feel something. That's what made those shows.'

230 and 231. Catwalk set, *Irere*,
Spring/Summer 2003
La Grande Halle de la Villette, Paris
Photographs by Anne Deniau

Opposite

232. *It's Only a Game*,
Spring/Summer 2005
Palais Omnisports de Paris-Bercy, Paris

233. Finale, *Natural Dis-tinction, Un-Natural Selection*, Spring/Summer 2009
Palais Omnisports de Paris-Bercy, Paris
Photograph by François Guillot

229

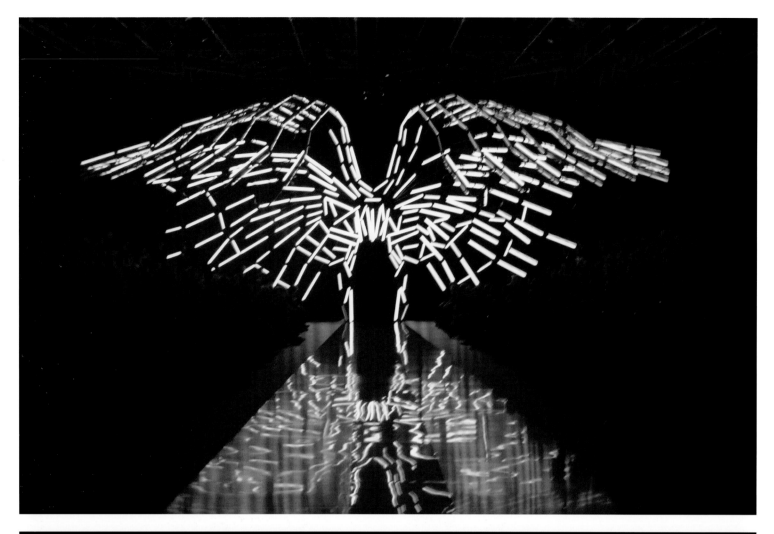

MAKING-UP

JANICE MILLER

———

'*To put on femininity with a vengeance suggests the power of taking it off*'
M. Russo, *The Female Grotesque: Risk, Excess and Modernity*, 1995

—

The strong cultural connections between femininity, hair-styling and make-up were exploited in Alexander McQueen's catwalk shows. It was hair and make-up that accentuated the cloned army of female warriors, inspired by Joan of Arc, which McQueen raised to present his collection *Joan* (Autumn/Winter 1998). Hairstylist Guido Palau used bald caps to give the models exceptionally high foreheads in medieval fashion (pl.243), or to provide a base on which to coil sparse plaits. On the models' faces, make-up artist Val Garland used 'a heavy layer of foundation', which was taken 'over the bald caps, concealing the eyebrows ... adding some red mascara to the lashes'.[1] The look was emphasized with red, custom-fitted contact lenses (pl.244). McQueen defied convention by coalescing hair-styling and make-up into an unforgiving, but striking, statement about feminine identity. *Joan* was a perfect reflection of his preoccupation with women's 'inner lives'.[2]

Other collections presented a figurative, if not literal, unmade-up face, with narratives embedded in the application of subtle textures and colours. For his historical and darkly Romantic collection *Sarabande* (Spring/Summer 2007), make-up artist Charlotte Tilbury mixed foundation with a white base, which was applied to the face, taken beyond the ears, down the neck, melting into light, visible brushstrokes towards the collarbone (pl.143).[3] This painterly technique referenced the works of Goya that formed its inspiration and also suggested a sense of life draining away. *The Widows of Culloden* (Autumn/Winter 2006) and *The Girl Who Lived in the Tree* (Autumn/Winter 2008) both used a nude make-up palette. In the case of the latter, burnished gold on the eyes and cheeks echoed the opulence of the clothes and

accessories in a show that told the story of a fairytale-like transformation of a girl into a princess (pls 245, 246).

McQueen was driven by a desire to push not only his own boundaries but also those of his audience, believing in fashion's ability to transform both individuals and social attitudes. In *The Overlook* (Autumn/Winter 1999), white stripes were painted, mask-like, across the eyes and eyelashes of the models, lending a semi-frozen appearance. Make-up is often likened to the mask as both share a capacity to transform the wearer, either by concealing or revealing the character within. Such connotations rendered the make-up for *The Overlook* undoubtedly strange, beautiful and wistful (pl.273). Far more troubling were the macabre clowns' faces that obscured the models' features in *What a Merry Go Round* (Autumn/Winter 2001). Here, the make-up was distorted, monstrous and emblematic of the nefarious characters that frequently inhabit children's stories (pl.239).[4] This juxtaposition of delicate, embroidered dresses with grotesque features mirrors the way McQueen oscillated between beauty and horror in his representation of women.

Thus it was often make-up that enacted the more complex aspects of human nature, which so fascinated McQueen. Many of his collections were bold in their attempts to question contemporary notions of beauty. Some exploited theatrical devices and techniques to tell this conceptual story but never to greater effect than in McQueen's last complete collection, *Plato's Atlantis* (Spring/Summer 2010), which chronicled an evolutionary transformation from sea to land. Guido Palau wove the models' hair into close-fitting braids inspired by the sinews of an anatomical drawing, or sculpted it into fin-like structures that rose up high from the top of the head (pls 240, 241). The make-up devised for the show by Peter Philips was at first simple, with blanked-out brows and an opalescent sheen on the skin provided by M·A·C pigment powders.[5] It evolved, however, across the last 15 models, gradually mutating them into 'creatures' by means of prosthetics on cheek and brow bones, resulting in an angular reconfiguration of the human face.

One of McQueen's most controversial collections, *The Horn of Plenty* (Autumn/Winter 2009), similarly tested the boundaries of the body by demonstrating that lipstick is perhaps the most emotive tool in a woman's make-up bag (pl.247). The possibility that painted red lips might be designed to mimic female genitalia is a popular notion, given credence by psychoanalysts such as Sigmund Freud[6] and Karl Abraham,[7] who identified a symbolic

relationship between mouths and vaginas in human libidinal development. Consequently, lipstick can be seen as a sexualized symbol. But, when it exceeds its margins, going beyond the natural boundary of the lip line, it creates a cavernous orifice that is both fetish object and threat. In *The Horn of Plenty* ripe, excessive and unnatural lips are lined and filled with red or black. Creator Peter Philips took inspiration from 'clowns, divas and Pierrot, with a bit of Joan Crawford thrown in'.[8] McQueen cited Terry Gilliam's film *Brazil* as an influence.[9] The result, however, is unmistakeably reminiscent of the work of performance artist Leigh Bowery (pl.242), whose experiments with the body had so influenced McQueen. Such lips suggest not just the genitalia but also the archetypal *vagina dentata* (or vagina with teeth), imbued in folklore with the terrifying capacity to devour or castrate.[10] Make-up in McQueen's shows confronted his audience with common fantasies and fears about women and female sexuality, demonstrating a unique ability to move, challenge and disturb.

Previous spread
239. Backstage, *What a Merry Go Round*,
Autumn/Winter 2001
Photograph by Anne Deniau

Opposite left
240. Detail of hair and make-up, *Plato's Atlantis*, Spring/Summer 2010
Modelled by Magdalena Frackowiak

Opposite right
241. Detail of hair and make-up, *Plato's Atlantis*, Spring/Summer 2010
Modelled by Yulia Lobova

Right
242. Leigh Bowery (left) and Fat Gill (right) as 'Miss Fuckit', Alternative Miss World, 1986
Photograph by Robyn Beeche

Below left
243. Jade Parfitt and Guido Palau backstage, *Joan*, Autumn/Winter 1998
Photograph by Robert Fairer

Below right
244. Detail of hair and make-up, *Joan*, Autumn/Winter 1998
Modelled by Jodie Kidd
Photograph by Alex Lentati

Opposite and above
245 and 246. Detail of hair and
make-up, *The Widows of Culloden*,
Autumn/Winter 2006
Modelled by Gemma Ward
Photograph by Anthea Simms

Overleaf
247. Magdalena Frackowiak and Sigrid
Agren backstage, *The Horn of Plenty*,
Autumn/Winter 2009
Photograph by Anne Deniau

GHOSTS

BILL SHERMAN

———

'Webster was much possessed by death
And saw the skull beneath the skin;
And breastless creatures under ground,
Leaned backwards with a lipless grin'
T. S. Eliot, *Whispers of Immortality*, 1919

—

Alexander McQueen was, like the Jacobean playwright John Webster, much possessed by death. But where Webster saw skeletons, McQueen also saw ghosts, and used his haunted vision to create theatre of great (if savage) beauty. Nowhere more dramatically, perhaps, than in the *coup de théâtre* that concluded the Autumn/Winter 2006 show, *The Widows of Culloden*, in Paris.

Inside a large glass pyramid, Kate Moss mysteriously appeared, suspended in the air and slowly rotating in a flowing, silk organza dress, as if swept up by underwater currents or caught by a slow-motion tornado (pls 248, 251).[1] Transparent and evanescent, a mythical woman in white, she wafted in and drifted out like a visitor from another world, stirring the audience into the kind of reverie associated not with the glamour of the modern catwalk but rather with the great nineteenth-century ghost stories of Edgar Allan Poe and Charles Dickens. And that, in fact, is precisely the world from which she was summoned: the optical illusion was widely described in the press as a 'hologram', but it used a much older optical technology called 'Pepper's Ghost'. Named after the popular Victorian chemist John Henry Pepper (1821–1900), it was devised in 1862 for a stage adaptation of Dickens's novella *The Haunted Man*.[2]

Theatrical 'phantasmagoria' had emerged as a sensation at the beginning of the nineteenth century. Part seance and part haunted house attraction, these shows used a so-called 'magic lantern' to project spectral images onto walls or transparent surfaces.[3] Building on the work of his fellow scientist Henry Dircks, Pepper found an affordable way to build these illusions into the very furniture of the theatre, with angled glass – invisible to the audience – reflecting projected images produced offstage (pl.250). While Pepper's invention formed part of his technical teaching at the Royal Polytechnic, it grew directly out of the same culture of artistic and scientific spectacle (in the wake of the Great Exhibition in Hyde Park's Crystal Palace) that produced the Victoria and Albert Museum itself. Pepper's own account, *The True History of the Ghost* (1890), began: 'When the Hyde Park second Great Exhibition in 1862 had closed its doors ... so that the halls and lecture rooms lately crowded with the numerous patrons of the old Royal Polytechnic were somewhat deserted, there came to the aid of the Institute a new invention, which people by common consent called "The Ghost".'[4]

And McQueen's glass pyramid (pl.252) also invoked another – less familiar and more private – Victorian invention for the display of ghosts. By the 1860s, post-mortem portraits were highly popular (see also pl.294), and photographer Henry Swan found a new way to produce three-dimensional pictures of absent, or deceased, friends and family. A hand-coloured photograph was placed within a small coffin-shaped box containing mirrors and prisms, known as Swan's Crystal Cube (pl.249). The effect, as a contemporary review put it, 'is a living being in perfect relief ... a very substantial ghost of the living and the departed.'[5]

These are tricks, to be sure, but they are meant to charm rather than deceive; they are objects of desire rather than dread. McQueen himself found the Victorian obsession with ghosts moving rather than depressing. When asked about his 'fascination with the macabre', he insisted that death 'is part of life ... I've always been fascinated with Victorian views of death ... when they used to take pictures of the dead. It's not about brushing it under the carpet, like we do today, it's about ... celebrating someone's life. And I don't think it's a bad thing. I think it's a very sad thing ... but I think it's [also] a very romantic thing because it means the end of a cycle and everything has an end ... it gives room for new things to come behind you'.[6]

Previous spread
248. Finale, *The Widows of Culloden*, Autumn/Winter 2006
Pepper's Ghost of Kate Moss wearing a silk organza dress
Photograph by Chris Moore

Right
249. Crystal cube miniature of Sarah Anne Bennett, *c*.1865
Hand-coloured photograph, prisms and mirrors
Casket Portrait Co., Ltd
V&A: E.3706-2007

Below
250. John Henry Pepper, 'Professor Pepper', performing his ghost illusion, 1860–1900

Right
251. Finale, *The Widows of Culloden*,
Autumn/Winter 2006
Pepper's Ghost of Kate Moss wearing
a silk organza dress
Photograph by Chris Moore

Below
252. Catwalk set, *The Widows of Culloden*,
Autumn/Winter 2006
Palais Omnisports de Paris-Bercy, Paris
Photograph by Michel Dufour

COUP DE THÉÂTRE

KEITH LODWICK

'There is nothing like a dream to create the future'
Victor Hugo, *Les Misérables*, 1862

—

When interviewed by David Bowie in 1995, and asked about the relationship between installation and theatre, McQueen replied, 'I hate the theatre, I used to work in the theatre, I used to make costumes for them and films'.[1] McQueen routinely expressed his dislike of theatre and yet in 1989 he worked for the most prestigious costumiers in the industry, Berman's & Nathan's Ltd. Berman's had an unrivalled collection of military wear spanning two centuries whilst Nathan's was known for its extensive period costume collection. Their merger in 1972 was a *coup de théâtre* and made it one of the largest costumiers in the world. It was in this world that McQueen found himself post-Savile Row. Berman's & Nathan's was located in Camden Street, north London and, by the mid-1980s, held over 700,000 items of costume. McQueen joined 160 permanent members of staff as an assistant pattern-cutter and was based in the Production Department in men's wardrobe, where a strict hierarchy was in place. Many of the staff had been there for their entire careers, wore carnations in their buttonholes, and addressed each other with the formal 'Mr' before their Christian names. Mr Lee was trained by head cutter Mr Frank Davidson (formerly head of men's tailoring at the National Theatre).

Berman's & Nathan's supplied costumes for large-scale West End musicals and major film and TV period dramas, and was the place to learn about cutting clothes for stage and screen. The common myth about costumes for the stage is that they are not well made as they do not have to last, but stage costumes have to survive the rigours of weekly performance, and endure sweat and quick changes in cramped spaces backstage. According to a former colleague, McQueen was 'fascinated by the row upon row of military coats and jackets ... he was very inquisitive about their cut and construction and wanted to learn as much as he could.'[2] Berman's & Nathan's collection of costumes, packed with examples of every major style, period and movement, fired his imagination.

One of McQueen's jobs was creating the coats and waistcoats based on the designs of Andreane Neofitou for the musical *Les Misérables*. Tailors worked from Neofitou's costume sketches, period pattern books and current production stock to recreate the memorable costumes of nineteenth-century France. When McQueen joined, *Les Misérables* (pl.255) was in its fourth year, had seen numerous cast changes, and had opened on Broadway and mainland Europe. The costumes had to be constantly re-made and re-styled. McQueen also worked on costumes for the musical *Miss Saigon* (premiered 1989) and the film *Black Heart White Hunter* (1990), directed by Clint Eastwood. At this stage he was trusted to create a frock coat for the star of the film *King of the Wind* (1990), Richard Harris, who portrayed King George II. The coat was based on a pattern taken from a 1720s coat in the V&A, illustrated in Norah Waugh's *The Cut of Men's Clothes 1600 – 1900*. McQueen used this example of his work and accompanying pattern in his application for Central Saint Martins (pl.258).

At this point, McQueen's career echoed that of fellow designer John Galliano. Galliano also had theatrical experience working backstage as a dresser on the National Theatre's 1982 production of Georg Büchner's French Revolution drama, *Danton's Death*, and was hugely influenced by this period. His graduation collection of 1984 was entitled *Les Incroyables*, based on the 1790s Directoire period. This era would also be reinvented and subverted by McQueen in his collections. The naval jacket designed for *Dante* (Autumn/Winter 1996), originally bought by his benefactress Isabella Blow and subsequently owned by Daphne Guinness, had all the trademark skill of expert tailoring and theatrical flair (pl.254). As Harold Koda identifies, the elongated collar 'evokes the style of *Les Incroyables*, the post-French Revolution dandies of the period, and their female counterparts, *Les Merveilleuses*, who took fashion to mannered extremes'.[3]

One of McQueen's most celebrated frock coats was created in collaboration with another artist who encompasses and transcends design and performance: David Bowie. The distressed Union Jack coat was worn on the cover of his 1997 *Earthling* album and subsequent tour. Bowie began his stage show with his back to the audience, a pose replicated on the album cover (pl.253). The coat was described as 'ruined, yet perfectly tailored, a pastiche of patriotism'.[4]

In *Joan* (Autumn/Winter 1998) the frock coat appears screen-printed with another revolutionary influence, this time the Romanov princess, Anastasia. Ten years later,

for *The Girl Who Lived in the Tree* collection, waistcoats and gold frogging would again evoke the heroines of the Paris boulevards, inspired by days spent in the revolutionary atmosphere of *Les Misérables* (pl.256).

Building on his skills gained on Savile Row, what McQueen then acquired at Berman's & Nathan's would become the hallmark of his craft. Whatever he felt about the environment, Berman's was unique and steeped in theatrical history. McQueen was surrounded by tailors who had created costumes for films such as *Lawrence of Arabia* (1962), *The Charge of the Light Brigade* (1968) and the entire James Bond catalogue.

Revolution was in the air when McQueen left Berman's & Nathan's. Within three years, the grand old costume house of the West End theatre world had been acquired by the costumiers Angels and eventually even the famous name of Berman's & Nathan's would be consigned to history.

Right
255. *Les Misérables*, Barbican
Theatre, London, 1985
Photograph by Michael le Poer Trench

Below left
256. Military jacket, *The Girl Who Lived in
the Tree*, Autumn/Winter 2008
Velvet with gold bullion cord
Modelled by Kamila Filipcikova
Photograph by Chris Moore

Below right
257. Military jacket, Givenchy Haute
Couture, *The Search for the Golden Fleece*,
Spring/Summer 1997
Velvet with gold bullion cord
Photograph by Chris Moore

Overleaf left
258. Pattern for coat in Norah Waugh, *The
Cut of Men's Clothes, 1600–1900*, London,
1964
V&A: National Art Library

Overleaf right
259. Frock coat, *Eye*, Spring/Summer
2000
Wool with silver embroidery
Photograph by Robert Fairer

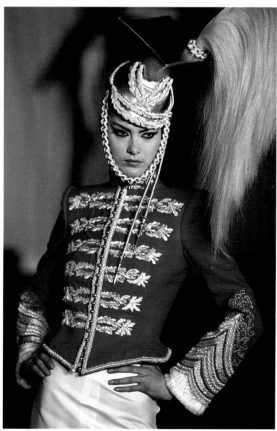

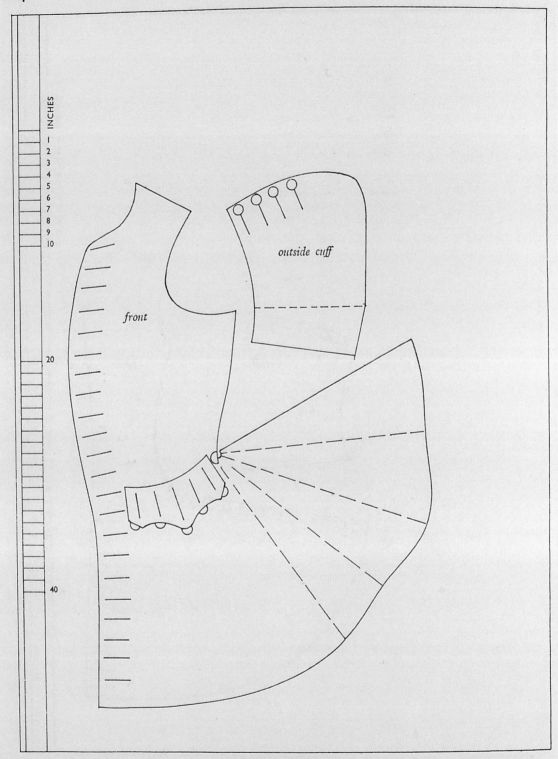

INCHES

1
2
3
4
5
6
7
8
9
10

20

40

front

outside cuff

DIAGRAM XVIII

COAT *c.* 1720–7. Heavy fawn silk. Button-holes worked in darker fawn silk to match basket-weave buttons. The last eight, also the back, button-holes are false. The deep cuff comes over the elbow and the back seam is open from X. Lined silk in a lighter shade. *Victoria and Albert Museum*

DANCE

JANE PRITCHARD

——

'His dresses were like clouds'
Sylvie Guillem, 2011

—

The intermingled history of the two art forms – couture and choreography – stretches back to Louis XIV, who established the couturiers' trade guild and the French ballet in the seventeenth century. A dancer, or performer, striving to capture motion, has a strong resonance with the world of fashion, especially the catwalk, where fabric and cut is best judged through movement. McQueen effectively blurred the boundaries between fashion and performance, proving that the one can be a fruitful source of inspiration for the other.

Given his early work with theatrical costumiers, such as Angels and Berman's & Nathan's, it is not surprising that Alexander McQueen was drawn into the world of dance. As is the case with many students of fashion, McQueen absorbed such references, which then consciously, or subconsciously, infiltrated his collections. The knights that appeared on a giant chessboard in his presentation for *It's Only a Game* (Spring/Summer 2005) showed the influence of the Ballets Russes designer Léon Bakst. Bejewelled bodices on tutu-shaped skirts in *The Girl Who Lived in the Tree* (Autumn/Winter 2008) suggested the costumes created for George Balanchine's ballet *Jewels* (1967), in turn inspired by the designs of jewellers Van Cleef & Arpels. McQueen's structured outfits sometimes recalled those for the abstractly geometric Bauhaus ballets of the 1920s,[1] while his use of tartan and tulle evoked the Romantic ballet *La Sylphide* (1832).[2] Indeed, many of McQueen's themes for collections would lend themselves to choreography (pl.10).

In his catwalk shows McQueen often mixed models and dancers. Famously he invited dance-rebel Michael Clark

to stage the catwalk show for *Deliverance* (Spring/Summer 2004), which was held at the Salle Wagram, a Parisian dance hall (pls 260, 263, 264). The fashion show-cum-performance was greeted with great enthusiasm. Inspired by America's Depression-era dance marathons, portrayed in the Sidney Pollack film *They Shoot Horses, Don't They?* (1969), 20 models were paired with 20 dancers.[3] The presentation comprised three parts: firstly, a 1930s ballroom scene, in which the movement was inspired by social dance; secondly, the marathon itself; and lastly, a representation of despair as the finalists, appearing broken and exhausted, struggled to stay on their feet.

The French ballerina Sylvie Guillem was an admirer of McQueen's creations, and McQueen was equally impressed when he first saw Guillem perform in ITV's South Bank Show Review of the Year (1993), claiming that she inspired his subsequent interest in dance. It was Guillem who invited McQueen to design the costumes for *Eonnagata* (2009), a collaborative creation between Guillem, the British choreographer/dancer Russell Maliphant, his lighting designer Michael Hulls, and the Canadian multi-disciplinary theatre artist and director Robert Lepage. McQueen, who had turned down previous offers to work in theatre, even from such hallowed institutions as the Paris Opera, jumped at the invitation. He had one condition, though: 'I wanted to bring my own mind to this collaboration. Otherwise, they didn't need me – they needed a costume department.'[4] It was Lepage who was responsible for the production's theme: the life of the intriguing Charles de Beaumont, Chevalier d'Eon, a career diplomat, spy and swordsman in pre-Revolutionary France, who switched between

Previous spread
260. Dress, *Deliverance*, Spring/Summer
2004
Printed silk
Modelled by Karen Elson
Photograph by Pierre Verdy

Left
261. Sylvie Guillem and Russell Maliphant
Eonnagata, Sadler's Wells, London, 2009
Photograph by Érick Labbé

Below
262. Russell Maliphant
Eonnagata, University of California,
Berkeley, 2009
Photograph by Érick Labbé

Opposite left
263. Jumpsuit, *Deliverance*, Spring/
Summer 2004
Silk
Modelled by Amanda Moore
Photograph by Anthea Simms

Opposite right
264. Ensemble, *Deliverance*, Spring/
Summer 2004
Jacket: silk; boots: Swarovski crystal and
synthetic
Photograph by Anthea Simms

dressing as a man and as a woman, so confounding attempts to ascertain his/her gender. The title of the production combined the Chevalier's name with *onnagata*, the term in Japanese kabuki theatre applied to actors who play female roles in a highly stylized manner.

The subject, with its multiplicity of influences, appealed to McQueen who brought elegance, refinement and imagination to the project (pl.261). In an interview with journalist Judith Mackrell, McQueen said: 'My designs are very eclectic, they have a lot of historical references ... I'm interested in the dark psychosis of [the character's] mind, there's a melancholy there that I like.'[5] Aware that dancers need costumes in which they can freely move, yet which are impressive sculpturally, McQueen produced preliminary designs early in the rehearsal process so that, with some modifications, they became integral to the production. The principal element was that of all-over body tights, slightly padded at hips and crotch to help disguise gender. To this McQueen added embroidered kimonos and Louis Quinze jackets, filtered through a twenty-first-century sensibility, together with crinolines that formed an exoskeleton around the dancers' bodies (pl.262). Their shapes remained visible

but as if trapped within a cage, signifying in McQueen's words 'de Beaumont's inner turmoil'.[6]

The extravagant costumes were beautifully crafted and the performers were concerned about damaging them. 'Alexander's designs are usually worn on the catwalk,' said Lepage. 'We are wearing these every day, sweating and stretching and falling on our knees.'[7] Maliphant also felt constricted by them. Used to dancing in little more than sweatpants and T-shirt, he found he was tripping over his skirts and finding it difficult to move in his jacket. 'At first I thought it was hopeless,' he said. But he came to see the magic of McQueen's creations. 'They moved so beautifully. They were really sculptural and the fabric was so good.'[8] Maliphant was still getting adjusted to the costumes when *Eonnagata* had its first preview performance in Québec City, Lepage's home, in December 2008. The Québec audience were unfazed by the show's exotic mix of modern dance, kabuki, theatre and sword fights. But backstage, things were chaotic. 'It felt like a fashion show, with a costume change every two minutes,' Maliphant said. But if the birth of *Eonnagata* had been complicated, the joy of it had been 'creating a shared aesthetic'.[9]

265. 'Blade of Light',
Numéro magazine, Spring/Summer 2004
Photograph by Nick Knight, art direction
by Alexander McQueen, choreography by
Michael Clark

No. 6

IMAGINATION

———

THE SHINING AND CHIC

ALISTAIR O'NEILL

'All work and no play makes Jack a dull boy'

JACK TORRANCE, *THE SHINING*, 1980

The work of Alexander McQueen was saturated with visual effects and film references, most clearly apparent in his fashion shows but also traceable in his fashion designs. McQueen was part of a generation of creatives who benefitted from the development of home cinema, and this way of watching films via VHS or DVD impacted on how he used film as a reference in his work. The role of the soundtrack was also significant, McQueen and John Gosling, his longstanding music collaborator, together producing 'a patchwork of ideas', a mix of references that might splice the main title recording for Stanley Kubrick's film *The Shining* (1980) with a 12-inch dance track by Chic. McQueen always wanted to stage fashion shows that could match the size, scale and ambition of feature films; this chapter charts how he achieved this transformation.

Some of McQueen's earliest press reviews noted the influence of film on the designer. *Nihilism* (Spring/Summer 1994), his second fashion show, had little to do with film, but journalists were quick to draw connections to cinema. Reviewing the show for the *Evening Standard*, David Hayes remarked that 'the newcomer also seemed to have spent much time in front of the television – after the watershed.'[1] Hayes cited Brian De Palma's film *Carrie* (1976) and the post-war British horror movies from Hammer Film Productions as likely influences on a collection that featured dried mud smears and dye seepages on sheer chiffon sheaths, alongside Edwardian-inspired tailoring with severe proportions and revealing cut-aways, typified by the 'bumster' trouser. *Nihilism* was driven by McQueen's desire to produce an ethnic-inspired fashion collection disconnected from the Western ideal of luxury clothing, in either material or finish. A frock coat in burnished and tarnished layers of gold was hand-printed by textile designer Fleet Bigwood, McQueen's first collaborator, who remembers being told by the designer to disrespect the cloth of gold he had produced (printed on poly cotton), 'so I threw every chemical I had in my studio at it.'[2] The sullied fabric was then hand-tailored into a coat which, when featured in an editorial in the *Observer* (pl.269), was described as 'based on the torn layers of a billboard.'[3]

McQueen's first commercial collection was titled *Taxi Driver* (Autumn/Winter 1993), in reference to Martin Scorsese's film of the same name (1976), and because his father drove a London black cab. His subsequent use of film as a reference was explicit and worn on the cuff – he continued to name collections in homage to the films by which they were inspired. *The Birds* (Spring/Summer 1995), for example, was an acknowledgement of the film of the same name directed by Alfred Hitchcock (1963). But there is also a much more layered and interconnected sense of film as a reference at play, as the medium permeated his designs and fashion shows in subtle and complex ways.

While McQueen regularly visited the Scala cinema in London's King's Cross in the early 1990s to see the films of Stanley Kubrick and Pier Paolo Pasolini on the big screen,[4] like many of his generation he also watched films on VHS tapes at home.[5] Film theorist Laura Mulvey has written widely on the influence of VHS, and in turn DVD, technology on how we engage with cinema, arguing that 'at the end of the twentieth century new technologies opened up new perceptual possibilities, new ways of looking, not at the world, but at the internal world of cinema.'[6] In McQueen's hands, this enabled him to integrate into his collections the techniques of VHS watching: fast-forward and rewind; slow motion, record, auto repeat; and repeated viewing.

Fast-forward

McQueen's Spring/Summer 1996 collection, *The Hunger*, takes a film's narrative and extends it, as if fast-forwarding past the film's end into an unscripted future scenario. It borrowed the title of Tony Scott's vampire movie (1983) starring Catherine Deneuve, Susan Sarandon and David Bowie (pl.272). The film's final scene is set in London, and as one vampire screams to be let out of her nailed coffin, another lights a cigarette and surveys the city from the balcony of her Barbican flat. This detail is not likely to have escaped the attention of McQueen, who had just moved his studio to Shoreditch, adjacent to the Barbican complex. His collection paraded the newly infected generation of London vampires that the film's ending proposed.

The credit sheet to the show featured a photograph of an open puncture wound on flesh, the means of contagion in the film (pl.270); and the fashion show made this exchange of bodily fluids visible in stylized form. For example, a latex bodice with hanging sleeves of silk brocade traces what looks like lines of blood dispersed across the body but which are in fact threads of felted yarn set into the rubber surface; while the decorative hanging sleeves frame the bodice, just like the grandiose interiors in the film that stage the blood-letting scenes (pl.267). In this collection, McQueen extended the meaning of a film through the conversion of its visual tropes and literary themes into another medium. As a form of mediation, his transformations are a creative conversation with film – part commentary, part intervention – through the processes of making and staging fashion.

Rewind

Much later, for *Sarabande* (Spring/Summer 2007), McQueen employed a live orchestra to play George Frederick Handel's Suite for Harpsichord No.4 in D Minor. But in this instance,

McQueen rewound the reference to an earlier use of Handel's piece in film, Stanley Kubrick's *Barry Lyndon* (1975). An adaptation of the nineteenth-century novel set in the eighteenth century by William Makepeace Thackeray, the film was famed for the director's use of lenses developed by NASA to film candlelight scenes (pl.280). McQueen's fashion show started with a lit candelabrum, hung low in the centre of the catwalk, which was then raised to signal the start of the show, a device drawn from the theatre of Thackeray's day when candles were lit just before the start of the performance (pl.268).

This reference to an eighteenth-century narrative through a twentieth-century film adaptation was McQueen's take on historicism. He signposted this most clearly by instructing the orchestra to play an arrangement of 'Paint it Black' by The Rolling Stones at the show's finale; a piece of music not only used by Kubrick in *Full Metal Jacket* (1987) but also by McQueen in *Dante* (Autumn/Winter 1996). Here the deployment of music is not only a commentary on its use in film, but also an illustration of how it is bound to the designer through its use in his fashion shows.

After securing financial sponsorship from American Express in 1997 to the tune of £20,000 per show (small change in film terms), McQueen was able to stage his shows in abandoned warehouses such as that in Gatliff Road, Victoria, which could be turned into what looked like a film set (that lasted a matter of days) for a fashion performance that lasted less than the duration of a short film. Reporting for a behind-the-scenes article on *Voss* (Spring/Summer 2001) in the *Observer*, Louise Davis stated: 'It's like the set for an eerie sci-fi Hollywood movie or a scene from *One Flew Over the Cuckoo's Nest*.'[7]

Slow-motion

In *Untitled* (Spring/Summer 1998), McQueen staged a Perspex catwalk filled with water that turned black with ink halfway through the show before 'rain' fell from the roof onto the models as they walked down it. These visual devices, developed by set designer Simon Costin, were not filmic per se (they were informed more by installation art); but McQueen asked for the fashion show's soundtrack, devised by John Gosling, to include the 'shark' theme to *Jaws* (1975) by John Williams, with which Gosling, also a music producer and recording artist, habitually opened his DJ set.

Previous spread
266. Plum Sykes backstage, *The Birds*,
Spring/Summer 1995
Jacket: silk with print of swallows
Photograph by Gary Wallis

Opposite
267. Ensemble, *The Hunger*,
Spring/Summer 1996
Top: silk brocade, latex and felted yarn;
trousers: silk brocade
Modelled by Stella Tennant
Photograph by Robert Fairer

268. Catwalk set, *Sarabande*,
Spring/Summer 2007

With the catwalk illuminated, and before the first model appeared, the show began with three minutes of recorded sound of thunder and lightning. When ink flooded the catwalk mid-show, there was first silence (the show music stopped), followed by 'I Can't Stand the Rain' by Ann Peebles, before the *Jaws* theme undercut it 20 seconds later. After a minute the rain descended and the fashion show resumed.

This treatment of sound is cinematic in form, as it makes use of the way film soundtracks build suspense or drama, mark duration and add to the film's intensity. McQueen uses this effect not to imply action or filmic movement, but to offer an audible element: it operates as a staging of cinematic effect within the span of a fashion show. In this sense, McQueen inserted a piece of film music to decelerate and extend the strict time-based formula of the fashion show. This device is most clearly used in *The Overlook* (Autumn/Winter 1999), the collection's title referencing the name of the hotel in Kubrick's horror film *The Shining* (1980). The invitation (p.310) was a simple sheet of A4 paper with the words 'All work and no play makes Jack a dull boy' repeated again and again, an echo of the film's chilling refrain. The show was staged inside a Plexiglas box that contained a winter woodland setting in which snow was falling, alluding to the final scene of the film (pl.275). Film references continued in the appearance of twin girls as models, evoking the film scene of twin girls from the past, glimpsed at the end of a corridor (pls 271, 276), and in the recurrence of hexagonal patchwork shapes, a panelled leather coat (pl.274) evoking the carpet pattern in the hallways of the Overlook Hotel.

The show was dedicated to the memory of Stanley Kubrick (pl.278) who had recently died, and it made use of one of the most noticeable temporal disturbances in the film's narrative in order to play with the idea of the duration of time. In the film Jack Torrance, played by Jack Nicholson, enters The Gold Room (the hotel bar) to find his fellow guests and staff transported to the 1920s. This entr'acte, a theatrical term for a performance between acts, dislocates time and space to disrupt the reality of the film, suggesting that all is not as it should be. The film's final reveal is a long tracking shot of a photograph of Jack in a group portrait of revellers at The Gold Room's 4 July celebration in 1921 (pl.277), destabilizing any sense of how long Jack really has been staying at the hotel. It is accompanied by the jazz standard 'Midnight, the Stars and You', sung by Al Bowlly accompanied by the Ray Noble Orchestra, which McQueen transposed into his fashion show to create another sense of rupture through a modern entr'acte – in this instance interrupting the fashion show with a three-minute ice-skating routine.

Although overall the connections to *The Shining* made in the fashion show are explicit, even unsubtle, the borrowing of Kubrick's leitmotif (in the sense of a space that dislocates narrative, and a song that displaces it even further) evidences a more nuanced referencing of film by McQueen. Even the doctored photograph of Jack in a tuxedo in The Gold Room in 1921, commissioned by Kubrick as a prop, which inserted Jack into an original photograph of partygoers from the 1920s with an overlaid fictitious title, is a model for the way McQueen blended

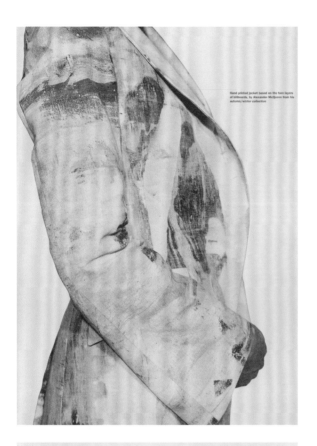

Hand printed jacket based on the two layers of billboards, by Alexander McQueen from his autumn/winter collection

Photograph by Gerhard Kircher for Alexander McQueen

the old into the new in his clothing designs. For example, a wool dress from *The Overlook* has a long sleeve bodice with a chevron of plaid that meets centre-front (pl.273) – a detail that references an earlier bodice design from *Highland Rape* (Autumn/Winter 1995) that conjoined tartan on the body in the same way. The plaid bodice is attached to a balloon hem skirt made from square patches of wool, not dissimilar to the jackets once made by trainee tailors using sample fabrics taken from out of date cloth-merchant sample books (connecting back still further to McQueen's tailoring apprenticeship). The dissonance that occurs between the two sets of checks where they meet is feathered-in on the dress, just like retouching the edges of a composite photograph, with wisps of felted wool that look like strands of wolf fur.

The collection marked a high point, not just for fashion as spectacle but also for the visual interpretation of narrative film in another medium. The *Evening Standard* noted the presence of Hollywood actresses in the front row: 'But even these experienced performers must have been impressed by the sheer scale of McQueen's latest production.'[8]

Record

Gosling remembers that, at the time, *The Shining* soundtrack by Wendy Carlos and Wendy Elkind was hard to source on vinyl, so the sound was ripped from VHS tapes (the soundtrack used was taken from the trailer for the film) before being transferred to 2-inch analogue tapes for mixing. The process of choosing the

Opposite above
269. Frock coat, *Nihilism*,
Spring/Summer 1994
Hand-painted, distressed, polycotton
Observer Magazine, 27 February 1994
Photograph by John Hicks

Opposite below
270. Credit sheet, *The Hunger*,
Spring/Summer 1996
Photograph by Gerhard Klocker
Courtesy of Alexander McQueen

Right
271. Lisa and Louise Burns as the
Grady twins
Stanley Kubrick, *The Shining*, 1980

Below
272. Catherine Deneuve as Miriam
Blaylock and David Bowie as
John Blaylock
Tony Scott, *The Hunger*, 1983

Opposite left
273. Dress, *The Overlook*,
Autumn/Winter 1999
Patchwork of wool, tweed and fur

Opposite right
274. Coat, *The Overlook*,
Autumn/Winter 1999
Leather

275. *The Overlook*, Autumn/Winter 1999
Photograph by Chris Moore

276. Ensemble, *The Overlook*,
Autumn/Winter 1999
Wool
Photograph by Chris Moore

show's soundtrack started at least two months beforehand, with Gosling being invited into the studio to look at research boards, prior to developing a set of tracks, most of which were rejected by McQueen who would then ask Gosling to return with a new selection. The collaborative edit was reworked over and over again. Gosling recalls that it was usually around version 13 that some agreement was reached: 'We'd start up with an idea here, and end up over there, and in-between there'd be loads of ideas rejected, but in them was enough to build up a patchwork of ideas.'[9]

This idea of patchwork as something pieced together from fragments not only represents how the music for the shows was created, and how some of the garments were constructed, but also how film is assembled. It chimes with something Alfred Hitchcock once said: 'One cut of film is like a piece of mosaic. To me, pure film, pure cinema is pieces of film assembled. Any individual piece is nothing. But a combination of them creates an idea.'[10] Like Hitchcock, McQueen also appreciated that sometimes the most effective fragment is the plainest, the one that almost seems as if it is missing.

Auto Repeat
McQueen's collection *Deliverance* (Spring/Summer 2004) set the bar for staging much higher, being based on the film *They Shoot Horses, Don't They?* (1969), directed by Sydney Pollack, which dramatized the phenomenon of dance marathons that took place during the American Depression (pls 281, 282). McQueen took the theme of the film as a means of exploring a range of fabrics connected to the era, such as sweatshirt jersey, denim and cotton madras. Patchwork was explored in honeycomb design coats and in cloth suiting pieced together from panels of checked and coloured fabrics, then topstitched in designs that followed the musculature of the body. A beige and red Prince of Wales check suit has flesh tone organza inlay panels set into it (the fishtail skirt has flesh tone lace inlays), so as to appear as though the seams of the garments are separating due to wear and tear.

The show music drew on the film's soundtrack, but mixed it with OST (original soundtrack) recordings of Francis Ford Coppola's *The Cotton Club* (1984) and Steven Spielberg's *The Colour Purple* (1985), together with singles by Nirvana, Portishead and Chic. McQueen and Gosling especially liked using Chic's 'Dance, Dance, Dance' as they loved the stage outfits worn by Chic on stage, which drew on the glamour of 1930s Harlem and formed a commentary on black social aspiration. Gosling had previously worked with the choreographer Michael Clark on his production of the ballet *I Am Curious, Orange* (1988) and had long wanted McQueen to collaborate with the dancer. Clark choreographed *Deliverance* using both dancers and fashion models, who exchanged the syncopation of the model walk for a dazed stagger produced by failing limbs, and whose dragging heels and lolling heads were manoeuvred by male dancing partners trying to keep pace with the race.

In Nick Knight's image of the collection (pl.265), the models are blown through the air like a gust of wind from a Hokusai print, replicating the circularity of the race and, in turn, the arc of the film as it segues into the fashion show and then back again. Here, fashion is presented as an unending cycle, as decorative as it is destructive. As a condensed and frozen image of McQueen's approach, it is representative of how he infused the fashion show with the inferences of film and the patterns of choreography. In so doing, he reinforced the centrality of the staging of a collection, from which all elements radiated.

If Knight's image offers a frozen interpretation of McQueen's fashion show, then a film-based project helps to make sense of how McQueen attempted to bring film and fashion closer together through staging in real time. In 1973, Annabel Nicolson presented *Reel Time* at the London Filmmakers Co-operative, an artist's film performance that involved running a long loop of 16mm film through a projector before it went through the needle plate of a sewing machine (pl.279). The more times the loop ran through the sewing machine, the more it was drilled with fine holes, which in turn affected the quality of the film's projection on the screen and its tendency to tear and snag. Nicolson sat at the sewing machine, also projected as a silhouette, patching each split before restarting the loop until it could no longer be played.

Nicolson's film performance drew on the shared qualities of sewing machines and projectors, and how they both utilize sprockets and gates to feed the materials they use. She inverted the logic of the sewing machine – so destabilizing the film rather than binding the elements together – to make a compelling live commentary, as it was projected, on visual disintegration. Like Nicolson, McQueen also inverted his materials. But he used the visual effects and references of film to destabilize the logical sequence of the fashion show and so suggest both visual disintegration and time-based transformation.

One aspect of McQueen's 'patchwork of ideas' that connects with this process is his interest in assembling his work into a unified whole and then unpicking it. He once remarked: 'You don't design a spaceship to go into space if it hasn't got wings, it doesn't make sense. In my own collection I like the spaceship not to have any wings because I want to see how it falls back to earth.'[11] McQueen was clearly motivated by wanting to design collections that went on a journey and were transformed by it. His shows unveiled this sense of discovery and change from the first to final look in time-based terms, but it is also evident in how the clothes themselves evolve across this span.

This is most aptly demonstrated in *Irere* (Spring/Summer 2003), a title that made use of the Amazonian word for transformation. The collection was inspired by the voyages of Christopher Columbus and Captain Cook into unknown territories where they encountered different cultures. The show invitation was a flick book that translated a model's face into that of an Amazonian boy (pl.284). Over the pages, the tribal adornments that pierce his face gradually emerge out of the model's skin, so that the final unaltered photograph of the boy is made stranger, appearing as artificial as a mannequin. Much more than the fashion show, the invitation makes it clear that journey and transformation are themes that McQueen wanted to explore, and not just on women's bodies; he also sought to investigate

Opposite above
277. 4 July ball, The Overlook Hotel, Oregon, 1921

Opposite centre
278. Stanley Kubrick filming *The Shining* in the Gold Room, Elstree Film Studios, Hertfordshire, England, 1978–9

Opposite below
279. Annabel Nicolson, *Reel Time*, 1973 London Filmmakers Cooperative

Above
280. Candlelit scene, Stanley Kubrick, *Barry Lyndon*, 1975

Right
281. Jane Fonda as Gloria Beatty and Michael Sarrazin as Robert Syverton Sydney Pollack, *They Shoot Horses, Don't They?*, 1969

282. *Deliverance*, Spring/Summer 2004
Photograph by Pierre Verdy

Opposite
283. Joan Fontaine as Mrs de Winter and
Judith Anderson as Mrs Danvers
Alfred Hitchcock, *Rebecca*, 1940

the idea of what it is to be a woman through exploring the representation of women, especially the construction of feminine types in film.

Repeated Viewing

McQueen's use of the films of Alfred Hitchcock is a central reference point in his work. His employment of their themes centres on representations of femininity and how they are challenged through transformation scenes. McQueen's collection *The Birds* makes no literal reference to the Hitchcock film's heroine. Instead, the first connection to the film is a black swallow design on an orange wool trouser suit, which begins block-black at the sleeve heads.[12] The birds then nosedive down the body of the jacket, moving into greater focus, the largest bird set at the base of the jacket's ventless back (pl.266). This is a reference to a scene in the Hitchcock film where birds invade the Brenner house by descending down the chimney en masse. Although sparrows were used for the film studio scene, it is based on an incident in 1960 in La Jolla, California, which involved swifts. The route of the birds down the chimney is also replicated in McQueen's print design, but not just on the jacket. Ten outfits after the appearance of the orange jacket, the print reappears, this time on a red silk skirt worn with a heavily corseted black jacket, made and modelled in the show by corset-maker Mr Pearl (pl.285). Across the span of the fashion show, the bird print travels – from top to bottom, and from female to male – translating femininity through artifice from one body to another. The jolt this performs is conveyed through the fall of the design, as it is unveiled through the fashion show. And what is so strange about the final figure is that he is so much more like Mrs Danvers in Hitchcock's *Rebecca* (1940) than any female role in *The Birds* (pl.283).

The reason for the link may be that both films are the only Hitchcock movies based on stories by Daphne du Maurier. In *Rebecca*, Mrs Danvers' unsettling presence prevents the young Mrs de Winter settling in to her new home by constantly reminding her of the clothes and effects of her dead predecessor. The scene in which Mrs Danvers fingers her deceased mistress's undergarments conveys, in feminist film theorist Tania Modleski's reading of the film, 'a femininity that remains alien and disturbing'.[13] And so Mr Pearl performs a similar role in McQueen's fashion show, for his appearance destabilizes the ordered sense of femininity unveiled by the procession of catwalk looks, through his visual dominance and exertion of bodily control.

McQueen went on to inhabit the space of Hitchcock's cinema in physical terms for *Eshu* (Autumn/Winter 2000) by staging it in the Gainsborough Film Studios in Hoxton, where Hitchcock shot a number of his early silent films. And McQueen's desire to match the scale of the director surfaced again in *The Man Who Knew Too Much* (Autumn/Winter 2005). The show invitation took the form of a film poster, appropriating Saul Bass's poster design for *Vertigo* (1958) and rewording the title in the same typography, which also spelt out the designer's name (p.316). If this offered

a clue, it lay in the kaleidoscope motif of the film poster, as McQueen telescoped and distilled the Hitchcock blonde, look after look. As a collection, it was informed by the logic of repeat viewing, aided by the choice of title as, of course, to have truly seen this Hitchcock film you would have had to watch it at least twice, as the director made two versions (1934 and 1956).

McQueen waited until this moment to pay homage to Edith Head's costume for Tippi Hedren, who plays Melanie Daniels in Hitchcock's *The Birds*. In McQueen's *The Man Who Knew Too Much* it surfaced like a curious imprint. If, like the femme fatale, the Hitchcock blonde is the figure of a discursive unease, then McQueen reproduced this in terms of a faithful copy, if a shade off, like a doppelgänger. McQueen's version (pl.287) is actually more faithful to Head's original sketch than the final costume worn by Hedren (pl.286).

McQueen considered another role for women, as portrayed in Hitchcock's films – that of the mother – for the invitation to *Natural Dis-tinction, Un-Natural Selection* (Spring/Summer 2009), a collection inspired by Darwin's theory of evolution. The digital composite double image was made by McQueen's nephew, Gary James McQueen, who has been employed as a print designer for McQ since 2006. He remembers, 'I used to pin all my work on a board behind me in the studio and one day Lee walked in and just saw it and said "Yeah, I want it".'[14] The digitally rendered human skull design was intended for a menswear print but McQueen appropriated it, deciding to produce a lenticular double image that segued between the skull design and a headshot portrait of himself to the same dimensions (p.320).

When asked about the invitation, McQueen claimed the skull was based on the desiccated head of Mrs Bates in Hitchcock's *Psycho* (1960), although this was not technically true in terms of the origin of the design. If the invitation was intended to advertise a collection that referenced Darwin's theory of natural selection, then McQueen's film reference marked these origins, in his account, as of an unnatural order; as in *Psycho*, the relationship between mother and son is far from simple, as Norman maintains her after death by embalming her and wearing her clothes. This makes the image less a memento mori, and much more a keepsake of darker drives raised by film.

McQueen returned to the idea of transformation for his subsequent collection, *The Horn of Plenty* (Autumn/Winter 2009), reworking the descending swallow print with its references to Hitchcock and also the work of graphic artist M.C. Escher.

A number of red silk dresses carried a print design that began with houndstooth at the neck, changed into birds that increased in scale

Opposite

284. Show invitation, *Irere*, Spring/
Summer 2003
Modelled by Tatiana Urina
Courtesy of Alexander McQueen
Photograph by Steven Klein

285. Ensemble, *The Birds*, Spring/
Summer 1995
Printed silk, cotton and leather
Modelled by Mr Pearl
Photograph by Chris Moore

286. Tippi Hedren as Melanie Daniels
Alfred Hitchcock, *The Birds*, 1963
Costume by Edith Head

Opposite
287. Ensemble, *The Man Who Knew Too
Much*, Autumn/Winter 2005
Jacket, top and pencil skirt: wool bouclé
and cashmere
Modelled by Inguna Butane
Photograph by Anthea Simms

as they flew down the body, and ended with a single magpie at the hemline (pl.288). While it is obvious that the print design is a reworking of a design from *The Birds* (Spring/Summer 1995), the transition from houndstooth (a reference to Christian Dior's use of the weave design for the Dior woman) to bird is more closely aligned to the kind of anthropomorphic transformation found in Greek mythology. Many of the transformation myths centre on young women in straightened circumstances who, pitied by the gods, are transformed into birds, thus enabling their escape. This fits with McQueen's longstanding intention to create clothes that make women feel protected and powerful.

This aim connects with cultural historian Ludmilla Jordanova's view of cultural products as forms of transformation in themselves, so 'made things may be treated as commentaries upon and interventions in specific situations.' According to Jordanova, creative practitioners produce artefacts that 'are in creative conversation with the contexts in which they are made and used'.[15] McQueen's contexts were the fashion show and the fashion studio, as well as the film theatre and home cinema. His great achievement lay in how he fused these contexts together for the staging of his collections.

In 1975, the cultural theorist Roland Barthes wrote a short essay, 'Leaving the Movie Theatre', which bemoaned the passivity of watching film at the cinema, of being in thrall to what he called 'the engulfing mirror' of the silver screen. Barthes composed

it just before home cinema technologies revolutionized film spectatorship, but his essay proposed 'another way of going to the movies' that could challenge its dictatorial rules of engagement. He proposed two ways of looking: one that gazed at the screen, and one that noticed everything about the environment of the cinema, 'ready to fetishize not the image but precisely what exceeds it: the texture of the sound, the hall, the darkness, the obscure mass of other bodies, the rays of light, entering the theatre, leaving the hall'.[16]

McQueen was unique in his desire to harness the scale and impact of film in his own work: from the outset he always said he wanted to work with people from the film industry when staging his fashion shows. In this he personified what film theorist Christian Metz termed the cinema fetishist: 'the person who is enchanted at what the machine is capable of, at the theatre of shadows as such.'[17] The fashion shows of Alexander McQueen made great and explicit use of film as a reference, but more than this, they embraced and made a fetish of those secondary aspects of watching film that Barthes wrote of, both in the cinema and beyond it. They turned a formulaic presentation with a sense of theatre into an immersive spectacle informed by the scale of cinema.

288. Dress, *The Horn of Plenty*,
Autumn/Winter 2009
Printed silk
Modelled by Aida Aniulyte

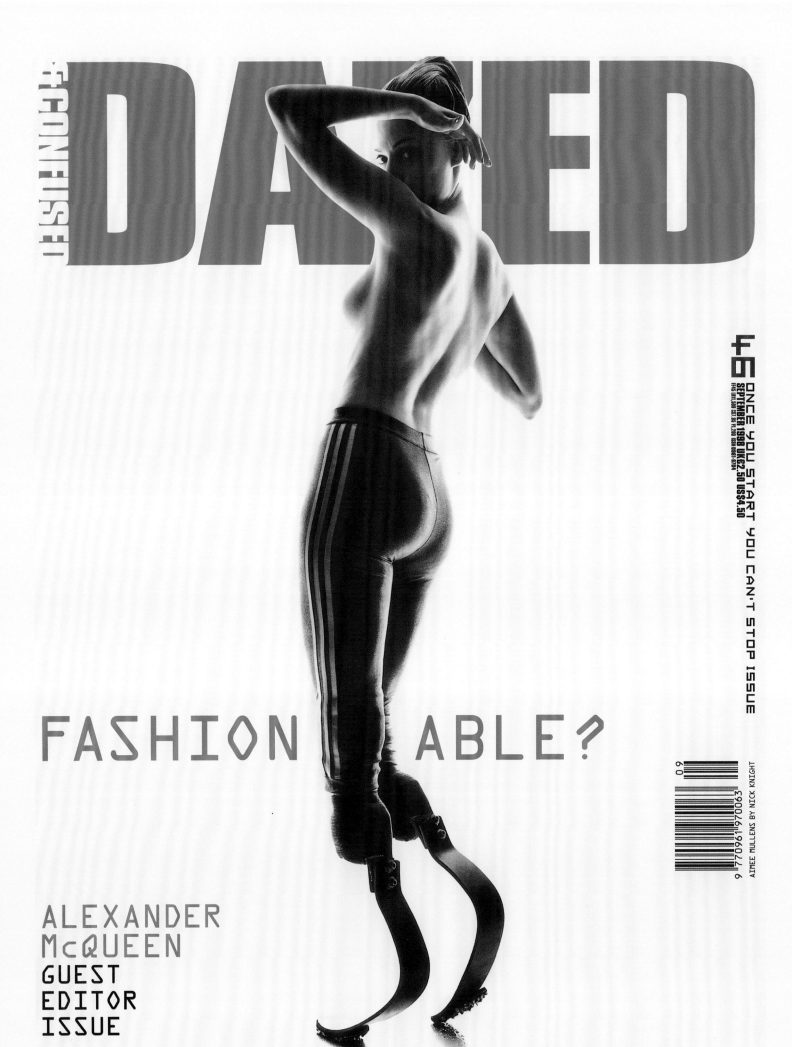

DAZED &CONFUSED

46

SEPTEMBER 1998 UK£2.50 US$4.50
IRE £3.80 S$7.95 ¥1,200 ISSN 0961-9704

ONCE YOU START YOU CAN'T STOP ISSUE

FASHION-ABLE?

AIMEE MULLINS BY NICK KNIGHT

ALEXANDER
McQUEEN
GUEST
EDITOR
ISSUE

FASHION-ABLE

JEFFERSON HACK

———

'Fashion is a big bubble and sometimes I feel like popping it'
Alexander McQueen, 2008

—

It is the summer of '98. Madonna's 'Ray of Light' is fighting it out in the charts with Massive Attack's 'Mezzanine'; France lifts the World Cup and the iPod is merely a twinkle in Steve Jobs' eye. Alexander McQueen has just shown his latest collection for Givenchy haute couture in Paris – a tribal collection inspired by royalty and the Amazon – and he is about to create the scene-stealing moment of September's London Fashion Week, when robot arms will spray-paint a white dress worn by stoic, revolving model, Shalom Harlow. Opening the show, *No.13* (Spring/Summer 1999), Paralympic athlete and amputee Aimee Mullins strides out on a pair of prosthetic legs, intricately hand-carved in wood.

Aimee Mullins was also the cover star for the September 1998 issue of *Dazed & Confused*, guest-edited by Alexander McQueen. Stylist Katy England, McQueen's creative right-hand and visionary fashion editor at *Dazed & Confused*, had spent months preparing the cover story that cemented the relationship between the designer and the athlete. Lee (as we called him) had seen a picture of Aimee, reached out to her and fell in love. As was the case with everything he did, he wanted to push the boundaries further, questioning narrow preconceptions of beauty, and so he began casting more people with disabilities, inviting his contemporaries such as Hussein Chalayan, Roland Mouret and Philip Treacy to design and customize pieces for them to wear. Photographed by the legendary Nick Knight using his now antiquated 10 x 8 film camera, 'Fashion-able', as the story was titled, was, Katy has since told me, 'the hardest thing I have ever done'. Katy, Nick and Lee believed sincerely in the beauty of the individuals they cast alongside Aimee (Jo Paul, Mat Fraser, Helen Mcintosh, Catherine Long, Alison Lapper, David Toole and Sue Bramley) and they worked painstakingly

with charity organizations and peer networks to navigate the hurdles that existed in mixing fashion photography with disability. 'We were entering into a different world,' explained Katy, 'and of course we had to tread very carefully, with extreme sensitivity.'

It was *Dazed*'s 'Never Mind the Bollocks'; it took us from being indie-outsiders to being one of the most talked about magazines on the planet that year. Inside, beyond the 'Fashion-able' story, you really feel like you're walking into the mind of McQueen at that time. Photographers Inez Van Lamsweerde and Vinoodh Matadin shot his Givenchy collection and Juergen Teller Grace Jones; Jack Webb documented underground sex clubs and the photographer and film director Robert Frank was profiled. Lee himself interviewed the actress Helen Mirren. I think the only person who Lee wanted in the issue that we couldn't get to shoot a story was Joel-Peter Witkin.

Soon afterwards, Lee became our fashion editor-at-large, forging a loyal and amazingly rich relationship with *Dazed*, resulting in a series of special photographic projects. What was incredible about working with him was that he never intellectualized his ideas or actions. When I asked him why he wanted to profile Helen Mirren, he just said, 'cause I like her'. He was a natural storyteller with an exceptional, childlike wonder for the world, coupled with a polemic anti-establishment ethos. Lee was truly fearless and never really gave a damn about what anyone else would think, or how they might perceive what he did. His concept of challenging conventions of beauty was never political, always punk. That's why this issue is as powerful and provocative today as it was then. It was Lee who taught me not to say, 'Why?' but more importantly, 'Why not?'.

Previous spread
289. *Dazed & Confused*, *'Fashion-able?'*,
issue 46, September 1998
Modelled by Aimee Mullins
Art direction by Alexander McQueen
Photograph by Nick Knight
Courtesy of *Dazed & Confused*

290. 'Access-able'
Dazed & Confused, *'Fashion-able?'*, issue
46, September 1998
Wooden fan jacket, Alexander McQueen
for Givenchy Haute Couture; suede T-shirt,
Alexander McQueen; crinoline, Berman's
and Nathan's
Modelled by Aimee Mullins
Art direction by Alexander McQueen
Photograph by Nick Knight

NIGHTMARES
AND DREAMS

SUSANNA BROWN

*'I think there is beauty in everything. What "normal" people would
perceive as ugly, I can usually see something of beauty in it'*

ALEXANDER MCQUEEN, 2003

Like the art of photography, McQueen's work explored the poetic relationship between light and shadow. The McQueen illusion was born of a marriage of opposites: horror and splendour, vulnerability and strength, the profane and the sublime, nightmares and dreams.[1] And, like a photographer, McQueen was focused on the creation of a potent final image, an aim he expressed in a discussion at the V&A in 2000: 'It's mainly to do with the end result as an image, and hopefully a lasting image. I don't like throw-away images; I like things to be stuck in the mind of people and maybe that's why my work can sometimes come across as aggressive or violent, because today maybe the world, to me, is a bit violent.'[2] He conveyed a similar desire to induce a visceral reaction a few years earlier: 'I don't see the point in doing anything that doesn't create an emotion, good or bad. If you're disgusted, at least that's emotion. If you walk away and you forgot everything you saw, then I haven't done my job properly.'[3] Just as the spectacular catwalk shows were the climax of McQueen's vision, the shoots for magazines and advertisements

were crafted to produce arresting two-dimensional interpretations of his designs. He formed friendships with numerous image-makers, among them Anne Deniau, Steven Klein, Nick Knight and Nick Waplington, and collaborated closely on shoots. McQueen also incorporated photographic images into his designs and collected photographs, framed and arranged with great sensitivity in his home. This chapter explores the crucial role played by the medium in his creative process.

McQueen stated on several occasions that, had he not been a designer, he would have liked to become a photojournalist. The greatest documentary pictures by the likes of Robert Capa, Henri Cartier-Bresson and Don McCullin possess narrative power and elicit an emotional response. Akin to a hunter or predator, the successful photojournalist needs intuition and lightning-fast reactions, as well as an artist's eye. In the twenty-first century photographs are produced at a staggering rate – currently more than 300 million are shared on Instagram every day, swiftly

Previous spread
291. Alexander McQueen in his
London studio
Harper's Bazaar, September 2008
Photograph by Don McCullin

Above
292. Hans Bellmer, *Les Jeux de la
Poupée*, 1937–8
Centre Georges Pompidou

Opposite above
293. Joel-Peter Witkin, *Leda*, 1986
Toned gelatin silver print

Opposite below
294. Memorial portrait of a woman,
c.1845–5
Daguerreotype in wood and embossed
leather case
V&A: E.642:1-2014

created and subsumed by the next snapshot. Yet connoisseurship and the serious collectors' market continue to grow, with photographs achieving ever-greater prices at auction.[4] The dichotomy between the fleeting and the carefully preserved might be paralleled with contemporary clothing production – cheap throw-away fashions at one end of the spectrum and handcrafted haute couture at the other.

One of McQueen's favourite books was *A New History of Photography* by Michel Frizot, first published in 1998. When compared to other encyclopedic tomes on the subject, Frizot's extraordinary book seems to place an emphasis on the more surreal examples from the past two centuries. The 775-page publication contains over 1000 images and reveals much about McQueen's relationship with the medium. It encompasses the elegiac, the hallucinatory and the macabre, and images range from Victorian nature studies – Adolphe Braun's *Flower Study* and Louis Rousseau's *Lizard* (both dating from the 1860s), and an early X-ray of a reptile (1896; pl.305) – to ghostly double exposures, 'spirit' photographs and Jules Duboscq's memento mori *Still-life* (1855). This stereoscopic daguerreotype depicts a bird of prey clutching a skull atop a fluted column. It is comprised of two slightly different views of the same subject which, when seen through a stereoscopic viewer, merge into a three-dimensional image. It is a vividly detailed reminder of life's transience and the connection to McQueen's aesthetic is instantly obvious. Interviewed by Nick Knight shortly before the unveiling of *Plato's Atlantis* (Spring/Summer 2010), McQueen spoke of his interest in Victorian photographs of the dead.

Examples of these poignant images exist at the V&A, home to one of the largest and most significant collections of photographs in the world. Memorial portraiture was popular in the nineteenth century when grieving families would commission a study of a recently deceased relative, photographed as if in a deep slumber or arranged to appear lifelike. The earliest examples were daguerreotypes, unique positive images formed on a highly polished silver surface and presented in Morocco leather cases lined with velvet (pl.294). In the age before the snapshot camera, these treasured objects were often the only visual record of the deceased. For McQueen, such portraits were 'about celebrating someone's life … I don't think it's a bad thing, I think it's a very romantic thing.'[5]

Some of the most memorable pictures in Frizot's book connect to motifs and materials central to McQueen's work. Linnaeus Tripe's careful arrangement of horn and ivory objects from India (1857), Felice Beato's samurai in chainmail and Charles Clifford's study of a helmet from Madrid's Royal Armory (both 1860s), and Alinari's advertisement for orthopaedic supplies (1905) relate to McQueen's fascination with animal forms, skeletons, armour and the distortion of the human body. Claude Cahun's photomontage *"H.U.M."* (1929–30), an amalgam of androgynous self-portraits, fragmented figures, birds and dressmaker's scissors, all floating before an X-ray of human lungs, might be construed as an abstract portrait of McQueen himself, were it not for its early production date. The Surrealist art movement explored unique ways of interpreting the world, turning to dreams and

the unconscious for inspiration. Herbert List, a photographer who worked briefly at *Harper's Bazaar*, explained that his dream-like photographs (pl.302) were 'composed visions where [my] arrangements try to capture the magical essence inhabiting and animating the world of appearances.'[6] McQueen shared with the Surrealists a fascination with extreme representations of the female body, fragmenting or distorting the human form with his designs. Surreal photographs occasionally inspired whole McQueen collections. *La Poupée* (Spring/Summer 1997) took as its starting point German artist Hans Bellmer's *Doll* project of the 1930s (pl.292), intended as a form of protest against the Nazi Party's cult of the perfect body. Bellmer created and photographed a series of partially dismembered and disturbing dolls, which embodied numerous qualities of the Surrealist object: 'subversive and erotic, sadistic and fetishistic … An erotic obsession, the *Dolls* incarnated his fascination for the corruption of innocence and for the writing of De Sade, whom he much admired.'[7] A figure from André Durst's surreal photograph of fashions by Schiaparelli was translated into three dimensions for *No.13* (Spring/Summer 1999), in which McQueen presented a model encircled by a vast wire coil.[8]

The surreal-infused image *Me + Cat* (pl.297) by Italian experimental photographer Wanda Wulz (1932) features in Frizot's book and was used in McQueen's *Eshu* (Autumn/Winter 2000). The image was printed on the back of a bodice, the fabric slashed into narrow vertical strips that swished as the model walked (pl.298). But it was far from the first time McQueen had incorporated photographs into his designs: his 1992 MA show included portraits of men and women collaged onto full, distressed-fabric skirts. *Dante* (Autumn/Winter 1996), the collection that centred on religion as the cause of war, featured garments photo-printed with Don McCullin's documentary pictures from war-torn Vietnam.[9] Many of the photographs McQueen appropriated were intended to provoke a reaction or make a political point. *Joan* (Autumn/Winter 1998), partly inspired by the murders of Joan of Arc in 1431 and of the Russian Imperial Romanov family in 1918, included portraits of the innocent, unsmiling Romanov children on tailored jackets and tops, overprinted onto clear sequins which made the images flicker and shimmer as if beneath a watery surface, visible but somehow out of reach. In *Dante*, other nineteenth-century portraits were printed onto high-collared cotton jersey coats, this time studies of a colony for the blind. Contemporary photographs were also incorporated into designs: a scarf made for *i-D* magazine's project opposing the Iraq War included two photographs of Prime Minister Tony Blair. McQueen christened the scarf 'Two Face' and intended it as an expression of his political disappointment.[10] When one begins to look for them, one can discover references – both direct and discreet – to well-known photographs in all of McQueen's collections.

After *Eshu* came *Voss* (Spring/Summer 2001). The models wore white head bindings, perhaps based on Adolf De Meyer's 1935 photograph for Elizabeth Arden, also reproduced in Frizot's book (pls 299, 300). But photography's influential role was most apparent in the show's spectacular final tableau, a scene inspired by Joel-Peter Witkin's *Sanitarium* (1983), which depicts a voluptuous 20-stone nude sucking in the breath of a monkey through transparent tubes (pl.296). Her pose is reminiscent of a reclining

299. Advertisement for Elizabeth
Arden, 1935
Gelatin silver print
Photograph by Adolf De Meyer

Opposite
300. Kate Moss backstage, *Voss*,
Spring/Summer 2001
Dress: silk chiffon
Photograph by Anne Deniau

Venus, presented in innumerable examples from the history of art, but over her face she wears a demonic winged mask; the overall atmosphere is disturbing in the extreme. Witkin's starting point for the sinister photograph was an article on anthrax and the exchange of disease between humans and animals. He sketched the initial idea before devising a stage plan and the creation of the image took a month from conception to final print. For his own interpretation, McQueen chose fetish writer Michelle Olley to play the role of the woman. He added living moths, bringing movement to an otherwise static scene (pl.295). In Andrew Bolton's words: 'Typical of McQueen's collections, *Voss* offered a commentary on the politics of appearance, upending conventional ideals of beauty. For McQueen, the body was a site for contravention, where normalcy was questioned and the spectacle of marginality was embraced and celebrated.'[11] Olley documented her experiences in a diary. A day after the show she wrote:

Wednesday 27th September 2000
I want people to know what I just went through wasn't a breeze and I did it for art. Yes, art. Because I believe it's worth going through that much palaver if it creates a strong image that conveys an important idea. And I believe that the idea that we are trapped by our 'civilised', socially approved identities is massively

important. It causes women so much suffering. Fear of ageing, fear of not being thin enough. Fear of not having the right clothes. Fear of our animal natures that we carry in our DNA – fish, bird, lizard, insect, mammal. We've never had it more techno, we've never needed it more human. We humans living now still cannot turn ourselves into perfect beings, no matter how long we spend at the gym, beauty parlour, shops, etc.[12]

Olley's comments on human fears and the futility of the beauty and fashion industries connect to another of the photographs that McQueen may have appreciated in *A New History of Photography*: Horst P. Horst's *Electric Beauty* (1939). Created when the world was on the brink of war, *Electric Beauty* (pl.301) was perhaps intended as a satirical comment on the increasingly extreme beauty treatments of the 1930s. The spot-lit model is seated next to a table filled with beauty instruments and appears to be undergoing several modern procedures simultaneously. The mask that obscures her face resembles that worn by Olley and renders Horst's model blind to her own bizarre appearance, unaware that she is dangerously close to being electrocuted. Wires from the mask and the electric massage device she holds in her hands encircle her body like serpents, preparing to suffocate or strangle her. The backdrop against which this scene takes place

enhances the threatening atmosphere. It shows an enlarged detail of *The Temptation of St Anthony* (*c*.1501), a triptych by the Flemish artist Hieronymus Bosch. Horst and his contemporaries at *Vogue* often used reproductions of historic paintings as backdrops, usually featuring classical architectural details or attractive landscapes.

In contrast, this eerie image is filled with the imaginary creatures and visual metaphors that typified Bosch's work. It depicts a bird-like monster on ice skates that wears the badge of a messenger and carries a letter. According to the complex symbolic code used by Bosch, the ice skates represent folly, while the funnel, twig and ball on the monster's head indicate wastefulness, promiscuity and merrymaking. Given Horst's keen interest in art, it is likely that he understood at least some of the messages encoded in the painting, and composed his photograph to serve as a caution against the vice of vanity.

The fantastical and grotesque elements of Bosch's work led him to be regarded as one of the forefathers of the Surrealists. McQueen cited Bosch, along with other Flemish painters Jan van Eyck and Hans Memling, among those he most admired. McQueen's final, unfinished collection was laden with religious iconography: Bosch's gruesome imagining of the torments of Hell (a panel from his triptych *The Garden of Earthly Delights*, *c*.1500) and works by Sandro Botticelli, Jean Fouquet and Stephan Lochner were printed onto heavy silks. When asked which artworks were on his wish list, McQueen replied: '[I] would love to buy a Memling, but I don't think I could ever [afford] it.'[13] Although that aspiration was never fulfilled, as soon as he had the means McQueen began to amass a personal art collection, which would ultimately include many photographs. The first piece he purchased was by Witkin: 'It was when I'd gone to Givenchy and I had a wage. I bought him from Pace/MacGill in New York and I just went mad. There are so many different ways that I look at Witkin … I don't find it extreme. I know it looks extreme to other people … I look at the whole thing and I find it poetic. It relates to my work.'[14] He went on to collect more than a dozen Witkin photographs and even had part of his house designed around them: 'There's one of three old people sitting in their armchairs with their heads cut open. I've had this frame built specially for it so that it's like a Byzantine triptych with little doors. But the weight of it is so vast that we've had to build a whole wall to support it.'[15]

Witkin asked him in 2003: 'What is your personal definition of beauty? I appreciate you collecting my work and would like to know what you consider beautiful in my work.' McQueen replied: 'I think there is beauty in everything. What "normal" people would perceive as ugly, I can usually see something of beauty in it. I appreciate your work with the same depth of feeling as that of Bosch. Your *Leda* is one of my favourite pieces (pl.293). I find the man so graceful.'[16] However, as Andrew Bolton has noted, McQueen's passion for Witkin's pictures would eventually wane: 'He felt he was about decadence, and not celebrating the idea of difference, which was one of Lee's mantras.'[17]

To display his photographs, McQueen worked with the framing company John Jones, a London family-run business founded in

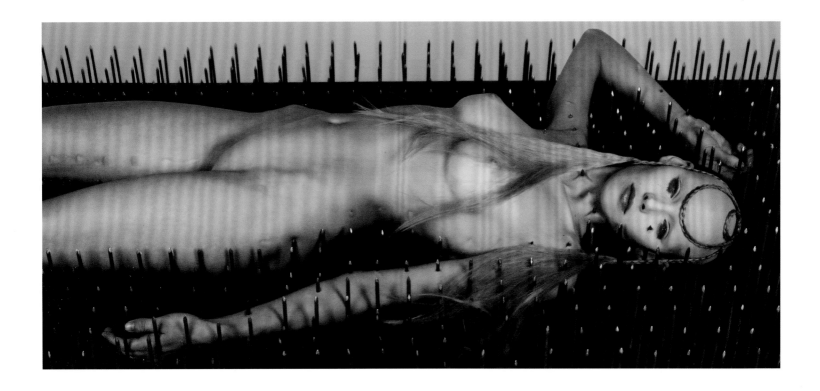

the 1960s. Tim Blake, the company's senior design consultant, recalled: 'We were fortunate enough to be introduced to work on Alexander McQueen's personal art collection by a mutual friend. We were asked to look mainly at reframing works by photographers including Joel-Peter Witkin, Abigail Lane, Sam Taylor-Johnson and Nick Knight. In the beginning there was really no personal input from McQueen. However, after we developed a unique understanding of how the work should be presented and best positioned in his house, McQueen became more interested in our vision and the design process … For McQueen, the frame designing was all about being simple and beautifully made … As the relationship grew, he brought in personal pieces such as Polaroids and sketches to be framed; we had a lot of fun. Throughout the whole working relationship, we were involved with the entire design and installation process. For every piece, we would look at the holistic context of the interior space to tailor the frame, complementing the piece and the space.'[18]

Images of McQueen's London home, taken by Ed Reeve and published in *ArtReview* in 2003, show a framed photograph of Lee Miller in Hitler's bathtub. Once a model, muse to Man Ray and star of Jean Cocteau's landmark film *The Blood of a Poet* (1930), the courageous Miller became a photographer in the 1930s and worked as *Vogue*'s war correspondent. David Scherman, her wartime lover, took the extraordinary portrait on 30 April 1945, while Hitler's Munich apartment was occupied by Allied forces. The Führer committed suicide in Berlin the day the shot was taken. Miller's heavy army boots are placed prominently in the foreground, still covered in the dust of Dachau, where she had photographed the previous day. From the black and white work of Miller, Bill Brandt and Walker Evans, to contemporary Brits

303. 'McKiller Queen', *The Face*, issue 15, April 1998
Modelled by Shirley Mallman
Art direction by Alexander McQueen
Photograph by Nick Knight

Opposite
304. *The Face*, issue 15, April 1998
Art direction by Alexander McQueen
Photograph by Nick Knight

THE FACE

PEED
rban Motor
hem

EX
nny
ghan
mie
akston

RE
dent Evil 2
Computer
or

GGRO
Springer
KO

No 15 APRIL 1998 £2.40 • US $7.50
LIRE 10700 • 14DM • 775PTAS • ¥1700 • 36 FF • CAN $7.95
10.75 HFL • 1.70LM • 100 AUST SCH

9 770263 121064
04 >

YOU'RE NOT GOING
OUT LIKE THAT!
Alexander McQueen
by Nick Knight

+

Jude Law
Cleopatra
**Monkey
Mafia**

Queen

s dead: Long live Alexander McQueen

Left
305. Eder and Valenta, *X-Ray Photograph of a Reptile*, February 1896
First published in *Versuche über Photographie mittelst der Röntgen'schen Strahlen*, Vienna, 1896
Röntgen Musuem, Remscheid, Germany

Below
306. Marc Quinn, *Winter Garden 10*, 2004
Pigment print on paper

Opposite
307. Fitting for *The Horn of Plenty*, Autumn/Winter 2009
Alexander McQueen, Sarah Burton, Judy Halil and model Polina Kasina
Clerkenwell Road studio, London, 2009
Photograph by Nick Waplington
V&A: E.259-2013

Mat Collishaw, Marc Quinn, Sam Taylor-Johnson and the Chapman Brothers, 'all the work in McQueen's art pantheon has had its influence on his fashion collections. Or to be more precise, on his shows.'[19] To some extent every collection reflects the personality of its owner and McQueen's mirrored the light and shadow of his genius. Collishaw's glowing *Ultra Violet Angels* (1993) – small light-boxes displaying silkscreen angels in ultraviolet ink – and Quinn's dazzlingly colourful ice gardens balanced the darker works in the collection (pl.306).[20]

Despite his love of photographs, McQueen rarely enjoyed being photographed himself. He told Don McCullin: 'I'm always nervous about having my picture taken. I'm not a great subject. Just don't ask me to smile; I'm not good at smiling.'[21] His friend Anne Deniau was one of the few photographers he happily sat for and she suggests his reticence to pose stemmed from the fact that 'he thought he wasn't beautiful.'[22] One of the earliest published portraits of McQueen was in *i-D* magazine, part of an article on recent graduates, and Terry Jones recalled, 'He wanted to be photographed from behind – that's how he wanted to present himself – so that's how we shot him.'[23] David Bailey was one of the few who managed to coax a smile from the designer '...because his jokes are so awful.'[24] In September 2008, *Harper's Bazaar* published a conversation between McCullin and McQueen. The two men, both masters of their chosen professions, found a common ground in their London roots and working-class childhoods. McQueen saw a connection in their solitary approach to work: McCullin's long hours in the darkroom and McQueen's propensity to lock himself away to work in isolation. He also believed they shared a desire to convey reality: '[I want] to depict the times I live in. That was the main thing that interested me about your work – you depict a time. Before, in art, it was always about painting. And photography, for me, is painting of the mind. Sometimes it's just the one image that creates the whole illusion for that particular period in time.'[25] Three portraits accompanied the article, the most intriguing of which is the shot of McQueen in his atelier (pl.291). Behind him research boards are plastered with dozens of reference images, predominantly fashion studies of sharply tailored women's suits and evening gowns from the 1930s and '40s, Horst's famous *White Sleeve* (1936) among them.

Anne Deniau began working with McQueen in the late 1990s. He allowed her enormous freedom to photograph whenever she wanted to, with 'no guidelines'. There was no contract between them, simply an agreement based on 'absolute trust'. The result of their friendship is an extraordinary body of work, described by McQueen as 'my life in pictures'. Between 1997 and 2010, Deniau captured the frenetic activity of every show, the intense preparations for each spectacular performance, work in the studio and portraits of the designer in reflective and joyous moments. Like McQueen, Deniau has a passion for the handcrafted and unique. She is fascinated by nineteenth- and early twentieth-century processes and employs printing techniques such as bromoil and gum bichromate, even handpainting on lith prints with watercolours and oils; one of her first portraits of McQueen was a striking blue cyanotype. A few days after each show, the pair would meet to look over the contact sheets together. Deniau

shot approximately 35,000 photographs in total, all on film. The book she produced in 2012, *Love Looks Not With The Eyes*, is a tribute to a collaboration that was, in her words, based on 'joy, creativity, love and excitement'.[26]

Another photographer to be given behind-the-scenes access was Nick Waplington, who was invited by McQueen to document the making of *The Horn of Plenty* (Autumn/Winter 2009; pl.307), with the intent of publishing the images as a book. 'I said sure, in a couple of years I would, but he said no, that it had to be me and it had to be now – this collection. He explained the idea behind the *The Horn of Plenty*, and why he wanted to document this collection particularly … He said he saw it as closing the door on his first 15 years; he saw it as his last collection as a young man.'[27] Waplington studied art at Trent Polytechnic and the RCA, and gained recognition early in his career for the project *The Living Room* (1991), which documents the daily lives of two close-knit working-class families in Nottingham in the late 1980s and early 1990s. Taken as a whole, his images of friends, places and events he has witnessed suggest a personal diary, yet also build up to provide a

308. Toni Frissell, *Weeki Wachee*, 1947
Underwater photograph
Library of Congress, Washington DC

Opposite
309. Film stills, *Irere*,
Spring/Summer 2003
Directed by John Maybury

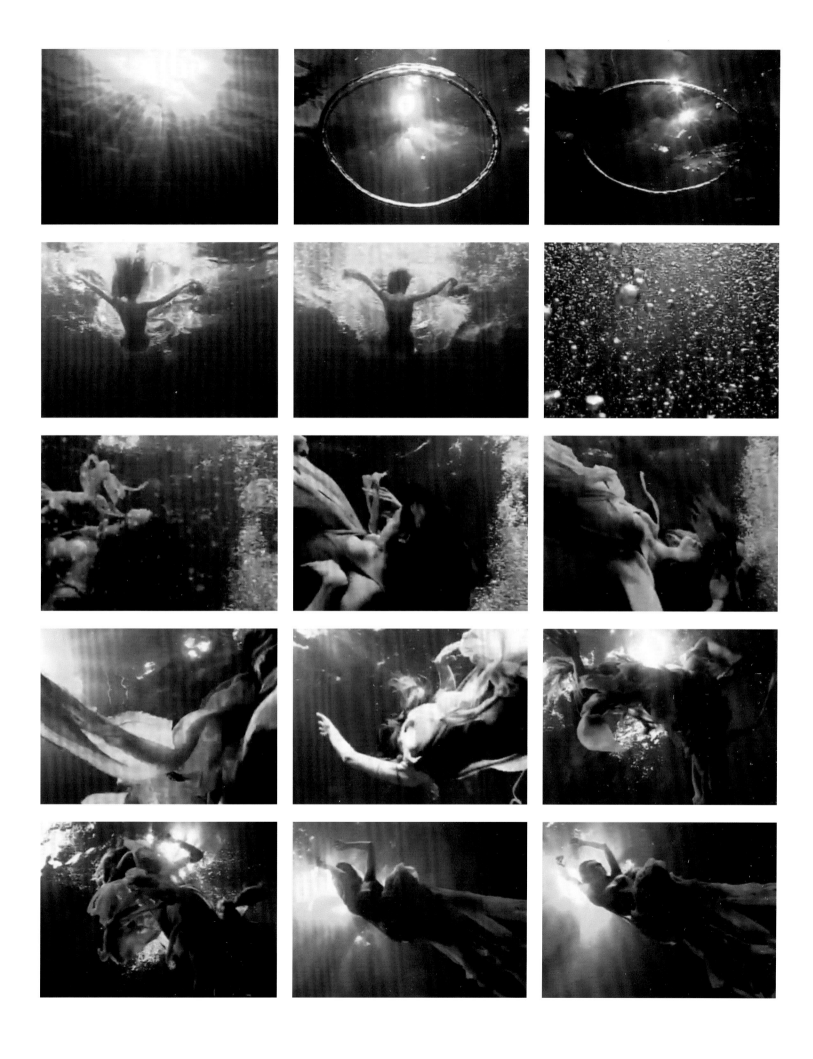

picture of our times, chronicling life on the streets of east London, or at festivals, street parties and demonstrations. Waplington often presents his work in book form. The photographs of *The Horn of Plenty* in different states of completion were to be interspersed with images by Waplington of recycling plants, rubbish dumps and landfill sites. The book was published in 2013 and the images were arranged in sequence by McQueen himself before he died. Waplington described how the project was a reflection of their shared interests:

> There was definitely a shared love of the aesthetic beauty of waste. I never told him that some of the photographs came from the Negev Desert. He just liked the pictures. The photographs related to the clothes because … he'd kept the sets from his previous collections and had created a huge pile of rubbish from them where the show was which he'd had sprayed black. The rubbish photographs were mixed with pictures of him sketching and making the clothes directly onto the model.[28]

Waplington compared McQueen's approach to that of a painter or photographer:

> He'd sit quietly, and then there would be these Svengali-like moments where someone would bring him a roll of fabric and he'd jump up and grab the rolls of cloth and drape them over the model and pin them and move them, and then someone would run off and sew them – and come back with them later. And it's these 'creation moments' after periods of inaction – just like a painter or a photographer; these are the little things that take you forward. His work was almost performance art – the grand gesture.[29]

One such breathtaking 'creation moment' was captured by Nick Knight for SHOWstudio in 2002. Titled 'The Bridegroom Stripped Bare', part of the *Transformer* series of live fashion stories created for the Internet, the film showed McQueen transforming a male model in white Yohji Yamamoto trouser suit into a bride (pl.310). Knight later described the electrifying performance:

> You hear all these stories about how the women in the Givenchy atelier were terrified when he got his scissors out, stories about how he hacks and cuts and slashes. So he cuts the suit up, pulls pieces down, gaffer tapes up the middle. Then he makes a train with the cloth. Then he gets white paint and throws it at the bottom half of the model and, with his hands, starts shaping it, moving the paint down the cloth. He's doing all this to incredibly loud techno music and he's sweating and slipping about in the paint and so focused, scarily focused, other-wordly. Finally, he puts a veil on him, ties his hands together and stuffs a tie into his mouth. There was a great sadness to it, I thought. I don't know how much of it was about Lee. By the end, this very handsome young man had been turned into a bride.[30]

McQueen found his collaborations with Knight exciting: 'Working with Nick is always exhilarating because he's always wanting to try to do new things … the work I do for SHOWstudio is always revolutionary … it's performance art and it's live on the net … it's fresh and it's new and Nick gives you carte blanche so it's cool.'[31]

In Knight, McQueen found a collaborator with the desire and the creative vision to see the world through his eyes[32] and together they produced fantastical and shocking images. One of their first projects was for *The Face* in April 1998 (pls 303, 304). Shot by Knight and art directed by McQueen, it marked his triumph with *Joan* (Autumn/Winter 1998) at London Fashion Week. It centered on the subjects of flesh and death and the most memorable of the series shows model Shirley Mallman on a bed of nails in which metal spikes appear to pierce her pale flesh and her eyes glow bright red. Knight worked with McQueen again soon after, on a special issue of *Dazed & Confused*, guest edited by McQueen (September 1998).

Much of Knight's image making over the past 20 years has exploited the latest advances in digital technologies and editing software. He manipulates and pushes his images to the extreme, an approach that McQueen embraced: 'I love to collaborate with people like yourself and David Sims … whenever we've worked together, I've always steered you away from the norm.'[33] Knight seemed capable of delving into McQueen's psyche in order to create the pictures the designer envisaged, which McQueen described as 'quite surreal moments … images made of nightmares and dreams.'[34] They worked with Ruth Hogben to create the mesmerizing film for *Plato's Atlantis* and the presentation of the collection was streamed live from Paris on the SHOWstudio website. Films were used in earlier shows, too: *Irere* (Spring/Summer 2003) included a film art directed by McQueen and directed by John Maybury (pl.309). The show told the story of a shipwreck and landfall in the Amazon and the film depicted a woman writhing through the water in a diaphanous chiffon dress. It evokes the late-1940s work of Toni Frissell, who photographed models underwater at Weeki Wachee Springs, Florida, for *Harper's Bazaar* (pl.308).[35] There is a sense of ambiguity in some of Frissell's pictures and in Maybury's film – are the women sinking into the sea's dark depths or swimming to the light at the surface? By live streaming *Plato's Atlantis*, McQueen was able to share the show in its entirety with the widest possible audience, but he also retained a passion for the still image, ever-aware of a photograph's power: 'I do it for the people who see the pictures in the press … I design the shows as stills and I think that if you look at those stills they tell the whole story.'[36]

310. 'The Bridegroom Stripped Bare', *Transformer*, July 2002
Alexander McQueen collaboration with SHOWstudio
Photograph by Nick Knight

ENCYCLOPEDIA OF COLLECTIONS

KATE BETHUNE

Alexander McQueen designed 36 collections for his London label, including his MA graduate collection; 35 of these were presented on the catwalk. Between October 1996 and March 2001 McQueen also produced two haute couture and two ready-to-wear womenswear collections a year – in addition to his London label collections – as chief designer for Givenchy womenswear. McQueen absorbed references as wide ranging as underground films and Gothic literature, Northern Renaissance art and war photography, and Victorian London and the Far East. Nature and autobiography also informed McQueen's approach to design, his collections reflecting his interest in the animal kingdom and the natural world as well as his East End roots, his Scottish heritage and distant ancestors in colonial Massachusetts. McQueen once said, 'Clothes don't come with a notepad ... it's eclectic. It comes from Degas and Monet and my sister-in-law in Dagenham' (*The Pink Paper*, April 1994). But perhaps the greatest repository of inspiration for McQueen was his own imagination. In his curious and complex mind he wove together myriad – and often divergent – themes, translating them into a coherent vision for each of his collections.

Cutting across taboos and conventions, McQueen was an iconoclast who consistently pushed the boundaries of fashion, both through the innovative cut, construction and material qualities of the garments he crafted and the often provocative, always spectacular, catwalk shows through which he presented them to the world. For McQueen, everything began with a concept for the catwalk presentation. As many of his colleagues have observed, he envisaged the collections as both garments and mise-en-scène. A tight-knit, trusted circle of art director, production designer, show producer, stylist, and music and lighting directors made this possible and enabled McQueen to turn his visions into a reality. McQueen's creative vision also extended to the ephemera and invitations that accompanied each show. Reproduced here, their diversity and graphic qualities reflect McQueen's breadth of vision for his collections and illuminate his creative collaborations.

All quotations are taken from publicity material and show notes issued by Alexander McQueen, unless otherwise stated.

JACK THE RIPPER STALKS
HIS VICTIMS

MA GRADUATE COLLECTION 1992
DUKE OF YORK'S HEADQUARTERS, LONDON; 16 MARCH 1992

McQueen's graduate collection – which he showed the day before his 23rd birthday under his given name Lee A. McQueen – marked the completion of his Master's degree in Fashion Design at Central Saint Martins. It was presented during London Fashion Week in the British Fashion Council tent at the Duke of York's Headquarters on the King's Road in Chelsea.

The collection was principally inspired by the East End felon Jack the Ripper and the prostitutes whom he savagely murdered in Whitechapel in 1888. Having grown up in London's East End, and with an ancestor who had supposedly owned an inn where one of the Ripper's victims lodged, McQueen was drawn to the darker aspects of the area's past.

The collection had a strong emphasis on tailoring. Victorian silhouettes were achieved by skilful cutting and were rendered in a sombre palette of predominantly black and maroon but with red and lilac silk linings. A deep-pink silk frock coat with barbed hawthorn print (by fellow student Simon Ungless), cut tight to the body and arms, showcased McQueen's skills, honed as an apprentice on Savile Row. Skirts echoing the Victorian crinoline were cut short, distressed with burn marks and overlaid with a bricolage of portraits from magazines, including that of a young Johnny Depp from the cult 1980s TV series *21 Jump Street*. A tight-fitting black jacket, with

peplum at the rear and dagger-shaped lapels, was lined with red silk. Strands of human hair were visible beneath the translucent linings of some of the garments, inspired by the Victorian prostitutes who sold their hair as love tokens. McQueen borrowed pieces from jewellery designer Simon Costin, including his 'Memento Mori' necklace (1986), which incorporated two bird's claws and three jewel-encrusted rabbit skulls.

Fashion editor Isabella Blow, who would become instrumental to McQueen's career, purchased the entire collection piece by piece.

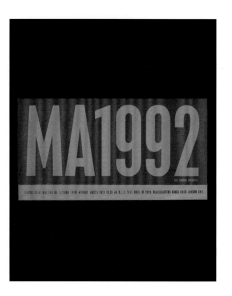

TAXI DRIVER

AUTUMN/WINTER 1993
THE RITZ, LONDON; MARCH 1993

McQueen was one of six new talents sponsored by the British Fashion Council via the newly launched NEWGEN initiative, which gave him the opportunity to present this, his first collection after leaving college, in a suite at The Ritz, London. The garments consisted of 13 new designs – made at a house in Tooting that McQueen shared with Simon Ungless. These were supplemented with others reworked from McQueen's graduate collection as well as some experimental pieces made in between. An enhanced collection of 26 pieces was subsequently presented under the name Alexander McQueen to buyers and journalists at the Covent Garden showroom of newly established fashion recruitment agents Alice Smith and Cressida Pye.

The collection demonstrated McQueen's early interest in accentuating parts of the female anatomy to create a new shape and marked the debut of one of his most important contributions to fashion, the 'bumster' trousers. These are described on a price list of the designs shown at Smith & Pye as 'French cut trousers (bumsters)'. The waistband was cut 5 cm below that of hipsters, so that they grazed the hipbone, elongated the torso and exposed the lower spine.

McQueen's interest in historical reinterpretation found expression in tailored angora Palazzo pants, trousers cut just above the ankle in 1950s style, and 'Korean-line' frock coats with Chesterfield collars. The traditional was suffused with modernity not only via innovative cutting, but also through the use of experimental materials and processes: tank tops with French partridge feathers encased in vinyl, and fabric edges dipped in latex as a substitute for seamed hems.

While the title perhaps referred to McQueen's father, who was a London cabbie, the explicit influence behind the collection was Martin Scorsese's film *Taxi Driver* (1976), which told the violent story of vigilante Travis Bickle (played by Robert De Niro). It manifested itself as a long line waistcoat, printed by Ungless with the image of De Niro's character.

McQueen's interest in the Victorian era was articulated in garments such as a corseted woollen riding jacket and a skirt printed with images of August Sander photographs (his notebooks for the collection also contained examples of photography from the era). Yet a couture coat made from silk suiting, with pleated and jewelled collar, shared the same name as Baroness Orczy's novel *The Scarlet Pimpernel* (1905) and hinted at McQueen's interest in Revolutionary France.

NIHILISM

SPRING/SUMMER 1994
BLUEBIRD GARAGE, LONDON; 18 OCTOBER 1993

McQueen's first professional catwalk show was presented at the Bluebird Garage on the King's Road, Chelsea, to the beat of American hip hop artist Cypress Hill's 'I Wanna Get High'. The building, formerly an Art Deco masterpiece, had acquired a reputation for drugs and violence. It was a fitting venue for McQueen's pioneering collection, presented by skinny, punkish models who were full of attitude.

Tailoring was technically precise and featured sharp lapels, hardened shoulders and frock coats that were cut away at the back. Lack of funding forced McQueen to be creative with his materials. An Edwardian jacket in corroded gilt and a frock coat with matching trousers made from cheap gold fabric, tarnished by chemicals that burned through the fibres, suggested defaced luxury. Many of the textiles McQueen utilized in his designs at this time, including a fabric screen-printed with a rusty resin paste of oxidized iron filings, were made with Fleet Bigwood, McQueen's former tutor at Central Saint Martins.

A strong ethnic undercurrent also prevailed. Pickled locusts sealed in liquid latex were embroidered onto a dress made from cling film, smeared in dirt. It was another co-project with Simon Ungless and served as a comment on famine in Africa. Other garments incorporated William Morris prints and hinted at McQueen's interest in the Arts and Crafts Movement. Although the collection was not intended as a commercial enterprise, McQueen was mindful to build his brand, his name appearing as a logo across the bust of a white shift dress.

McQueen's debut show aroused the attention of the fashion press. Critics identified perversity in models dressed in cling-film knickers and muslin tops smeared with a blood-like residue. Although Marion Hume of *The Independent* branded the show 'a catalogue of horrors', she conceded that McQueen's 'shocking' innovation was instrumental for safeguarding London's creative supremacy.

McQueen created the show invitations with pages torn from an encyclopedia that were hand-stamped with the date and venue.

BANSHEE

AUTUMN/WINTER 1994
CAFÉ DE PARIS, LONDON; 26 FEBRUARY 1994

Staged at the Café de Paris, a historic nightclub in the heart of London's West End, *Banshee* unfolded to a soundtrack of Celtic pipe music, which gave way to hard club beats and a female rapper swearing.

The prevailing mood of the collection, named after the spirit from Gaelic mythology (Bheansidhe) who wailed whilst washing the blood-stained clothes of men approaching a violent death, was one of romance undercut with tragedy. McQueen resurrected the image of a post-shipwreck seascape through dresses of tattered tulle and jackets with gold piping on collars and cuffs in reference to a drowned captain's uniform.

However, as the collection notes stated, McQueen's models were 'no banshees of the deep', rather 'survivors, women who [were] proud to wear their beauty'. He presented his strong women, among them Isabella Blow, via controversial designs and irreverent styling. Over-sized sleeves resembled those on a straitjacket; a sheer black dress with an Elizabethan neckline was modelled by a pregnant young woman, her shaven head stencilled with the word 'McQueen'. The designer instructed her to pose like the bride in one of his favourite paintings, Jan van Eyck's *The Arnolfini Portrait* (1434).

While a painterly theme found expression in gauzy black dresses dripping with metallic prints that evoked molten silver and suggested dark romance, McQueen honed in on the erogenous zones with necklines cut to reveal the nipples and knitwear made by Julien MacDonald that exposed the breasts.

McQueen's interpretation of contemporary Britishness also shone through in his combinations of heavy pea-jacket melton mixes with spider-web silver lace, thick flannels paired with glossy latexes and sequinned tops. Drawstring 'leg-ups' and a jacket held in place by 3 cm of silver thread emphasized McQueen's inventiveness with cut and cloth, alongside a continuing interest in unlikely materials and silhouettes. Here he first experimented with moulded designs that emphasized the form of the body beneath – in this instance a breastplate crafted from plaster of Paris.

THE BIRDS
SPRING/SUMMER 1995
BAGLEY'S WAREHOUSE, LONDON; 10 SEPTEMBER 1994

McQueen's Spring/Summer 1995 collection was presented at Bagley's warehouse, a rundown party venue in an insalubrious part of King's Cross, London. The collection was made with the assistance of Andrew Groves and David Kappo. Jewellery designer Simon Costin, who worked on McQueen's set for the first time, provided accessories. *The Birds* was the first show styled by Katy England, who was assisted by Alister Mackie. Fashion journalist Plum Sykes, then assistant at British *Vogue* and 'It Girl', modelled.

This collection initiated McQueen's love of birds as expressed through his designs, their gracefulness and profile in flight consistently informing his silhouettes from this point. Dramatic prints of swallows – produced by Simon Ungless – flew across burnt-orange tailored suits and tight-fitting red skirts. The graphics had been reworked on the computer by Groves to create the impression of a sinister flock that surrounded and engulfed the wearer. The image, informed by Hitchcock's 1963 suspense thriller, *The Birds*, after which the collection was named, connected McQueen's fascination with ornithology with his passion for film.

Road kill provided another inspiration for the collection and its staging. The show invitation featured an image of a small bird squashed on a road. Costin, who had trained in theatre design as well as jewellery, painted the catwalk to look like a road, with models entering via a long, dark tunnel. Tyre-tread prints – again a direct reference to *The Birds* – violated crisp white suits and cellophane tops, and were echoed in the models' body and face make-up, generating fresh criticisms of the

designer's representation of women. McQueen subverted his catwalk collection in new ways by inviting corsetier Mr Pearl to model a tight-fitting jacket and skirt, which drew attention to his cinched waist; the svelte silhouette was inspired by Tippi Hedren's wardrobe for the film.

HIGHLAND RAPE
AUTUMN/WINTER 1995
NATURAL HISTORY MUSEUM, LONDON; 13 MARCH 1995

Considered McQueen's breakthrough collection, *Highland Rape* was presented on a catwalk scattered with heather in the British Fashion Council tent outside the Natural History Museum in South Kensington, London.

The controversial collection, which was delivered to dance music overlaid in places with the knell of a church bell, made reference to McQueen's Scottish ancestry. Garments fashioned from the MacQueen clan tartan of red and black shot through with yellow invested the designs – and designer – with a sense of heritage, while the inclusion of plumes from wild birds acknowledged the Scottish game-keeping tradition. But there was nothing romantic or idealistic about this collection. It was precisely McQueen's intention to subvert any sense of nostalgia with designs that shocked and cut against romanticized notions of Scotland's past.

The contentious use of 'rape' in the title unsurprisingly aroused criticism and accusations of misogyny from the press. McQueen, however, insisted that the collection was a commentary on the Highland Clearances levied against Scottish communities in the nineteenth century and the 'rape' of a culture by English aggressors. Still critics identified violence in the savage cutting of the clothes, which were ripped and torn to expose flesh and breasts, and vulgarity in the silver watch chains – made by jewellery designer Shaun Leane – that hung from the pubic region of skirts. Aside from the uncomfortable title, the designer provoked his audience further with a graphic invitation that depicted a surgical wound with scabs left by the suturing needle.

The clothes complemented the political atrocity that served as the base inspiration for the collection. Any sense of romantic fragility inherent in garments crafted from chiffons and laminated laces was transformed by the aggressive way in which they were presented. But this was not intended to debase the women who wore them. McQueen's models, some styled with dark make-up and black and mirrored contact lenses, were not vulnerable victims but fearless women whom he had galvanized through the strength of his designs.

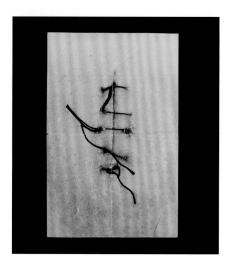

THE HUNGER

SPRING/SUMMER 1996
NATURAL HISTORY MUSEUM, LONDON; 23 OCTOBER 1995

Presented as the finale to London Fashion Week in the East Lawn tent outside London's Natural History Museum, *The Hunger* was the first McQueen catwalk show produced by creative consultant Sam Gainsbury; Gainsbury had commenced her working relationship with McQueen as casting director for *The Birds*. It would result in a longstanding collaboration, with Gainsbury producing every subsequent show (from 1997 together with business partner Anna Whiting). *The Hunger* also cemented McQueen's collaboration with Shaun Leane, who produced the single 'Tusk' earring for the collection. Other collaborators included the Icelandic musician Björk, who produced the soundtrack. McQueen dedicated the collection to his friend – by now his creative director – Katy England.

The collection was inspired by Tony Scott's dark, sexualized horror film of the same name (1983), which starred Catherine Deneuve, David Bowie and Susan Sarandon and told the story of a love triangle involving a doctor and a vampire couple. The spectre of the insatiable vampire was translated via tailoring that featured aggressive cut-outs, sharp collars developed from his graduate collection, and flesh-like designs, including a top that incorporated strands of red yarn that echoed human veins. McQueen harnessed sexual undertones with themes of mortality and decay in a visceral, moulded corset – constructed from worms sandwiched between sheets of transparent plastic – which emphasized the breasts and hinted at decomposing flesh. Other designs included thorn and feather prints which were applied to slim silhouettes.

The ensemble comprising red bumsters and a floral brocaded top with hanging sleeves was selected by fashion editor Tamsin Blanchard as 'Dress of the Year' for 1996; an annual award conferred since 1963 by the Fashion Museum, Bath.

In his early collections, McQueen sometimes included a small number of male models. However, *The Hunger* featured 28 menswear designs out of a total of 95.

DANTE

AUTUMN/WINTER 1996
CHRIST CHURCH, LONDON; 1 MARCH 1996

McQueen's Autumn/Winter 1996 collection – dedicated to Isabella Blow - was presented in the dramatic setting of Nicholas Hawksmoor's Christ Church in Spitalfields, east London. The Baroque edifice was a pertinent choice of venue, for McQueen had learned from his mother that his family had descended from the Huguenot immigrants who had moved to the area in the 1680s. The fashion press were anxious to see what McQueen would present in a place of worship. They were not disappointed. Guests, among whom a skeleton was seated, overlooked a runway in the shape of a cross; the sound of a missile gave way to club beats mixed with organ music and salvos of gunfire. The first McQueen show to feature Kate Moss as a model, it set a new theatrical precedent for the designer.

Ostensibly named after Dante, the fourteenth-century Florentine poet, who presented in his *Divine Comedy* an allegorical vision of the afterlife, the collection was a commentary on religion, war and innocence. Religious iconography and brutal images of conflict abounded. Black and white photographs of social pariahs, including a nineteenth-century colony for the blind, and Don McCullin images of the Vietnam War were printed on jackets and coats, creating a poignant contrast to the luxurious fabrics beneath. McQueen also borrowed from his favourite photographic artist Joel-Peter Witkin, in particular the mask with the figure of Christ crucified, which he took from Witkin's *Portrait of Joel, New Mexico* (1984). Fourteenth-century Flemish paintings – a genre McQueen greatly admired – also found expression in

the slashed sleeves, erect collars and layered clothes that he assimilated from figures in paintings by Jan van Eyck and Hans Memling.

Statuesque models draped in black lace veils, and a corset of black lace and jet beading laid over a ground of soft purple (the colour of Victorian 'half' mourning), signified McQueen's ability to find beauty in death as the soundtrack gave way to Samuel Barber's 'Adagio for Strings'. McQueen, however, harnessed the melancholic with the energy of British street culture by pairing his creations with frayed and bleached denims.

Accessories were integral. A Philip Treacy headpiece of stag's skull and antlers and a lace cap with withered hand by Simon Costin invoked memento mori, while a crown of thorns by Shaun Leane connected with the collection's religious undercurrent. Whereas some models appeared as innocents with nails seemingly driven through their hands, others looked fierce with spikes projecting through scraped back hair and metal thorns that appeared to burst through the skin. *Dante* was presented twice, the second show staged in a disused synagogue on New York's Lower East Side on 30 March.

BELLMER LA POUPÉE

SPRING/SUMMER 1997
ROYAL HORTICULTURAL HALL, LONDON; 27 SEPTEMBER 1996

McQueen provoked more controversy with his Spring/Summer 1997 show at London's Royal Horticultural Hall, in which models descended from a staircase onto a catwalk flooded with water. Out walked model Debra Shaw, shackled at the elbows and knees to a square metal frame. The uncomfortable vision of a black model in shackles led to accusations of McQueen glamorising slavery, but he insisted he had chosen the piece for the manner in which it restricted the model's movement, making her appear puppet-like.

The marionette reference was connected to the show's primary inspiration, the work of German Surrealist artist Hans Bellmer. Bellmer's 1934 photographic series *Poupée, variations sur le montage d'une mineure articulée* ('The Doll, Variations on the Assemblage of an Articulated Minor') presented dissected and reconstructed dolls, offering a response to Nazi theories of eugenics and Aryan ideals.

The collection – the first on which Sarah Burton worked – fused the 'purity of Far Eastern culture with the sharp punk elements of the West'. Revealing zips on tops and trousers were paired with 'sculpted jackets' sprayed with graffiti in 'bright and icy tones'. The effect was mimicked in the glistening make-up on the models' faces, which appeared to have been sprayed through a stencil. A Surrealist theme was manifested in a pink silk brocade cheongsam with a funnel neck that concealed the lower part of the wearer's face. Branch-like headpieces by designer Dai Rees, fashioned from porcupine quills, also featured.

McQueen was again praised for innovative tailoring. While a jacket was cut away at the rear to form a soft cowl back, a coat took on a trapezoidal form suggestive of origami. In another jacket, an inner metal frame held the arms outstretched, suggesting entrapment in the stocks, while the fantail at the back hinted at the possibility of escape through flight.

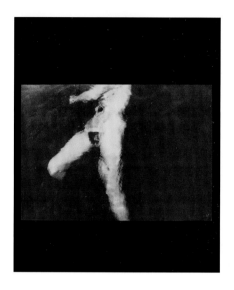

IT'S A JUNGLE OUT THERE

AUTUMN/WINTER 1997
BOROUGH MARKET, LONDON; 27 FEBRUARY 1997

For his next collection, Autumn/Winter 1997, McQueen drew the fashion press to Borough Market in south London. The backdrop was a set constructed from wrecked cars and a screen of corrugated iron, littered with holes to look like bullet marks. Simon Costin, who designed the set, identified a scene from the Irvin Kershner thriller *The Eyes of Laura Mars* (1978) as a primary reference. Set to an eclectic soundtrack, which featured howling sirens and excerpts from The Prodigy's 'Breathe', an anarchic scene ensued as one of the cars accidentally caught fire. Jodie Kidd modelled.

In this collection McQueen paid tribute to the animal kingdom, citing the African mammal, Thomson's Gazelle, as his primary inspiration. McQueen considered the gazelle to be the food chain of Africa and he drew comparisons between it and human life. It was also a metaphor for urban life, and especially the fashion industry, in which only the strongest survive.

McQueen's theme was conveyed in the gazelle's beautiful markings that were mirrored on the models' faces and in the black contact lenses that emulated mammals' eyes. Several garments were fashioned from skin and horn. For example, a pair of curved, impala horns sprouted from wooden blocks concealed in the shoulders of a ponyskin jacket. Elsewhere McQueen's touch was softer, as seen in dresses punctured with cut-outs of delicate flowers, or pastel embroidery applied to a Prince of Wales check silk jacket and gauze sheaths. Some models, however, appeared more predator than prey,

in harnesses and skin-tight black leather dresses, face pieces crafted from metal and chains, and with long, silver talons that protruded from the hands.

McQueen's engagement with Old Master paintings offered an unexpected contrast in a jacket with sharp, wide shoulders, printed with a detail from Robert Campin's painting depicting the *The Thief to the Left of Christ* from the Flémalle panels (c.1430), which appeared centrefold on the rear. The exaggerated shoulders were inspired by the work of McQueen's assistant designer, Catherine Brickhill.

McQueen collaborated with Nick Knight on the invitation which featured a digitally altered image of the model Debra Shaw.

UNTITLED

SPRING/SUMMER 1998
GATLIFF ROAD WAREHOUSE, LONDON; 28 SEPTEMBER 1997

McQueen's Spring/Summer 1998 collection was the first to be presented at the Gatliff Road warehouse, a rundown former bus depot in London's Victoria neighbourhood. A Central Saint Martins fashion graduate, Sebastian Pons, had joined the design team as McQueen's assistant. It was the first show for which McQueen received financial support from American Express, which was about to launch a new gold credit card. The collection was presented as *Untitled* because the sponsors were uncomfortable with the implicit sexual connotations of the original title, 'The Golden Shower'.

The set, in which a runway had been positioned above clear Perspex tanks lit from below, engaged with McQueen's interest in the transformative qualities of water. Thunder and lightning flashes created drama and anxiety, indicating that change was imminent. Halfway through the show the tanks beneath the catwalk filled with pools of black ink as Ann Peebles' 'I Can't Stand the Rain', overlaid with the John Williams' soundtrack to *Jaws* (1975), filled the air. Sinister undertones, however, gave way to lightness for a finale of designs in white. As rain poured from the ceiling, drenching the models and causing black mascara tears to run down their faces, gauzy cottons became transparent.

Tailoring was simple, precisely cut and featured diagonal and flag panelling. While pinstripes and Prince of Wales checks were shot through with accents of gold and yellow, gold and silver glitter shone through latticed leathers.

McQueen's love of nature and metamorphosis was identifiable in amphibious designs such as a tight python-skin dress, which formed a second skin over the model to merge human with animal. Hybridization was further reflected in Shaun Leane's 'Spine' corset, which was cast from a human skeleton and extended into a tail-like structure, worn over a sparkling black dress. The uncomfortable fusion of human and animal was inspired by Richard Donner's horror film *The Omen* (1976), in which a jackal gives birth to a child. A sense of brutality was also carried through in Leane's 'Jaw Bone' mouthpieces, which were worn by male models and were suggestive of the reconstructive surgery that was pioneered on Second World War soldiers. A silver headpiece by Sarah Harmarnee offered commentary on the impact of weapons on the body; the metal blade that ran down the nose sitting threateningly close to the delicate skin of the face.

JOAN

AUTUMN/WINTER 1998
GATLIFF ROAD WAREHOUSE, LONDON; 25 FEBRUARY 1998

Joan was the second of McQueen's catwalk shows to be presented at the Gatliff Road warehouse. Guido Palau styled the female models' hair for the first time, the white blonde hair and severe fringe of some echoing that of the school children in Wolf Rilla's sci-fi horror film *The Village of the Damned* (1960). Mira Chai Hyde styled the male models' hair and Val Garland was the make-up artist. The show was dedicated to McQueen's friend and muse, Annabelle Neilson.

The stark, industrial feel of the venue provided a foil to catwalk sets that were growing in complexity and intensity. Whereas McQueen toyed with water in his previous show, this time he invoked fire. McQueen had been struck by a Richard Avedon photograph that appeared in an editorial in the *The New Yorker* in November 1995 called 'In Memory of the Late Mr and Mrs Comfort'. It inspired his most dramatic finale to date, in which a satanic ring of flames encircled a lone masked model in a red ensemble, which echoed flayed flesh, while the bugle bead skirt suggested dripping blood.

Themes of martyrdom and persecution prevailed in a collection saturated with blood and violence. Glossy red snake skins and leathers hinted at bloodshed; tartans referenced the execution of Mary, Queen of Scots; haunting prints of the murdered Romanov children flickered over sequins on coats and dresses. Medieval references were present in chainmail garments and tailoring with features incorporated from ecclesiastical dress and double-fronted clerical coats with *trompe l'oeil* effect capes. The martyrdom

of Joan of Arc was manifested in an articulated armoured creation by Sarah Harmarnee that suggested portraits of the French heroine in her battle dress; it also recalled a Thierry Mugler armoured suit from 1995 titled 'Robot Couture'.

The collection was presented by models that appeared aggressive and untouchable in dark, powerful silhouettes. Red contact lenses lent an air of menace, as did the hooded tops, which bore a resemblance to bondage masks. The presence of such strong, fearless, sexualized women served as a counterpoint to the murder of innocents.

The invitation featured a detail from Jean Fouquet's *Melun Diptych*, c.1452, which had been tinted red.

NO.13
SPRING/SUMMER 1999
GATLIFF ROAD WAREHOUSE, LONDON; 27 SEPTEMBER 1998

McQueen's thirteenth collection, simply titled *No.13*, was presented on a pared down, unvarnished wooden runway conceived by Joseph Bennett, who had joined the team as production designer. Underpinning the collection was a concern with the handcrafted, inspired by the late Victorian Arts and Crafts Movement, with designs constructed from wood, leather, lace and raffia. Plywood skirts, in natural tones, splayed out to mimic the spines of a fan, while winged bodices of the same wood connected the use of organic materials with the celestial and the sublime. The emphasis on the natural and the traditional stood in stark contrast to a soundtrack by American hip hop artists the Beastie Boys.

Paralympic athlete Aimee Mullins entered wearing a pair of wooden prosthetic legs, hand-carved in ash, which were reminiscent of the filigree qualities of Baroque carver Grinling Gibbons. Once again, McQueen experimented with the manipulation of bodily forms. Hard, leather bodices with high necks formed restrictive carapaces that forced models to adopt an erect posture. One model, wearing a mesh dress, appeared as though suspended in a spiral of wire, recalling 'Models in a Surreal Landscape', a feature photographed by André Durst for British *Vogue* (15 January 1936). Surgical undertones were implicit in lacing that appeared as crude stitches, and in moulded bodices and pants with leather buckles that evoked medical corsetry. These designs were inspired by the workshops at Queen Mary's Hospital, Roehampton, which were instrumental in pioneering prostheses for casualties of the First World War. Yet this hardness was tempered by soft, tiered lace skirts and

trousers – suggestive of the ruffles on a flamenco dancer's skirt – that harmonized the aesthetic into images of romance and beauty. Recognition of this achievement was marked by the award of 'Dress of the Year' (for the second time), *The Independent*'s fashion editor Susannah Frankel selecting McQueen's lace dress with moulded brown leather collar.

In spite of the understated backdrop, there was no shortage of spectacle. Models rotated on plinths like fragile music-box dolls. The finale was the most arresting of any McQueen show yet. Former ballerina Shalom Harlow stood centre stage between two Fiat car robots, which appeared to interact with her in a gentle dance before turning predator and firing sprays of black and acid-yellow paint at her pure white trapeze dress. The sequence, inspired by a Rebecca Horn installation *High Moon* (1991), was perhaps intended as a counterpoint to William Morris's anti-industrial ethic, thereby provoking comment on the interaction between man and machine at the turn of the twenty-first century.

THE OVERLOOK
AUTUMN/WINTER 1999
GATLIFF ROAD WAREHOUSE, LONDON; 23 FEBRUARY 1999

McQueen's Autumn/Winter 1999 collection was again presented at the Gatliff Road warehouse, this time transformed into a frozen landscape set within a giant Plexiglas cube. Midway through the show, skaters wearing white ballerina skirts, some made of lace and feathers, glided across the ice around frosted silver birch trees set in banks of snow, under ultraviolet lights. Al Bowlly's 'Midnight, The Stars and You' played softly in the background. It was a vision of pure romance.

The audience – who had been warned to dress warmly – were no doubt expecting a rupture to the charming frozen scene; the collection having been named after the ill-fated hotel in Stanley Kubrick's psychological horror film *The Shining* (1980). McQueen had intimated that the show would have a darker side: the invitation repeated the film's chilling refrain 'All work and no play makes Jack a dull boy'; the soundtrack – borrowed from the film – was overlaid with baying wolves and howling wind; the presence of two young red-headed models recalled the haunting ghosts of the murdered sisters in the film; and the final looks were presented in a blizzard that recalled the film's final scene.

However, McQueen drew not on the violent plot of the film but on the isolated, snowbound setting. Beauty and elegance intensified in glistening stiff lace dresses evocative of spun cobwebs, an aluminium skirt with cut-out Gothic script and curlicues, and an exquisite quartz bodice by Kees van der Graaf. Luxurious furs, chunky knits and Icelandic parkas

in soft pinks offered a vision of modern luxury. As usual, McQueen intrigued with his tailoring, this time manifested in a frock coat with a fantail silhouette, which attested to his interest in asymmetry and birds. The collection also engaged with native and tribal cultures. While the models' plaited hair, and frosted white stripes painted across the eyes, served as reference to the Native-American burial site underneath The Overlook hotel in the film, Shaun Leane's spectacular coiled corset, made from individual rings of aluminium that fitted precisely to the curves of the wearer, found its inspiration in the Ndebele women of South Africa.

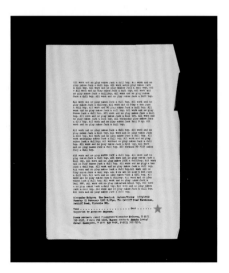

EYE

McQueen presented his Spring/Summer 2000 collection in New York to the American press and buyers who often would not attend London Fashion Week. It was a controversial decision but was seen as a shrewd financial move. The show, which was almost cancelled on account of Hurricane Floyd, was held at Pier 94 on Manhattan's West Side. Models walked through water over a black catwalk, the liquid symbolizing Middle Eastern oil. For the finale, McQueen aimed high, with models suspended from ropes over a spiked catwalk that recalled a bed of nails.

McQueen stated that the initial inspiration for the collection came from Turkish music that he had heard on a taxi radio. Islamic overtures were strong, and McQueen developed the theme in a design that suggested the burka. It was cut short at the front and worn with a pair of embellished knickers, creating a provocative statement. A yashmak by Shaun Leane, consisting of jewelled metal plates linked by chains, fused the Islamic with the medieval in a piece that spoke of the clashing of Western and Middle Eastern cultures during the Crusades. McQueen brought this up to date with examples of American sportswear printed with Arabic and crescent moon motifs and overlaid with Middle Eastern jewellery.

New shapes emerged in long scarf sleeves and trousers with high, scooped hems. Fabrics included brocades and embroidered leather, decorated with gold bells, Islamic coins and ruffled ribbon. While traditional embroidered tunic tops with bell-shaped sleeves were cut high to expose the midriff – serving as comment on the concealment of the Middle Eastern female body – fetishistic studded leather harnesses, which exposed the breasts, attested to Western liberalization.

The collection received mixed reviews. McQueen, who never intended to show in New York in the long term, returned to London the following season.

ESHU

McQueen returned to his East End roots and presented his collection for Autumn/Winter 2000 in a building in Shoreditch that formerly had been home to a power station and the old Gainsborough Film Studios. A runway covered in broken slate provided an apposite backdrop for a collection centred on primitivism, while tribal drums invoked the voodoo diaspora of sub-Saharan Africa.

Inspired by the story of a Victorian lady who settled in Africa, *Eshu*, named after an earth deity worshipped by the Yoruba peoples, brimmed with references to tribal customs. The full-face mask of a spirit-god replete with bushy mane, animal skins and fake monkey furs, wooden beads and hooped jewellery stacked high on the neck, all reinforced a vision of Africa prior to colonial intervention. Transformative designs, including a distressed denim dress with Edwardian high neck and leg-of-mutton sleeves, its skirt smeared with terracotta, hinted at the impact of turn-of-the-century missionaries on the African topography.

Once again, McQueen experimented with materials and developed new silhouettes. Bleached, felt roses formed a soft skirt beneath a raffia-moulded bodice, while a synthetic horsehair dress was beaded and corseted to create a fitted silhouette. A one-shouldered earth-coloured leather dress, its skirt punctured with a feathered design, sat asymmetrically over an exposed metal crinoline.

Eshu also told a story of survival through aggressive jewellery that pulled back the lips to expose the teeth. Whereas the visceral qualities of previous collections had focused on blood and flesh, here they were channelled through the material properties of skin, fur and hair. A detail of hair, streaked with colour, featured on the invitation.

VOSS

SPRING/SUMMER 2001
GATLIFF ROAD WAREHOUSE, LONDON; 26 SEPTEMBER 2000

McQueen had always declared that he wanted his shows to elicit a strong audience reaction. *Voss*, one of his most celebrated, achieved that result. An enormous clinical glass box formed the centrepiece, constructed to resemble a padded cell in a psychiatric hospital with white tiled floors and walls formed from surveillance mirrors. From the outset the mood was tense; the audience forced to endure an hour-long wait, staring at their own reflections whilst listening to the unnerving pulse of a heartbeat. Eventually, the light levels in the glass box rose to reveal models trapped in the cube, who were unable to see the audience.

Depictions of madness and incarceration were the principal inspirations behind the collection's presentation. While the psychiatric hospital was most readily identifiable, Frank Darabont's film *The Green Mile* (1999), which told the stories of inmates on death row, provided an alternative notion of confinement.

Voss, like so many of McQueen's collections, harnessed multiple, disparate themes which coalesced into the designer's unique vision of beauty. The title – the name of a Norwegian town renowned as a wildlife habitat – suggested the collection would celebrate nature. Bodices, skirts and dresses constructed from razor-clam, mussel and oyster shells astonished the audience with their elegance and ingenuity. McQueen's love of birds found expression in feather skirts, and in a headdress composed of taxidermied hawks, which hovered perilously above a model and appeared to claw her hair through the bandages that swathed her head.

The notion of medical scrutiny was starkly conveyed in a vermillion ensemble, modelled by Erin O'Connor, which comprised a skirt of dyed ostrich feathers and bodice of microscope slides hand-painted red to hint at the blood beneath the skin. The sharp glass of the slides hanging delicately from the bodice also mimicked the soft feathers on a bird's chest.

McQueen's fascination with the Orient was explicit in designs featuring appliquéd chrysanthemum roundels; an embroidered grey silk ensemble with real amaranthus dangling from the rectangular headpiece; and a dress that incorporated the panels of an antique Japanese silk screen atop a skirt constructed from 80 polished black oyster shells. The look was completed by a neckpiece of silver branches, adorned with clusters of Tahitian pearls.

The finale was the most transgressive of any of McQueen's catwalk shows: a recreation of Joel-Peter Witkin's *Sanitarium* (1983). As the models dispersed and the soundtrack of a pulsing heartbeat gave way to a flat-line monotone, the glass box shattered to reveal the voluptuous, naked figure of fetish writer Michelle Olley, reclining on a horned chaise longue in the graceful pose of a Botticelli painting, her masked head bowed and attached to a breathing tube. Moths fluttered about her before the lights dimmed and left the audience to ponder the meaning of beauty.

WHAT A MERRY GO ROUND

AUTUMN/WINTER 2001
GATLIFF ROAD WAREHOUSE, LONDON; 21 FEBRUARY 2001

McQueen's final presentation at the Gatliff Road warehouse was the stuff of childhood nightmares. A macabre circus emerged on a set constructed to resemble a carousel. The lighting rig recalled that in the marble hall of the Berlin zoological gardens, where German Expressionist vampire film *Nosferatu* (1922) had premiered. Gothic, dark and disturbing, the theme was not the nostalgia of youth, but childhood fear and vulnerability. McQueen cited the character of the sinister Child Catcher from the family classic *Chitty Chitty Bang Bang* (1968) as a primary inspiration. In addition to informing a number of designs, the character's idiosyncratic voice was incorporated into the soundtrack.

Any traces of sentimentality, discernible in the set and the sounds of children playing, were violated by the latex-clad carousel horses and models that pole-danced around the stage to a conflicting recording of metal and hard rock. Inspired by Bob Fosse's *Cabaret* (1972), and styled to resemble German dancers of the 1930s, with dark lips and hair in waves set tight to the head, some models wore black leather great coats and Kaiser Wilhelm caps.

A tableau of automated toys and dummies, dusty through neglect, and dotted about with skeletons, provided a backdrop for models caked in clowns' make-up; the delicate, 1920s flapper style and embroidered dresses worn by some were in stark contrast to their grotesque features. This juxtaposition of the beautiful and the vulgar was also

channelled through accessories, which combined precious Tahitian pearls and lacquered pheasant claws.

In spite of the sinister undertones, *What a Merry Go Round* was a consolidating collection that revisited a number of designs from previous collections including *Joan*, *Eshu* and *Voss*. It was also a commercial collection. While bias-cut jersey dresses appealed for their wearability, the skull that appeared with crossbones on a black chunky knit would soon be transformed into a signature brand motif.

French undertones were also present; overtly in the characters of Harlequin and Pierrot, which informed the make-up, and more subtly in designs that echoed French Revolutionary uniforms. McQueen also invoked Eugène Delacroix's *Liberty Leading the People* (1830) in a gauzy, silver bias-cut dress that exposed one breast. The engagement with French culture and pointed references to liberty were hardly incidental, for McQueen had recently parted from French fashion conglomerate LVMH to broker a deal with the Gucci Group (Kering). He would show in Paris for the rest of his career.

THE DANCE OF THE TWISTED BULL

SPRING/SUMMER 2002
STADE FRANÇAIS, PARIS; 6 SEPTEMBER 2001

McQueen's Spring/Summer 2002 show was the first of his own-label collections to be presented in Paris. In contrast to many of his preceding shows, which had steadily increased in intensity and complexity, this was a calm, even casual presentation for the designer. Models walked through a smokescreen behind which a video of a bullfight played to an eclectic soundtrack of electronic music, acoustic Spanish guitar and the haunting vocals of Björk.

There was not the usual harmonizing of myriad divergent themes, rather a unified aesthetic that coalesced around Spanish dance. This was manifested both in the figure of the flamenco dancer and in the matador. Other elements of Spanish culture were incorporated via architectural cut-outs on a white top that recalled the work of Antoni Gaudí, and through colours that attested both to the Mediterranean and the dark Romanticism of the painter Francisco de Goya.

Flamenco and matador tropes – and their associated connotations of sex and death – were harmonized in dramatic polka dot gowns that captured the passion inherent in bullfighting and dancing. One ensemble incorporated long banderillas (decorative spears used in bullfighting), which appeared to lance the body and catch the edge of the ruffled skirt that hung from the spears to form a train. The models were portrayed as strong, sexualized women with exposed breasts and seductive smoky-eyed make-up. Sombre black

suits with flared trousers, and heavily embellished short jackets with padded shoulders, served as a complement to the seductive flamenco dancers, conveying the sex appeal of the matador rather than his masculinity and bravery, qualities for which he is lauded in Spanish culture.

Historicism was again invested in the designs. While eighteenth-century features were incorporated into modern all-in-one ensembles via integrated corsets and a corset used as outerwear, black silk and woollen breeches suggested that McQueen had turned to Juan de Alcega's *The Tailor's Pattern Book* (1589) for inspiration.

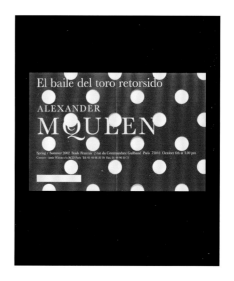

SUPERCALIFRAGILISTIC-EXPIALIDOCIOUS

AUTUMN/WINTER 2002
LA CONCIERGERIE, PARIS; 9 MARCH 2002

McQueen's collection for Autumn/Winter 2002 heralded a return to the theatrical. The venue, the vaults of La Conciergerie, the medieval palace where Marie Antoinette was incarcerated prior to her execution in 1793, provided a suitably dramatic backdrop.

Among McQueen's inspirations was Tim Burton, director of dark, Gothic fantasy films such as *Beetlejuice* (1988) and *Edward Scissorhands* (1990). McQueen wanted the collection to have a 'Sleepy Hollow-esque feel'; the film *Sleepy Hollow* (1999) being Burton's reinterpretation of Washington Irving's tale of the headless horseman, set in 1790s rural New York. The drama inherent in the literary tale was translated by McQueen into the figure of an eighteenth-century highwayman replete with mask, tricorn hat and billowing cape.

Burton designed the lighting for the show and also the invitation: an ink-blotted school exercise book filled with his signature, quirky illustrations of children with scrawny necks and bulging eyes. The classroom motif extended into the collection with tight, pencil skirts that signified sex and seduction. Models, who appeared as schoolgirls-gone-bad with untamed hair and make-up that echoed American rock band Kiss, wore bowler hats of the type worn in Stanley Kubrick's 1971 adaptation of Antony Burgess's disturbing novel, *Clockwork Orange*. In the

same vein as *What a Merry Go Round*, this catwalk show subverted adolescent norms with its sexual overtones and implied sadomasochism.

McQueen returned to several of the themes elaborated in his Autumn/Winter show from the year before, such as children's literature and cinematography; the title was borrowed from Walt Disney's *Mary Poppins* (1964). Unlike the film, McQueen's show was far from saccharine and instead bore closer approximation to a Grimm's fairy tale. An alternative vision of the figure of Little Red Riding Hood was presented by a model wearing an eighteenth-century-inspired hooded cape of lilac leather with wolverine dogs at her sides. Teutonic references also persisted, this time through an engagement with Germanic Puritanism that was articulated in neutral suits bound in fetishistic brown leather harnesses.

McQueen also referenced the ill-fated Marie Antoinette in high-waisted dresses with sheer tops, reminiscent of paintings by the French queen's favourite portraitist Elisabeth Vigée- Lebrun, and in deep red leather creations that hinted at the blood shed at the guillotine. These were complemented by empire-line ensembles that evoked the classically inspired dress of the *Merveilleuses* and epitomized the liberties associated with the infant republic.

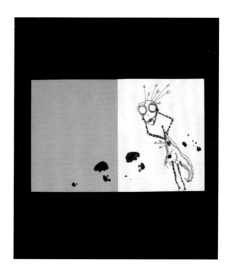

IRERE

SPRING/SUMMER 2003
LA GRANDE HALLE DE LA VILLETTE, PARIS; 5 OCTOBER 2002

For his Spring/Summer 2003 collection, McQueen once again looked to water for inspiration. The show opened with an underwater film directed by John Maybury that showed a girl in a torn chiffon dress plunge into the sea and appear to drown. But this was not a poignant film of a lost innocent, for *Irere*, meaning 'transformation' in one of the indigenous Amazonian languages, was to tell the story of the girl's metamorphosis from shipwreck survivor to Amazonian princess in a tale of redemption and survival.

The collection was inspired by the Roland Joffé film *The Mission* (1986), in which a Jesuit missionary in eighteenth-century South America attempts to protect a native tribe from Portuguese forces. McQueen referenced the periods of European discovery and the great explorers – Christopher Columbus and Captain Cook – with modern renderings of historic dress. A gold Elizabethan-style doublet with lacings down the back and ruffles at the cuffs was brought up to date with sharp cut-outs that exposed the white ground underneath.

Irere was presented in three sequences. The first models walked out as pirates who had survived the shipwreck, their hair wet and make-up smudged. Micro-mini chestnut leather skirts, worn with tattered organdie shirts and knee-high brown leather boots with curved Portuguese heels, referenced the pirate aesthetic. Fragile femininity was conveyed in McQueen's 'Oyster' gown, constructed from a bodice of boned tulle and shredded chiffon, its skirt consisting of hundreds of circles of chiffon arranged on the bias to replicate the folds on an oyster shell. This was followed by the torn chiffon dress seen on the drowning girl in the film, hinting that she had survived and was to be transformed.

Then came a sequence of designs in black – leather shirts above chiffon skirts, laser-cut harness dresses and bodysuits. One model wore an embellished cape and cone-shaped hat with buckle that evoked the seventeenth-century period of exploration. Styled with untamed hair that lent a punkish attitude, black eyes that suggested a masquerade mask, and walking to a cover version of 'Son of a Preacher Man' and David Bowie's 'Jean Genie', these models embodied the mischievous black sprites that the drowning damsel encountered in the forests on the island. The giant screen at the rear projected images in night vision, the sprites glowing an eerie shade of green.

Darkness gave way to a riot of colour for the final section, as models emerged as birds of paradise in chiffon gowns, some with bold feathered prints by Jonathan Saunders. Here McQueen pushed technological boundaries, projecting onto the screen thermal images of the models that were saturated with the vibrant colours of the tropical rainforest.

SCANNERS

AUTUMN/WINTER 2003
LA GRANDE HALLE DE LA VILLETTE, PARIS; 8 MARCH 2003

McQueen replaced tropical climes with the frozen Arctic tundra in his Autumn/Winter 2003 presentation. At ground level, a rubble-strewn wasteland set against an icy mountain was covered with rocks and a dusting of snow, while an enclosed wind tunnel supported by industrial scaffolding focused attention above. The invitations for the presentation were illustrated with scans of McQueen's brain, hence the title.

The collection engaged with McQueen's interest in Eurasian culture and was presented as a journey of displaced travellers, from West to East, from dark to light, across the harsh plains of Siberia through Tibet and on to Japan, the land of the Rising Sun. Strong, opulent designs stood in stark contrast to the barren set. Voluminous silhouettes conveyed modern luxury: over-sized, hooded, fur-trimmed jackets were belted tightly at the waist and paired with full skirts. Russian influences were strong. Embroidered panels and hems, and padded skirts trimmed with fur, suggested folk dress. The traditional was brought up to date, however, with khaki waistcoats and A-line skirts constructed from neoprene.

McQueen's fascination for Japanese culture also shone through in designs that incorporated familiar kimono shapes and the reds and whites of the Japanese flag. In *Scanners*, he pursued this interest further. While some designs were inspired by manga cartoons, he experimented in others with the forms of fourteenth- and fifteenth-century samurai armour: a dress constructed from panels of embroidered leather atop a delicate, silk petticoat stood out for its hardened beauty.

A different aesthetic emerged in models sporting punkish designs. Black and white checkerboard patterns were mixed with embellished black leathers that hinted at Ridley Scott's dystopian sci-fi classic *Blade Runner* (1982). Police sirens wailed in the background as Tiffany's 1980s pop hit 'I Think We're Alone Now' played out, perhaps a parody of tense international relations between East and West during the third phase of the Cold War (1985–91).

Attention shifted from ground level to the tunnel above the catwalk as a model wearing a black and white bodysuit struggled against the wind, a parachute of printed pink silk billowing out behind her. A final sequence of Japanese inspired outfits in reds and whites appeared on the ground to the sound of The Sparks' 'This Town Ain't Big Enough for the Both of Us' – a further comment on East-West relations – before wind howled though the tunnel once more and a model wearing an enormous kimono, embroidered with kabuki motifs, battled against the gales.

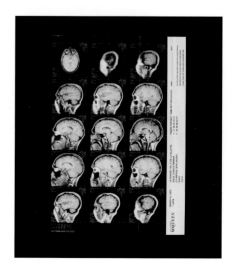

DELIVERANCE

SPRING/SUMMER 2004
SALLE WAGRAM, PARIS; 10 OCTOBER 2003

McQueen set a new precedent for performativity in the staging of his Spring/Summer 2004 catwalk show. This time he collaborated with dancer Michael Clark, who choreographed a routine that paid homage to one of McQueen's favourite films, Sydney Pollack's *They Shoot Horses, Don't They?* (1969), which was based on the dance marathons held in America during the Depression. The concept was a 'dance to the death', the gruelling nature of which rooted the narrative to the unforgiving contemporary fashion industry. McQueen's choice of invitation, a cardboard medication packet, provided further comment on the exhausting pace of the fashion sector, and the pressures and expectations it places on contemporary designers.

The venue, the Salle Wagram, was a nineteenth-century Parisian dance hall replete with red velvet curtains, crystal chandeliers, wood panelling and frescoes; a McQueen touch was the addition of a mirrored disco ball. It was a pertinent choice for a show that incorporated professional dancers alongside McQueen's familiar catwalk models.

The show unfolded in three sequences. In the first, couples danced under spotlights to big band sounds in 1930s bias-cut dresses that evoked Hollywood glamour, an antidote to the Depression era. As a disco track by Chic cut in, the intensity amplified with dancers executing high kicks that thrust the feathered and sequinned skirts high into the air. Glamorous eveningwear designs in satins, lamés and sequins gave way to a second sequence with a sportswear aesthetic. Skin-tight bodysuits, sequinned hot pants, racing stripes and trainers all reinforced the quickening speed of an elimination dance, as contestants raced around the room to a beating soundtrack with undertones of Nirvana's 'Smells Like Teen Spirit' before slumping to the floor.

In the final sequence, the now exhausted dancers staggered across the room to the distorted sounds of Billie Holiday. One model, in a floating chiffon gown printed to look like a delicate watercolour painting, was caught by her partner as she fell, before being carried off. Karen Elson, modelling the same design as that from the opening sequence except that its sparkling sequins were now tarnished, appeared to expire on stage. As Portishead's 'Strangers' played out, the dishevelled dancers expended any residual energy in attempting kicks that sent them to the ground. In this final sequence McQueen replaced the luxurious gowns that glistened with energy at the show's beginning with utilitarian denims, jerseys and patchworks (fabrics rooted to the 1930s) that served as a sartorial signifier of exhaustion and despair.

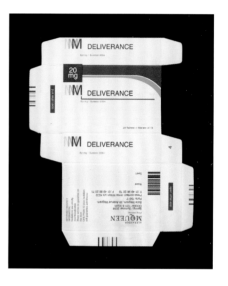

PANTHEON AD LUCEM

AUTUMN/WINTER 2004
LA GRANDE HALLE DE LA VILLETTE, PARIS; 5 MARCH 2004

McQueen took a pause from spectacle for the presentation of his Autumn/Winter 2004 collection. Although he stated that he wanted to focus attention on purity of design rather than showmanship, *Pantheon ad Lucem* ('Towards the Light') was not completely devoid of theatre. As scenes from space were played out in the background, models styled to look like androgynous inhabitants from another planet – with pale skin, elongated eyes and hair pulled into short, tight curls – emerged from what appeared to be the door of a spacecraft onto a circular, illuminated catwalk.

Like most McQueen collections, *Pantheon ad Lucem* fused multiple, disparate elements. The show centred on a futuristic narrative inspired by sci-fi films such as Steven Spielberg's *Close Encounters of the Third Kind* (1977) and Stanley Kubrick's *2001: A Space Odyssey* (1968) – the soundtrack sampled Richard Strauss's theme tune 'Zarathustra'. Yet the title and pared down presentation connected the collection to Ancient Greek dress, which had inspired a number of ethereal, draped jersey gowns that skimmed the body in the manner of 1930s designer Madeleine Vionnet. Some appeared to suggest Princess Leia's costumes in George Lucas's *Star Wars* films of the 1970s, thus further harmonizing the futuristic with the classical past. These delicate creations were offset by thick tweed suits, shearling coats, and a gold and bronze boxy jacket decorated with a pattern reminiscent of crop circles.

Other cultures and historical eras were referenced, too. While black gowns with long sleeves and embellished yokes hinted at Plantagenet queens, high-necked, feathered shoulder capes with glass beads pointed to Native American culture. The final looks – presented in darkness and lit by LED lighting – re-focused attention on the future and McQueen's development of new silhouettes. A gold dress overlaid with a geometric pattern extended upwards from the bodice to form a funnel covering the model's chin and outwards at the hips to shift attention from the waist. The final showpiece was a staggering frothy gown of lengths of pleated silver tulle arranged on the diagonal. An ornate silver shoulder piece by Shaun Leane, with neck collar and orchid detailing, rose out of the funnelled bodice, which offset the cinched waist and balanced the A-line skirt that flowed out into a voluminous, scalloped train.

IT'S ONLY A GAME

SPRING/SUMMER 2005
PALAIS OMNISPORTS DE PARIS-BERCY, PARIS; 8 OCTOBER 2004

Initially McQueen's Spring/Summer 2005 show appeared the most conventional yet. The first models walked to the sounds of Frankie Goes To Hollywood's 'Relax' on a white catwalk with white walls at the rear. Absent were the theatrics of water, Plexiglas cubes and giant projections. Yet as the first wave of models failed to leave the catwalk, and instead formed a line down the centre, it emerged that McQueen was experimenting with theatre of a new kind.

The initial group of six blonde models wore tailored, Edwardian designs inspired by the schoolgirls in Peter Weir's period thriller *Picnic at Hanging Rock* (1975). The second tranche to form a line on the catwalk were Asian models wearing neutral tones that were lifted with colourful prints and embroidery. Next came a group of redheads in pale green and white designs, ahead of Latin American models in sunny shades of yellow. Ostensibly McQueen was curating his models into types, while once again drawing a distinction between East and West. Contemporary Western culture was referenced in sportswear designs. Whereas one ensemble incorporated the helmet and shoulder pads of an American footballer, another bore an approximation to a motocross jumpsuit. These were matched by designs inspired by the East. A lilac embroidered silk dress with high collar twisted from the bodice into a puffball skirt and was pulled in at the waist by an obi sash that trailed to the ground. Another Japanese robe fused Western and Eastern cultures via a camouflage print in tones of lilac and soft green.

Once again McQueen experimented with body shapes and moulded designs. A dress with an appliquéd carousel motif extended at the rear into a bustle-like form, which sat beneath a brown, moulded leather bodice with high neck and stitching down the back that echoed designs from *No.13*. McQueen advanced this idea further in moulded leather ensembles that rose upwards from the neck into helmets from which ponytails sprouted, and downwards over exaggerated hips to end in horsehair skirts. The restriction imposed on the models by the hard carapace was reinforced by a metal bar across the mouth that evoked both sports helmets and braces used in corrective dentistry.

Whilst McQueen had thus far chosen to draw attention to the designs, next came the spectacle. As the final models lined up, the soundtrack changed to Frankie Goes To Hollywood's 'Two Tribes', suggesting that a confrontation was to come. As the lights came back up, a giant checkerboard appeared. It was now apparent that McQueen had delivered his models as chess pieces, which turned to face each other, ready to engage in a game. The set was inspired by contemporary artist Vanessa Beecroft's performance photographs and the chess scene at the end of *Harry Potter and the Philosopher's Stone* (2001). Choreographed by Les Child, the models responded to instructions from a robotic voice and started to eliminate their opponents from the game as the overture from the film played in background.

THE MAN WHO KNEW TOO MUCH

AUTUMN/WINTER 2005
LYCÉE CARNOT, PARIS; 4 MARCH 2005

McQueen's collection for Autumn/Winter 2005, staged in a school hall, was a tribute to one of his favourite film directors: Alfred Hitchcock. Although McQueen had already alluded to Hitchcock in *The Birds* (Spring/Summer 1995) and *Voss* (Spring/Summer 2001), *The Man Who Knew Too Much* was saturated with overt references. While the title shared its name with Hitchcock's classic thriller (1934 and 1956) – a film McQueen had loved as a child – and the show's invitation was based on the advertising poster for *Vertigo* (1958), the film set backdrop – with the hall windows illuminated in purple at the end of an orange-lit runway – hinted at the voyeurism of *Rear Window* (1954). A Hitchcock aesthetic was also referenced in the collection, with designs inspired by Edith Head's costumes for Hitchcock heroines, such as Tippi Hedren, and McQueen's first handbag named after another of the director's leading actresses, Kim Novak.

The collection was conventional – both in terms of the designs and their presentation – and hugely successful commercially. It was also extremely nostalgic. Brimming with vintage silhouettes from the late 1950s and early '60s, models walked to upbeat tracks from the era by artists including Johnny Kidd and the Pirates, Alan Vega, Dusty Springfield, Elvis Presley, and Martha Reeves and the Vandellas.

McQueen was particularly fascinated by the precise manner in which Hitchcock heroines were dressed. He referenced the figures of Hedren and Novak – with their neat suits and debonair styling – via pencil skirts and jackets with three-

quarter length sleeves that were perfectly coordinated with leather gloves, seamed stockings, crocodile sling-backs and large, round sunglasses. Bouffant hair and bright red lips injected sex into an image of prim sophistication. While a model evoking screen icon Marilyn Monroe wore a sexy, lace top and tight-fitting skirt, a second wearing a mohair jumper and leopard-print skirt sported the tousled hair of Brigitte Bardot, another of the decade's sirens.

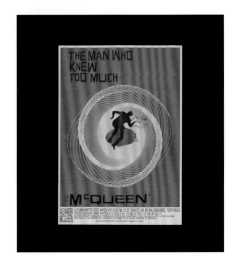

When McQueen ventured into eveningwear he looked to Anglo-American couturier Charles James. A pillar-box red satin gown with sweeping fishtail demonstrated an architectural quality reminiscent of the couturier. A glamorous nude cocktail dress encrusted with crystals that shimmered under the lights echoed the infamous dress designed by Jean Louis and worn by Marilyn Monroe when she sang 'Happy Birthday' to President John F. Kennedy in 1962. Ironically, whereas McQueen had previously been criticized for being too edgy and overshadowing his designs with theatrics, on this occasion he was rebuked by fashion editors for playing it too safe.

NEPTUNE

SPRING/SUMMER 2006
IMPRIMERIE NATIONALE, PARIS; 7 OCTOBER 2005

The trend of pared down catwalk shows continued with *Neptune*, which was presented at an industrial warehouse in the Paris suburbs. The title – the name of the Roman god of the sea – teased the audience, which anticipated a return to McQueen spectacle. Instead, a plain, 30 ft runway with a narrow, bright strip of light evoked the sparse feel of early shows like *Nihilism* when McQueen was without the funds to invest in elaborate shows.

Neptune was a collection of glamorous, body-conscious silhouettes designed for the confident, metropolitan woman. 1980s power dressing provided a strong influence. The work of controversial French fashion photographer Guy Bourdin, and that of graphic designer and film director Jean-Paul Goude, responsible for the hard, androgynous look of 1980s icon Grace Jones, were cited by McQueen as inspirations. Further references to 1980s dress were evidenced in figure-hugging designs reminiscent of Azzedine Alaïa and Gianni Versace, and in shiny, pleated skirts that echoed signature Issey Miyake creations.

Tailoring was predominantly in black and featured very short skirts, shorts, culottes and jackets with hard shoulders. Sheer panels, chiffon shirts and visible underwear invested the looks with sex appeal. Leather shorts were toughened up with embellished wrestling belts; short, figure-hugging dresses were given harness tops and paired with gladiator-style sandals; and a skin-tight pair of leather trousers was worn with a short leather jacket that exposed the mid-riff, all consolidating the hardened, sexy look. The occasional design

in silver, or a Grecian robe in white – one with a gold chain belt – brought glamour to the predominantly monochrome palette. Short chiffon dresses encrusted with jewels, as well as revealing swimwear in tones of gold and silver, channelled sex appeal. This was complemented by a show invitation that featured an image of a woman in a bath, partially covered by bubbles which distorted the figure.

The hard-edged collection was presented to a rock soundtrack that incorporated Siouxsie Sioux and the Banshees, Suzi Quatro, and Ike and Tina Turner's hit 'Nutbush City Limits'.

THE WIDOWS OF CULLODEN

AUTUMN/WINTER 2006
PALAIS OMNISPORTS DE PARIS-BERCY, PARIS; 3 MARCH 2006

McQueen's audiences had waited several seasons for a return to a theatrical show. They were not disappointed with *The Widows of Culloden*. The show – once again dedicated to Isabella Blow – was loaded with emotion. While the title appeared in Gaelic on the invitation – Bantraich de cuil lodair – as memoir to a diminishing culture, the emotive soundtrack incorporated an eclectic mix of tracks from Michael Nyman's score for *The Piano* (1993), bagpipes overlaid with drums from a Scottish pipe band, punk rock and the howling winds of the Highlands. Models walked the rough wooden boards of a square catwalk in romantic designs that stood out for their exquisite craftsmanship.

McQueen revisited his interest in his Scottish ancestry and the historic subjugation of Scotland at the hands of its English neighbours. This time the inspiration was the Jacobite Risings that culminated in the Battle of Culloden (1746), the collection a memorial to the widows who had lost their husbands in the bloody conflict.

Despite the emotive subject matter, *The Widows of Culloden* was a more composed and less aggressive rendering of Scotland's past than McQueen's *Highland Rape* collection. It was filled with the now familiar MacQueen tartan, although this time its application was more refined. A tartan dress was draped over one shoulder and around the neck in traditional Scottish style but accompanied by a tulle underskirt and a top of flesh-coloured net appliquéd with black lace. A black belt with Celtic buckle cinched the waist to emphasize the female

form. Once again, McQueen celebrated the Scottish game-keeping tradition, this time with neat tweed suits paired with plumes from grouse and partridge. An exquisite headdress by Philip Treacy and Shaun Leane comprised a bird's nest filled with seven soft blue, speckled eggs encrusted with Swarovski gemstones and flanked by mallard wings.

The collection was striking for the level of craftsmanship inherent in each of the designs. An evening gown constructed from tiers of pheasant feathers demonstrated a lightness of touch and an ingenuity of construction. McQueen, who was interested in the concept of heirlooms, wanted to invest every piece with emotional content. His intention was poignantly conveyed in a majestic lace dress with ruffled skirt, modelled by Raquel Zimmermann, and worn with resin antlers draped with an antique lace veil.

The collection captured a sense of melancholy that was not only transmitted in the fragility of the designs but also consolidated in its memorable finale. As the lights dimmed, Kate Moss emerged as an ethereal apparition from within a glass pyramid, slowly dancing in the air in a delicate chiffon dress to John Williams' haunting soundtrack from *Schindler's List* (1993). The sequence, produced by Baillie Walsh and art directed by McQueen, was inspired by the Lumière brothers' film *Danse Serpentine* (1896), based on the dance made famous by Loie Fuller in 1891. It was another technological feat for McQueen, this time with roots extending to the nineteenth-century stage mechanics of 'Pepper's Ghost'.

SARABANDE
SPRING/SUMMER 2007
CIRQUE D'HIVER, PARIS; 6 OCTOBER 2006

Sarabande was another collection that epitomized fragile beauty undercut with a sense of decaying grandeur. The set, designed to look like a deserted theatre, was dominated by a magnificent chandelier that evoked a scene from Stanley Kubrick's eighteenth-century drama *Barry Lyndon* (1975). Presented in the round, models walked the bare wooden boards of a nineteenth-century theatre to a live chamber orchestra that played 'Sarabande', the fourth movement of the harpsichord suite in D minor by George Frederick Handel, which also featured in the Kubrick film.

Darkly romantic and quintessentially feminine, the collection notes cited the portraits of Francisco de Goya, indigenous Mexican dress, and English country garden flowers as key inspirations. The influence of the eccentric patron and socialite Marchesa Luisa Casati – famed for wearing live snakes as bracelets and for declaring her desire to be a living work of art – was also apparent in a white dress with a floor-length grey mantilla that recalled Ignacio Zuloaga's 1922 portrait, and in a showpiece constructed from frozen flowers. As the model walked, blooms fell to the floor, exposing the transience of living things. While the image of French actress Sarah Bernhardt in her coffin, her body strewn with flowers, is discernible in the gown, McQueen cited the photographic compositions of decaying fruit by his friend Sam Taylor-Johnson and Marc Quinn's frozen flower installation *Garden* (2000) as further inspirations.

Once again, McQueen translated for his audience the beauty inherent in death and decay. The collection was an elegy to

nature, with delicate birds recalling Audubon prints hand-painted onto a moulded leather dress, florals embroidered on soft tulle gowns, and petals trapped inside layers of chiffon that alluded to designs by his one-time mentor Koji Tatsuno. A sense of melancholy pervaded the collection, with models draped with mourning veils, their skin ghostly pale, some with silvered wispy hair in suggestion of faded beauty, others with plaits that suggested Henri Cartier-Bresson's poignant portrait of a mother and child, *Mexico City* (1934). The prevailing colour palette – the dusky pink and mauve tones of lavender and heather – lent an antique quality and recalled the hand-coloured sepia prints of Pre-Raphaelite photographer Julia Margaret Cameron.

The collection was also dark in places. While McQueen's interest in Flemish Gothic was discernible in a Philip Treacy black silk hat that recalled the hood in Jan van Eyck's self-portrait (1433), the opening look – a high-waisted black redingote with a black silk hat in the form of a giant rose – was suggestive of the costumes worn by Silvana Mangano in Luchino Visconti's Edwardian-era film *Death in Venice* (1971). The Rolling Stones' 'Paint it Black' reinforced the theme.

IN MEMORY OF
ELIZABETH HOW, SALEM 1692
AUTUMN/WINTER 2007
LE ZENITH ARENA, PARIS; 2 MARCH 2007

McQueen revisited dark drama in the presentation of his Autumn/Winter 2007 collection, the last show styled by Katy England. A 45 ft inverted black pyramid suspended over a blood red pentagram, traced in black sand, set the stage for a collection that combined the religious persecution meted out by seventeenth-century Puritans with ancient Egyptian paganism. A film co-directed by McQueen and Daniel Landin of locusts, naked bodies suspended in limbo, an owl's face, and skulls engulfed in flames provided a dramatic backdrop to a show that starkly contrasted with the softer, romantic qualities of the designer's two preceding catwalk presentations.

Once again, McQueen drew on his family history. He had learned from his mother, an amateur genealogist, that a distant relative – Elizabeth How – had been hanged during the notorious Salem Witchcraft Trials of 1692, falsely accused of practising witchcraft. Warrior-like moulded bustiers in brown leather suggested a defiance against persecution, while an advancement of the moulded bodice – this time extending downwards over the hips into a flat skirt panel and upwards from the neck to conceal the mouth, nose and brow – hinted at the suppression of religious freedoms.

Symbols of pagan worship were referenced by headpieces in the form of a crescent moon and star, encrusted with Swarovski crystal and gemstones. Joseph L. Mankiewicz's

film *Cleopatra* (1962), which starred Elizabeth Taylor as the ill-fated Egyptian queen, was another discernible influence. The film provided the inspiration for the make-up – dramatic cobalt blue eyes framed with heavy eyeliner – which brought a touch of Hollywood glamour to an otherwise dark collection.

The palette for a collection centred on the dark arts and folk culture of the puritanical New British World was understandably sombre. There was also a Gothic undertone, identifiable in a green and black taffeta evening gown with a cross of embroidered crystals on the bodice. Blacks, dark browns and maroons were, however, offset by origami-style cocktail dresses in iridescent blues and golds that recalled the precious lapis lazuli and gold of Egyptian sarcophagi. A bold contrast was provided by a bodysuit of gold paillettes, inset with a moulded golden bodice with drooping breasts. A further touch of glamour was injected by a black gown dripping with silver beading that recalled flowing hair, evoking Jean Cocteau's linear designs for Elsa Schiaparelli.

McQueen also intrigued with cocoon-like designs that deviated from the Victorian silhouette to create new womanly shapes, this time suggesting the contours of the ovum. Praised for his characteristic juxtaposition of hard and soft in designs that connoted fertility and protection, the collection was criticized by some for its macabre theatrics.

LA DAME BLEUE

SPRING/SUMMER 2008

PALAIS OMNISPORTS DE PARIS-BERCY, PARIS; 5 OCTOBER 2007

Following the death in May 2007 of Isabella Blow, McQueen joined forces with long-time collaborator Philip Treacy to deliver a collection in tribute to the stylist who had been instrumental in the early stages of both designers' careers. At the end of a reflective catwalk appeared a huge pair of flapping, outstretched wings, their shape traced by neon tubes of light. The invitation, an illustration by Richard Gray, showed a winged Blow ascending to heaven in a chariot, wearing a dusty pink, feathered trapezoidal gown and a Philip Treacy headdress comprising a halo of black spears.

According to the collection notes, Spring/Summer 2008 was inspired by 'extreme glamour'. The collection was delicate in places, theatrical in others. Moreover, an engagement with nature and its transformative qualities was conveyed in designs that echoed Blow's passion for reinventing herself through her wardrobe.

The show opened with tailored designs that invoked McQueen's characteristic Savile Row sensibility. Strong hip and shoulder lines created structured silhouettes rendered in traditional menswear fabrics including plaid mohair and Prince of Wales check. McQueen distilled his inveterate fascination with Japan and the East; this time into silk designs with kimono sleeves and obi belts that reflected the Japanese-themed couture collection he designed for Givenchy (Autumn/Winter 1997), and shoes that drew inspiration from geta. Japanese symbolism also was evident in a striking Philip Treacy headdress comprising a flutter of red butterflies made from

hand-painted turkey feathers; the butterfly was revered in Japan as the personification of the soul.

As with many of McQueen's collections, there was a strong avian presence. Whereas a padded leather jacket with wings formed from reworked trainer moulds referenced McQueen's collaboration with Puma, feathers applied to gowns charted a shift towards opulence. Some models appeared as bird-woman hybrids with feathers applied to the face. While the final looks included vibrant printed chiffon gowns that summoned up the birds of paradise creations in *Irere*, a pair of unfurled wings were placed – inverted – over the bodice of a parachute dress made from soft blue silk, creating a statement unique to the show.

In this collection McQueen presented two alternative visions of femininity. Whereas ethereal chiffon gowns in soft colour palettes hinted at goddesses and conveyed the image of a fragile, delicate woman, black and neon designs incorporated fencing masks and shoulder pads, projecting fierceness and strength. The two aesthetics were tempered by creations that incorporated metallic paillettes in dusty tones and suggested soft armour, and in a geometric pink python-skin dress attached to a silver body grid by Shaun Leane – another close friend of Blow – which formed a protective cage around the face.

THE GIRL WHO LIVED
IN THE TREE

AUTUMN/WINTER 2008

PALAIS OMNISPORTS DE PARIS-BERCY, PARIS; 29 FEBRUARY 2008

McQueen's Autumn/Winter 2008 collection centred on a fairy-tale narrative devised by McQueen about a girl who descends from a tree to marry a prince and then become a queen. It was inspired by a 600-year-old elm tree in the garden of the designer's Sussex home. At the centre of the set stood a giant tree swathed in fabric, inspired by Bulgarian artist Christo, who is renowned for wrapping buildings with material.

The collection notes listed the inspirations to be 'The British Empire, Queens of England, the Duke of Wellington. Toy soldiers and punk princesses.' These themes found expression in two distinct sequences. The first featured romantic designs with a predominantly slender silhouette that was emphasized by jackets with nipped-in waists and S-bend corseted tops above ballerina skirts. Here emerged McQueen's punk princess to the orchestral soundtrack of American grunge band Nirvana's 'Come As You Are', styled with unruly back-combed hair and dressed in rags, hand-knitted mohair and washed tweeds. The dark palette was lifted in places with striking decorative touches. While some designs were scattered with intricate snowflakes, another was lifted by a yoke of glistening jewels. A third was decorated with a silver print of the elm tree, which appeared embossed in cream on the gold show invitation. The sequence closed with a white tulle dress embroidered with two black peacocks in profile, a reference to the national bird of India.

What followed was beautiful and majestic. Opening to a suite of regal music by Haydn and Mozart, the second sequence continued the story of the princess as she leaves the darkness of the tree, meets her prince, and is greeted by the riches of the world. McQueen, who had spent a month in India with friend and collaborator Shaun Leane, looked to the twilight years of the British Raj. Offset against regimental-style jackets trimmed with gold frogging, gowns of feathers, tulles encrusted with Swarovski crystal, rich satins and crimson velvets were given tight-fitting bodices and exaggerated ballerina-style skirts. With their New Look silhouettes, they hinted at the haute couture creations of designers such as Hardy Amies and Norman Hartnell for the young Queen Elizabeth II. Columnar dresses crafted from sumptuous, patterned sari silks referenced the grandeur of Maharajas, while a regal cape of red silk with high ruffled neck was paired with an 'Empire' bag.

Styling for these designs was delicate, with a light touch to make-up, jewelled diadems, and individual hand-crafted slippers adorned with embroidery and jewels that recalled Roger Vivier's creations for Dior. Yet a sense of anarchy prevailed in a silk ballerina-style dress with a 'bastardized' Union Jack print.

NATURAL DIS-TINCTION, UN-NATURAL SELECTION

SPRING/SUMMER 2009
LE 104, 5 RUE CURIAL, PARIS; 3 OCTOBER 2008

McQueen's Spring/Summer 2009 collection was presented on a catwalk filled with antique taxidermy – including an elephant, giraffe, tiger, zebra and polar bear – in an art space that was formerly a Paris morgue. It was a fitting venue for a collection that was to interrogate the impact of humanity on the environment. Mounted on a plinth at the back of the sloping concrete catwalk stood a metal globe onto which images of a glowing sun, silver moon and the earth rotating on its axis were projected. The show invitation featured a lenticular by Gary James McQueen, the designer's nephew, in which the image of McQueen's face morphed into a human skull, hinting at the vulnerability of life.

The primary inspirations behind the collection coalesced around Charles Darwin, the Industrial Revolution and, in particular, the impact of the destructive nature of man. McQueen divided the collection into two sequences to convey his message. The first featured organic shapes, soft colours and natural fibres digitally printed with images of the earth's natural materials – wood grains and meadow flowers – that were engineered for each garment. These designs placed the natural and the technological in provocative juxtaposition. While dresses cut from a single piece of fabric connoted historical simplicity, silk flowers trapped in tulle referenced Victorian specimen jars. Although decorative touches were predominantly soft – whitework embroidery and beetle-wing sequins – metallic buttercups on mini dresses dripped with acid-yellow enamels and provided a point of contrast.

The second sequence continued to draw inspiration from natural forms – flowers, crystals and minerals – but here they were engineered with a hard edge and enhanced to convey the synthetic qualities associated with modernity and the human touch. Prints were angular and invoked crushed crystal, metallic structures such as the Eiffel Tower and a granite mountain that was borrowed from a Dan Holdsworth triptych. In one design a diamond print morphed into a human skeleton. Dresses shaped like bell-jars and bodysuits encrusted with jet, gold and silver Swarovski crystal conveyed harsh lines in material form. Sharper silhouettes were complemented by a colour palette that incorporated black and white as well as vivid pinks and sapphires, and synthetic materials that included Lycra and bonded leather.

Whilst McQueen stated in the collection notes that he was 'not aiming to preach', his belief that 'we're in danger of killing the planet through greed' was fundamental.

THE HORN OF PLENTY

AUTUMN/WINTER 2009
PALAIS OMNISPORTS DE PARIS-BERCY, PARIS; 10 MARCH 2009

McQueen returned to drama with his Autumn/Winter 2009 collection and a set that was both theatrical and exuberant. *The Horn of Plenty* (dedicated to his mother) revisited McQueen signature collections as well as referencing and subverting iconic designs in fashion history. Far from a nostalgic retrospective, the concept of re-invention was instead explored through irony and parody. At the centre of the set stood a giant rubbish tip sprayed black, composed of props from past shows: a broken merry-go-round horse, crushed car parts and the chandelier from *Sarabande*. Added to these were broken televisions and chairs, a washing-machine pipe and even a kitchen sink, echoing the show's subtitle, 'Everything and the kitchen sink'. This collection was a powerful comment on the excesses of fashion in a modern consumer age. Sharing its name with the pub in which Jack the Ripper's final victim Mary Kelly was reputedly last sighted, *The Horn of Plenty* – with its connotations of excess – also suggested impending disaster.

Political undertones were implicit in the collection. A catwalk formed of shattered glass alluded to the nation's collapsed economy following the crisis of 2008. McQueen's use of exaggerated forms – oversized M.C. Escher prints of magpies and ubiquitous houndstooth checks – hinted at the pressure placed on contemporary designers to produce bigger and better collections to sell to mass markets and cement commercial success. Where McQueen invoked the haute couture classics of Chanel, Dior and Givenchy, he subverted them by developing the references and motifs

to the point of hyperbole, at once paying respect to and lampooning the revered designers. McQueen also inverted his own signature creations, with trousers that were transformed into jackets and gowns that were reworked into coats. In characteristic McQueen style, luxury was mixed up with baser elements, most notably in a paper nylon 'rubbish sack' gown with lacquered silk 'bubble wrap' opera coat. Shaun Leane accessories from past collections, including neck coils and claw earrings, also were recycled in the collection; the silver yashmak from *Eye* reinvented as the hooded bodice of a silk ballgown, printed with the image of a red milk snake.

A strong Gothic vein also ran through the collection. This was most starkly manifested in a darkly romantic 'black swan' gown, the duck feathers enveloping the wearer in a bow-like form. A Gothic aesthetic carried through into the styling, which was aggressive and teetered on the precipice between the grotesque and the farcical. Models with faces whitened by Peter Philips and dark, oversized, clown-like lips appeared at once drag queen caricatures and homages to Leigh Bowery and Marilyn Manson, as they walked out to the American rock star's 'Beautiful People' and a compilation of tracks from former McQueen shows. While the hair and make-up was inspired by the consumer-driven world of Terry Gilliam's *Brazil* (1985), Philip Treacy hats transformed mundane household goods, including refuse sacks, tyres and sprayed hub caps, into objects of beauty whilst hinting at the disposability of fashion in the twenty-first century.

PLATO'S ATLANTIS

SPRING/SUMMER 2010
PALAIS OMNISPORTS DE PARIS-BERCY, PARIS; 6 OCTOBER 2009

McQueen's final runway presentation was widely acclaimed as his finest collection. Fittingly, he returned to what inspired him most: nature. This time McQueen merged Darwin's nineteenth-century theories of evolution with twenty-first-century concerns over global warming. *Plato's Atlantis* – a reference to the legendary island described by the Greek philosopher, which sank into the sea – prophesied a future world in which ice caps would melt, seas would rise, and humanity would need to evolve in order to survive. It was pure fantasy.

McQueen delivered his models as an androgynous army of other-worldly beings –human-animal-alien hybrids. Two cameras on giant robotic arms moved along the catwalk, scrutinizing these specimens and projecting their images onto a white-tiled backdrop that resembled a clinical laboratory. Model Raquel Zimmermann appeared on an LED screen, writhing in sand and covered by vibrantly coloured snakes.

As evolution advanced and each model charted the progression from life on land to life under the sea, their features changed. Hair was either plaited tight to the head in mounds or sculpted into fin-like peaks, while the contours of models' faces were distorted with prosthetic enhancements, both features connoting biological adaptation. Colours and textures shifted with the transition from species to species. Camouflage prints of roses, and jacquards depicting moths in green and brown tones, referenced life above the sea; amphibious snake prints suggested a transition to water; and designs in blues and purples incorporated images of ocean creatures, such as stingrays and jellyfish. Here McQueen

perfected the use of digital printing techniques with each design engineered specifically for individual garments.

McQueen developed a host of new shapes, tailored to mimic marine features: pronounced hips and shoulders gave way to amorphous forms; a fluted miniskirt resembled the folds of a jellyfish; puffed sleeves were folded and pleated to connote gills.

Cinematic references to sci-fi and fantasy films including Ridley Scott's *Alien* (1979), James Cameron's *The Abyss* (1989) and John McTiernan's *Predator* (1987) found expression not only in aspects such as the show invitation and colour palette but also shoe designs. The models stalked the catwalk in 25 cm heels, the 3D printed 'Alien' design inspired by the artwork of H.R. Giger (a member of the special effects team for *Alien*). The 'Armadillo' boot created a form entirely without apparent reference to the natural anatomy of the foot, the scaly surface of designs rendered in python skin invoking the armoured shell of the animal after which the shoe was named.

As the show came to a close Zimmermann re-appeared on screen, slowly disappearing beneath the waves, and the cameras now focused on the audience. McQueen broke new ground not only with his superlative collection but also through its multi-media presentation. In collaboration with photographer and web publisher Nick Knight, the show was the first to be streamed live over the Internet, enabling an interactive dialogue between fashion and technology.

AUTUMN/WINTER 2010
—
HÔTEL DE CLERMONT-TONNERRE, PARIS; 10 MARCH 2010

The collection that followed McQueen's death in February 2010 – unofficially and posthumously titled 'Angels and Demons' – was presented in an appropriately sombre manner. It was shown in private to seven select groups in the parqueted salon of an ornate eighteenth-century Parisian mansion.

Sixteen designs had been cut on the stand by McQueen and were nearing completion at the time of his death. These were selected for the collection and finished by Sarah Burton – then McQueen's head of womenswear design – and her team. The final collection under McQueen's hand drew inspiration from Byzantine art and Old Master paintings. In particular, McQueen honed in on religious iconography, borrowing from paintings and altarpieces by artists such as Hans Memling, Hieronymus Bosch, Sandro Botticelli, Jean Fouquet, Hugo van der Goes, Jean Hay and Stephan Lochner. Entire artworks and specific details were captured digitally and then woven into jacquards, or once again printed and engineered to fit individual garments. Renaissance statuary also provided an influence and was expressed in a pale chiffon gown printed with images of grisaille angels from the *Portinari Altarpiece* by Hugo van der Goes, c.1475. The fluted skirt recalled carved alabaster.

McQueen harnessed the historical with the modern through his innovative techniques. Despite many designs being digitally rendered, there was a strong emphasis on handcraft that contrasted with the ultra-technological outlook of the

preceding collection. There was also an overriding simplicity; some designs were cut from a single bolt of fabric and many involved minimal seams. Yet the collection was ornate in places. Shoes crafted from crocodile skin, with gilded, hand-carved wooden soles, featured ivy adorned with acorns and evoked the work of Baroque carver Grinling Gibbons. While a silver pair embroidered with wings featured a heel sculpted into the shape of an angel, the signature McQueen skull found expression on an ankle boot.

The styling of the collection was also classic McQueen. This time each model wore a burnished metallic skullcap, in some cases bisected with a Mohican of golden feathers. They walked like birds to a suite of classical music by Haydn and Beethoven.

The poignancy of a collection that engaged with the themes of religion and the afterlife, and which was crafted from the most luxurious of materials and techniques, rich silks, duchesse jacquards, satin organzas, gold-painted goose feathers, matelassé and *fil coupé*, was self-evident. As the collection notes that were handed to the audience read, 'Each piece is unique, as was he'.

ENCYCLOPEDIA OF COLLECTIONS CREDITS

Jack the Ripper Stalks his Victims, Autumn/Winter 1992
Catwalk image: Photograph by Niall McInerney
Show invitation: Courtesy of Central Saint Martins Museum Study Collection

Taxi Driver, Autumn/Winter 1993
Above: 'The Real McQueen', *Observer Magazine*, March 1993
Below: 'With a Little Help from my Friends', Hilary Alexander, *Sunday Telegraph*, 7 March 1993
Modelled by Alice Smith
Photograph by Sean Knox

Nihilism, Spring/Summer 1994
Catwalk image: Photograph by Brendan Beirne
Show invitation: Courtesy of Chris Bird

Banshee, Autumn/Winter 1994
Catwalk image: Photograph by Niall McInerney
Show invitation: Courtesy of Fleet Bigwood
Photograph by Rankin

The Birds, Spring/Summer, 1995
Catwalk image: Photograph by Chris Moore
Model: Jade Parfitt
Show invitation: Courtesy of Fleet Bigwood
Design by Silvia Gaspardo Moro

Highland Rape, Autumn/Winter 1995
Catwalk image: Photograph by Robert Fairer
Show invitation: Courtesy of Fleet Bigwood
Photograph by Nicola Schwartz,
Design by Silvia Gaspardo Moro

The Hunger, Spring/Summer 1996
Catwalk image: Photograph by Robert Fairer
Show invitation: Courtesy of Alexander McQueen
Photograph by Gerhard Klocker

Dante, Autumn/Winter 1996
Catwalk image: Photograph by Robert Fairer
Show invitation: Courtesy of Alexander McQueen
Photograph by Nicola Schwartz

Bellmer La Poupée, Spring/Summer 1997
Catwalk image: Photograph by Chris Moore
Show invitation: Courtesy of Fleet Bigwood

It's a Jungle Out There, Autumn/Winter 1997
Catwalk image: Photograph by Niall McInerney
Modelled by Jodie Kidd
Show invitation: Courtesy of Mark C. O'Flaherty
Modelled by Debra Shaw
Photograph by Nick Knight with art direction by Alexander McQueen

Untitled, Spring/Summer 1998
Catwalk image: Photograph by Anthea Simms
Modelled by Gisele Bündchen
Show invitation: Courtesy of Alexander McQueen

Joan, Autumn/Winter 1998
Catwalk image: Photograph by Anthea Simms
Modelled by Debra Shaw
Show invitation: Courtesy of Alexander McQueen
Photograph by Phil Poynter

No.13, Spring/Summer 1999
Catwalk image: Photograph by Anthea Simms
Show invitation: Courtesy of Alice Smith and Cressida Pye
Photograph by Richard Green

The Overlook, Autumn/Winter 1999
Catwalk image: Photograph by Anthea Simms
Show invitation: Courtesy of Alice Smith and Cressida Pye

Eye, Spring/Summer 2000
Catwalk image: Photograph by Chris Moore
Backstage pass: Courtesy of Anne Deniau

Eshu, Autumn/Winter 2000
Catwalk image: Photograph by Anthea Simms
Show invitation: Courtesy of Tracy Chapman

Voss, Spring/Summer 2001
Catwalk image: Photograph by Anthea Simms
Modelled by Jade Parfitt
Show invitation: Courtesy of Alexander McQueen

What a Merry Go Round, Autumn/Winter 2001
Catwalk image: Photograph by Chris Moore
Show invitation: Courtesy of Alexander McQueen
Photograph by Ferdinando Scianna

The Dance of the Twisted Bull, Spring/Summer 2002
Catwalk image: Photograph by Chris Moore
Modelled by Laura Morgan
Show invitation: Courtesy of Alexander McQueen
Design by Michael Nash Associates

Supercalifragilisticexpialidocious, Autumn/Winter 2002
Catwalk image: Photograph by Anthea Simms
Modelled by Carmen Kass
Show invitation: Courtesy of Alexander McQueen
Illustration by Tim Burton
Design by Michael Nash Associates

Irere, Spring/Summer 2003
Catwalk image: firstVIEW
Modelled by Lettícia Birkheuer
Show invitation: Courtesy of Alexander McQueen
Photograph by Steven Klein
Design by Michael Nash Associates

Scanners, Autumn/Winter 2003
Catwalk image: Photograph by Chris Moore
Modelled by Eugenia Volodina
Show invitation: Courtesy of Alexander McQueen
Artwork by Michael Nash in collaboration with Spencer Wallace at Nirvana CPH

Deliverance, Spring/Summer 2004
Catwalk image: Photograph by Anthea Simms
Modelled by Erin Wasson
Show invitation: Courtesy of Alexander McQueen
Design by Michael Nash Associates

Pantheon ad Lucem, Autumn/Winter 2004
Catwalk image: Photograph by Anthea Simms
Modelled by Tiiu Kuik
Show invitation: Courtesy of Alexander McQueen

It's Only a Game, Spring/Summer 2005
Catwalk image: Photograph by Chris Moore
Modelled by Ajuma Nasanyana
Show invitation: Courtesy of Alexander McQueen
Design by Michael Nash Associates

The Man Who Knew Too Much, Autumn/Winter 2005
Catwalk image: Photograph by Chris Moore
Modelled by Shannan Click
Show invitation: Courtesy of Alexander McQueen
Design by Michael Nash Associates

Neptune, Spring/Summer 2006
Catwalk image: Photograph by Chris Moore
Modelled by Valentina Zelyaeva
Show invitation: Courtesy of Alexander McQueen
Photograph by Gerhard Klocker
Design by Michael Nash Associates

The Widows of Culloden, Autumn/Winter 2006
Catwalk image: Courtesy of Swarovski Archive
Model: Snejana Onopka
Show invitation: Courtesy of Alexander McQueen
Photograph by Julia Margaret Cameron (Royal Photographic Society)
Design by Michael Nash Associates

Sarabande, Spring/Summer 2007
Catwalk image: Photograph by Chris Moore
Modelled by Elise Crombez
Show invitation: Courtesy of Alexander McQueen
Photograph by Nick Knight
Design by Michael Nash Associates

In Memory of Elizabeth How, Salem 1692, Autumn/Winter 2007
Catwalk image: Photograph by Chris Moore
Modelled by Magdalena Frackowiak
Show invitation: Courtesy of Alexander McQueen
Photograph by Joel-Peter Witkin

La Dame Bleue, Spring/Summer 2008
Catwalk image: Photograph by Chris Moore
Modelled by Raquel Zimmermann
Show invitation: Courtesy of Alexander McQueen
Illustration by Richard Gray

The Girl Who Lived in the Tree, Autumn/Winter 2008
Catwalk image: Photograph by Anthea Simms
Modelled by Alyona Osmanova
Show invitation: Courtesy of Alexander McQueen

Natural Dis-tinction, Un-Natural Selection, Spring/ Summer 2009
Catwalk image: Photograph by Anthea Simms
Modelled by Jourdan Dunn
Show invitation: Courtesy of Alexander McQueen
Artwork and photograph by Gary James McQueen

The Horn of Plenty, Autumn/Winter 2009
Catwalk image: Photograph by Chris Moore
Modelled by Alla Kostromichova
Show invitation: Courtesy of Janet McQueen
Photograph by Hendrik Kerstens

Plato's Atlantis, Spring/Summer 2010
Catwalk image: Photograph by Chris Moore
Modelled by Magdalena Frackowiak
Show invitation: Courtesy of Alexander McQueen
Artwork by Gary James McQueen

Autumn/Winter 2010
Catwalk image: firstVIEW
Modelled by Polina Kasina
Show invitation: Courtesy of Alexander McQueen

Alexander McQueen, 1994
Photograph by Gary Wallis

CHRONOLOGY

1969   Born Lee Alexander McQueen on 17 March in Lewisham, London.

1979–84   Rokeby School for Boys, Stratford, London.

1984–8   Tailor's apprentice on Savile Row, first with Anderson & Sheppard (1984–7), then Gieves & Hawkes (1987–8).

1988–9   Works for theatrical costumier Berman's & Nathan's, Camden, London.

1989–90   Spends three months working as a pattern-cutter for Koji Tatsuno, Mayfair, London.

1990   Spends nine months working as a pattern-cutter for Romeo Gigli in Milan; begins MA in Fashion Design at Central Saint Martins, London.

1992   Completes MA in Fashion Design and presents graduate collection, *Jack the Ripper Stalks his Victims*, during London Fashion Week in March.

1993   Presents first professional catwalk show, *Nihilism* (Spring/Summer 1994), at the Bluebird Garage on the King's Road, Chelsea, London.

1996   Appointed chief designer at Givenchy, Paris; continues to show collections under the McQueen label in London; awarded British Designer of the Year.

1997   Awarded British Designer of the Year; American Express commences sponsorship of catwalk shows with *Untitled* (Spring/Summer 1998); McQueen's work is displayed at the V&A in the exhibition *The Cutting Edge: 50 Years of British Fashion*.

1998   Commences collaboration with Swarovski.

1999   First Alexander McQueen store opens at 47 Conduit Street, Mayfair, London.

2000   The Gucci Group (now Kering) purchases a 51 per cent stake in the Alexander McQueen company.

2001   Awarded British Designer of the Year by the British Fashion Council; McQueen leaves Givenchy; participates in the V&A exhibition *Radical Fashion*.

2002   Opens flagship store on West 14th Street, New York.

2003   Awarded British Designer of the Year; receives the Council of Fashion Designers of America (CFDA) Award for Best International Designer; awarded a Most Excellent Commander of the British Empire (CBE) by Her Majesty the Queen for services to the fashion industry; flagship London store opens on Old Bond Street, Mayfair, London; launches first fragrance, 'Kingdom'.

2004   Launches menswear line; organizes the American Express *Black* show, which commemorates the fifth anniversary of the Centurion credit card and comprises a retrospective of 40 McQueen designs as well as a restaging of iconic catwalk show moments.

2005   Launches second fragrance 'My Queen'; commences collaboration with PUMA, designing for their menswear and womenswear lines.

2006   Launches McQ, a diffusion line that encompasses menswear, womenswear and accessories.

2008   Flagship stores now open in Las Vegas, London, Los Angeles, Milan and New York; awarded GQ Menswear Designer of the Year; launches a make-up line for M•A•C Cosmetics in collaboration with make-up artist Charlotte Tilbury.

2009   *Plato's Atlantis* (Spring/Summer 2010) becomes the first fashion show to be live-streamed on the Internet via fashion website SHOWstudio.

2010   Dies, aged 40, on 11 February 2010 in London. The final collection (Autumn/Winter 2010) comprised 16 designs, all completed by Sarah Burton, McQueen's head of womenswear since 2000 and now creative director. The memorial service is held on 20 September at St Paul's Cathedral, London.

NOTES

In Search of the Sublime
Andrew Bolton
1   *Time Out*, London (24 September – 1 October, 1997).
2   Ibid.
3   *WWD*, 12 February 2010.

Edward Scissorhands
Claire Wilcox
1   http://showstudio.com/project/in_camera/session/alexander_mcqueen; accessed October 2014.
2   BBC documentary *The Works*, series 3, episode 9: Alexander McQueen 'Cutting up Rough', July 1997.
3   As a result, the format of Fashion in Motion was changed from walking models around the galleries of the Museum to runway presentations in the Raphael Gallery, where it still takes place today.
4   Alexander McQueen interview, Fashion in Motion, Victoria and Albert Museum, London, 2000: 'The V&A never fails to intrigue and inspire me'; https://www.youtube.com/watch?v=buPyMyog8Jo and http://www.vam.ac.uk/content/articles/f/fashion-in-motion-alexander-mcqueen/; accessed August 2014.
5   Nick Knight, in conversation with Claire Wilcox, 10 September 2014.
6   Alexander McQueen (cited note 4).
7   Arnie Witton-Wallace, in conversation with Claire Wilcox, 6 October 2014.
8   *Radical Fashion*, Victoria and Albert Museum, 18 October 2001 – 6 January 2002. The exhibition included Azzedine Alaïa, Hussein Chalayan, Comme des Garçons, Jean Paul Gaultier, Helmut Lang, Maison Martin Margiela, Alexander McQueen, Issey Miyake, Junya Watanabe, Vivienne Westwood and Yohji Yamamoto.
9   Katy England, in conversation with Claire Wilcox, 17 July 2014.
10 Ruth Hogben, in conversation with Claire Wilcox, 18 September 2014. All subsequent Hogben quotations are from this conversation.
11 Tracy Chapman, in conversation with Claire Wilcox, 19 September 2014.
12 Alexander McQueen, 'Paris Modes', Paris Première TV channel, January 2004, http://www.youtube.com/watch?v=hOA-osK6aHo.
13 Sarah Burton in conversation with Tim Blanks, in *Alexander McQueen: Savage Beauty*, exh. cat., The Metropolitan Museum of Art (New York, 2011), pp.229–30.
14 'Paris Modes' (cited note 12).
15 Adam Phillips, in conversation with Claire Wilcox, 23 July 2014.
16 'Paris Modes' (cited note 12).
17 Ibid.
18 Georg Simmel, 'Die Mode', *Fashion*, 1911, p.41.

Su[i]ture: Tailoring & the Fashion Metropolis
Christopher Breward
1   Alice Cicolini and Christopher Breward, *21st Century Dandy* (London, 2003).
2   James Sherwood, *The London Cut* (Venice, 2007), p.74.
3   James Sherwood, 'Going for Bespoke', *How To Spend It* magazine, *Financial Times* (July 2002).
4   Alan Hollinghurst, *The Line of Beauty* (London, 2004), p.200.

5   Sherwood (cited note 2), p.73.
6   Judith Watt, *Alexander McQueen: Fashion Visionary* (London, 2012), p.15.
7   Sherwood (cited note 2), p.36.
8   Watt (cited note 6), p.15.
9   Sherwood, 'Going for Bespoke' (cited note 3).
10 Alice Cicolini, *The New English Dandy* (London, 2005).
11 Christopher Breward, *Fashioning London: Clothing and the Modern Metropolis* (Oxford, 2004).
12 Angela McRobbie, *British Fashion Design: Rag Trade or Image Industry?* (London, 1998), p.177.
13 Watt (cited note 6), p.15.
14 Caroline Evans, 'Fashion Stranger than Fiction: Shelley Fox' in C. Breward, B. Conekin and C. Cox (eds), *The Englishness of English Dress* (Oxford, 2002), p.209.
15 Peter Ackroyd, 'London Luminaries and Cockney Visionaries', London Weekend Television Lecture 1993, published by LWT Action & BT in the Community. Delivered at the V&A, London, 7 December 1993 and broadcast by LWT, 19 December 1993. See Evans (cited note 14).
16 Caroline Evans, *Fashion at the Edge: Spectacle, Modernity and Deathliness* (Newhaven CT and London, 2003), p.141.
17 Watt (cited note 6), p.27.
18 Judith Walkowitz, *City of Dreadful Delight: Narratives of Sexual Danger in Late-Victorian London* (London, 1992), p.228.
19 Evans (cited note 16), p.145.
20 Evans (cited note 16), p.142.
21 Ibid.
22 Watt (cited note 6), p.39.
23 Ibid.
24 *AnOther Man*, Autumn/Winter 2006, p.143.

Clan MacQueen
Ghislaine Wood
1   Alexander McQueen, interview as part of BBC2 series *British Style Genius*, October 2008; http://www.bbc.co.uk/britishstylegenius/content/21860.shtml; accessed 2014.
2   *Time Out*, London (24 September – 1 October, 1997).
3   McQueen interview (cited note 1).
4   McQueen owned a copy of Robert Wilkinson Latham's *Scottish Military Uniforms* (Newton Abbot and New York, 1975).
5   Susannah Frankel, *Visionaries* (London, 2001). p.19.

Central Saint Martins
Louise Rytter
1   Central Saint Martins College of Art and Design is part of the University of the Arts London, and was formed in 1989 as a merger of St Martin's School of Art (founded in 1854) and the Central School of Arts & Crafts (founded in 1896). The college was located at 107–109 Charing Cross Road until 2011 when it moved to King's Cross. http://www.arts.ac.uk/csm/about-csm/history/; accessed 1 November 2014.
2   BBC documentary, *The Works*, series 3, episode 9: Alexander McQueen, 'Cutting up Rough', July 1997.
3   *Purple Fashion* magazine, Spring/Summer 2007, issue 7, http://purple.fr/magazine/s-s-2007-issue-7/106; accessed 21 August 2014.
4   http://www.bbcattic.org/britishstylegenius/content/21856.shtml; accessed 7 April 2013. This

is also the source of the quotation by Alexander McQueen with which this feature opens.
5   Bobby Hillson, telephone interview with Louise Rytter, 21 August 2014.
6   Louise Wilson, interview with Susannah Frankel, in *Alexander McQueen: Savage Beauty*, exh. cat., The Metropolitan Museum of Art (New York, 2011), p.15.
7   Fleet Bigwood, interview with Claire Wilcox, Kate Bethune and Louise Rytter, 18 August 2014.
8   Simon Ungless, interview with Louise Rytter, 10 September 2014.
9   Natalie Gibson, interview with Louise Rytter, 21 August 2014.
10 Audio guide transcript, Andrew Bolton, http://blog.metmuseum.org/alexandermcqueen/coat-jack-the-ripper; accessed 21 August 2014.
11 *McQueen and I*, Channel 4 Television Corporation, 2011.
12 BBC documentary, *The Works* (cited note 2).

Drawing a Line
Abraham Thomas
1   Simon Ungless, interview with Louise Rytter, 10 September 2014.
2   Alexander McQueen, interview with Nick Knight for SHOWstudio, http://showstudio.com/project/in_fashion/alexander_mcqueen; acccessed October 2014.

The Early Years
Susannah Frankel
1   Isabella Blow also took credit for McQueen's use of his middle name, calling him 'Alexander the Great'.
2   The Gucci Group is now known as Kering, and is the majority stakeholder in McQueen, the company, today.
3   Press release written by fashion recruitment agents Alice Smith and Cressida Pye, 1993.
4   Simon Ungless, interviewed by Susannah Frankel, October 2014. This applies to all subsequent Ungless quotes, unless otherwise cited.
5   The 'bumster' was first mentioned in the price list for *Taxi Driver* (Autumn/Winter 1993).
6   Janet Fischgrund, interviewed by Susannah Frankel, September 2014. This applies to all subsequent Fischgrund quotes, unless otherwise cited.
7   Katy England, interviewed by Susannah Frankel, September 2014. This applies to all subsequent England quotes, unless otherwise cited.
8   Trino Verkade, interviewed by Susannah Frankel, in *Alexander McQueen: Savage Beauty*, exh. cat., The Metropolitan Museum of Art (New York, 2011).
9   Sebastian Pons, interviewed by Susannah Frankel, August 2014.
10 Sam Gainsbury, interviewed by Susannah Frankel, London, September 2014. This applies to all subsequent Gainsbury quotes, unless otherwise cited.
11 Janet Fischgrund, interviewed by Susannah Frankel, in *Alexander McQueen: Savage Beauty*, exh. cat., The Metropolitan Museum of Art (New York, 2011).
12 Sarah Burton, interviewed by Susannah Frankel, September 2014.

Plato's Atlantis: Anatomy of a Collection
Claire Wilcox

1 Alexander McQueen's sister, Tracy Chapman, said: 'Lee went through all the elements and then said he'd run out of them.' In conversation with Claire Wilcox, 14 October 2014.
2 Alexander McQueen, 'Paris Modes', Paris Première TV channel, January 2004, http://www.youtube.com/watch?v=hOA-osK6aHo.
3 The aquarium was founded in 1903 under the supervision of zoologist and ethnographer Alfred Cort Haddon (1855–1940). Haddon was a correspondent of Phillip Henry Gosse (1810–1888), the Victorian naturalist consulted by Charles Darwin. Gosse set up the first marine aquaria in Britain and also wrote the first descriptive catalogue of British marine invertebrates.
4 'Paris Modes' (cited note 2).
5 Isabella Blow, *Tatler*, February 2004, p.96.
6 'The Girl From Atlantis', *Vogue Nippon*, May 2010, modelled by Alla Kostromichova, photograph by Sølve Sundsbø.
7 The box was first filled with black sand to which glitter was added, but then replaced with yellow sand. An animal handler provided the (non-venomous) snakes and eels. Ruth Hogben in conversation with Claire Wilcox, 18 September 2014.
8 Hogben (cited note 7).
9 Nick Knight, in conversation with Claire Wilcox, 10 September 2014.
10 Sam Gainsbury, in conversation with Claire Wilcox, 11 September 2014.
11 J. Harris, 'Digital Skin: How Developments in Digital Imaging Techniques and Culture are Informing the Design of Futuristic Surface and Fabrication Concepts', *Textile: The Journal of Cloth and Culture*, 11 (3) (Oxford, 2013), pp.242–61.
12 Annabelle Neilson, quoted in Anne Deniau, *Love Looks Not With The Eyes* (New York, 2012), p.337.
13 Annabelle Neilson, in conversation with Claire Wilcox, 11 June 2014.
14 Anne Deniau, email correspondence with Claire Wilcox, October 2014.
15 A further sheet, written in McQueen's hand, lists: 'sharks and aquatics; manta ray (back of jackets); whale noise; killer whales marks; barnacles as embroideries; look at marine fish markings?; whales (blue) moth pleats; bubble (print) (embroidery); storms thunder; sunrise-sunset; rain-wind-waves; pearls stringed; travel from one destination to another; dolphin greys bottle nose'. Source: McQueen Archive.
16 Anne Deniau, in conversation with Claire Wilcox, 6 October 2014.
17 Sarah Burton quoted in Bolton, p.229.
18 *The Atlantis Dialogue, Plato's Original Story of the Lost City and Continent*, trans. Benjamin Jowett, 1892 (Los Angeles, 2001).
19 Sarah Burton (cited note 17).
20 Sarah Burton (cited note 17), p.228.
21 Sarah Burton (cited note 17), p.229.
22 Ibid.
23 Jakob Schlaepfer is a Swiss supplier of innovative fabrics to the fashion trade. The gauze is so fine it is able to remove impurities from water, it is said.
24 With thanks to Malin Troll, senior designer womenswear, Alexander McQueen, 10 June 2014.
25 Averyl Oates, quoted in https://www.youtube.com/watch?v=Ied41Il0YCg; accessed October 2014.
26 Grateful thanks to John Clarke. Also see *The Guardian* (27 July 2011), http://www.theguardian.com/lifeandstyle/2011/jul/26/alexander-mcqueen-pet-dogs.
27 *i-D* Magazine, October 1998.

Givenchy
Edwina Ehrman

1 Grace Bradberry, 'French fashion has designs on Britons', *The Times* (9 October 1995).
2 Hilary Alexander, '"I do like to see aggression", Alexander McQueen has had a new lease of life following his split from Givenchy', *Daily Telegraph* (7 June 2001).
3 Alexander (cited note 2).
4 Avril Groom, 'All Hail the Man who is Putting the Tart into Tartan', *The Scotsman* (8 July 1997).
5 In sixteenth- and seventeenth-century theatre, the area below the stage symbolized hell while the area above it stood for heaven.
6 Susannah Frankel, 'Fashion: Predictable? Moi?', *Independent* (21 July 1999).
7 Christa D'Souza, 'McQueen and Country', *The Guardian* (4 March 2001).
8 Suzy Menkes, 'McQueen Brings Poetry to Britpop Showmanship', *New York Times* (29 September 1998).

Walking Out
Helen Persson

1 The chopine-style shoes for *Eclect Dissect* were made by John Lobb, the London shoemaker founded in 1866 and now part of the Hermès Group with an ultimate bespoke service in Paris.
2 Judith Watt, *Alexander McQueen: Fashion Visionary* (London, 2012), p.187.
3 Sarah Leech, assistant footwear and jewellery designer for Alexander McQueen, interview with Claire Wilcox and Kate Bethune, London, 10 June 2014.
4 The 'Armadillo' never went into production and only 21 samples remain in existence. Andrew Leahy, global communications director Alexander McQueen, email correspondence with Kate Bethune, 13 August 2014.

Refashioning Japan
Anna Jackson

1 The word 'kimono', which means 'the thing worn', was not generally used until the late nineteenth century. The more correct term is 'kosode', which means 'small sleeve', a reference to the opening at the wrist.
2 'Ukiyo', or 'floating world', is the contemporary term used to describe the culture of pleasure and entertainment that developed in urban Japan in the Edo period. Woodblock prints of the subject are known as 'ukiyo-e', 'pictures of the floating world'.

Nature Boy
Jonathan Faiers

1 Gilles Deleuze and Félix Guattari, '1730: Becoming-Intense, Becoming-Animal, Becoming-Imperceptible ...' in *A Thousand Plateaus* (London, 1992), p.238.
2 Deleuze and Guattari (cited note 1), p.245.
3 See Dilys E. Blum, *Shocking! The Art and Fashion of Elsa Schiaparelli* (Philadelphia, 2003) for further discussion of Schiaparelli's use of fur and feathers.
4 An overlapping abbreviation of Bondage and Discipline (BD), Dominance and Submission (DS), and Sadism and Masochism (SM).
5 Deleuze and Guattari (cited note 1), p.239.
6 Deleuze and Guattari (cited note 1), p.305.
7 Alexander McQueen, quoted in Andrew Bolton, Preface, *Alexander McQueen: Savage Beauty*, exh. cat., The Metropolitan Museum of Art (New York, 2011), p.13.

A Gothic Mind
Catherine Spooner

1 Chris Baldick, *The Oxford Book of Gothic Tales* (Oxford, 1992), p.xix.
2 Andrew Bolton, Preface, *Alexander McQueen: Savage Beauty*, exh. cat., The Metropolitan Museum of Art (New York, 2011), p.13.
3 Catherine Spooner, *Fashioning Gothic Bodies* (Manchester, 2004).
4 Catherine Spooner, 'Costuming the Outsider in Tim Burton's Cinema, or, Why a Corset is Like a Codfish', *The Works of Tim Burton: Margins to Mainstream* (New York, 2013).
5 Mark Salisbury, *Burton on Burton* (London, 2006), p.106.
6 Kelly Hurley, *The Gothic Body: Sexuality, Materialism, and Degeneration at the Fin de Siècle* (Cambridge, 1996), p.4.
7 Alexander McQueen, centrefold, *AnOther* magazine, A/W 2002.
8 Julia Kristeva, *Powers of Horror: An Essay on Abjection*, trans. Leon S. Roudiez (New York, 1982), p.4.

Memento Mori
Eleanor Townsend

1 Alexander McQueen, as cited by Tamsin Blanchard, 'Electric Frocks', *Observer* (7 October 2001).
2 A reference to John Webster's play, *The Duchess of Malfi* (1612–13); T.S. Eliot, 'Whispers of Immortality', 1918–19, http://www.poetryfoundation.org/poem/236778; accessed August 2014.
3 Another aspect of McQueen's own anatomy made an appearance in a 2005 collaboration with Puma. Inspired by the muscles and skeletal structure of the foot, McQueen's My Left Foot Bound trainers incorporated an imprint of the designer's foot inside the transparent rubber sole. Other designs featured latticework and rubber tendons mirroring the musculature and sinews of the foot. See Jess Cartner-Morley, 'Boy done good', *The Guardian* (19 September 2005); Samantha Conti, 'McQueen Puts Best Foot Forward', wwd.com, 20 September 2005; accessed 28 October 2014.
4 In 2004, McQueen collaborated with American Express on Black, a one-off event inspired by the black Centurion Card, which saw him show in London for the first time in many years. Conceived as a retrospective of McQueen's collections, it took place at Earl's Court exhibition hall, which had been transformed into a luxurious black chandeliered ballroom for the occasion.

5 Alexander McQueen in *Time Out*, London (24 September – 1 October 1997).

6 Isabella Blow, *Cutting Up Rough*, BBC documentary, 1997.

7 Alexander McQueen in *Time Out* (cited note 5).

8 Caroline Evans, *Fashion at the Edge: Spectacle, Modernity and Deathliness* (New Haven CT and London, 2003), p.223.

9 See for example, *A Thousand Years* (1990), featuring flies feasting on an ox's head and being killed by an Insect-O-Cutor, *Sensation*, exh. cat., Royal Academy (London, 1997), p.94 (ill.); p.213, cat. no. 34.

10 Damien Hirst, cited in 'We're Here for a Good Time, not a Long Time', interview with Alastair Sooke, *Daily Telegraph* (8 January 2011).

11 http://www.damienhirst.com/for-the-love-of-god; accessed August 2014.

12 Alexander McQueen, interviewed by by Nick Knight for SHOWstudio, 2009; http://showstudio.com/project/platos_atlantis/interview; accessed August 2014.

Layers of Meaning
Kirstin Kennedy

1 *The Guardian* (20 April 2004).

2 I am grateful to Lois Oliver for sharing her thoughts with me on the identification of the source paintings. Lois Oliver, 'Tailoring the Image', unpublished paper delivered to Sherborne Decorative and Fine Arts Society, 27 February 2014.

Wasteland / Wonderland
Zoe Whitley

1 Kate Abbott, 'Tracey Emin and Sarah Lucas: How we made The Shop', *The Guardian* (12 August 2013).

2 Abbot (cited note 1).

3 http://www.tate.org.uk/context-comment/video/roselee-goldberg-live-culture-talk-view-here-one-hundred-years-performance-art; accessed 30 August 2014.

4 Jake Chapman, interview with Zoe Whitley, London, 11 September 2014. All subsequent Jake Chapman quotations are from the same interview.

Museum of the Mind
Lisa Skogh

1 McQueen's interest in nature's possibilities (*naturalia*) and fine craftsmanship (*artificialia*) can also be seen in his celebration of his muse Aimee Mullins and his commission of the lavishly carved prosthetic legs for the collection *No.13* (Spring/Summer 1999). See Jefferson Hack's essay in this volume on McQueen's role as guest editor for *Dazed & Confused*, special issue 46, September 1998.

2 Patrick Mauriès' *Cabinets of Curiosities* (London, 2002) is a good visual resource, a tip of the iceberg of vast scholarly literature on the topic. The existence and development of the scholarly field of early modern history of collecting is mainly due to the efforts of Arthur MacGregor and Oliver Impey, with their edited volume *The Origins of the Museum. The Cabinet of Curiosities in Sixteenth- and Seventeenth-Century Europe* (Oxford, 1985 and 2001) and subsequently the *Journal of the History of Collections* (Oxford Journals, 1989–), edited by Arthur MacGregor and Kate Heard.

3 The Habsburg collections referred to here were formed by Holy Roman Emperor Rudolf II (1552–1612) in Prague, and were later in the seventeenth century moved to the Kunsthistorisches Museum, Vienna, where they still reside; the other belonged to Archduke Ferdinand II of Tyrol, and remains in Ambras Castle, near Innsbruck. Other images from Patrick Mauriès' *Cabinets of Curiosities* (2002), used by McQueen on research boards, showed amongst many *Kunstkammer* objects a selection of ivories from the Green Vault, Staatliche Kunstsammlungen, Dresden, which had been turned into complex mathematical shapes.

4 A sculpture goblet in the shape of Daphne, made in gilt silver and a coral branch by Abraham (1555–1600) and Wenzel (1508–1585) Jamnitzer, Nuremberg, c.1580–6, is in the Grünes Gewölbe of the Staatliche Kunstsammlungen, Dresden. See also interview with Philip Treacy, audio guide to The Metropolitan Museum of Art, New York, 2011.

5 Hans-Olof Boström, *Det underbara skåpet: Philipp Hainhofer och Gustav II Adolfs konstskåp* (Uppsala, 2001), amongst others.

6 The two most important so-called *Natternzungen Kredenze*, or serpent-tongue table pieces, are today in the *Kunstkammer* of the Kunsthistorisches Museum and in the Schatzkammer of the Deutscher Orden, both in Vienna.

7 Philip Delves Broughton, 'In the Palace Fit for McQueen', *The Times* (1 November 1997), p.10.

8 Polly Morgan, email interviews with Lisa Skogh: 19 July 2014, 30 July 2014, 3 August 2014, 17 September 2014.

9 Christine Göttler and Wolfgang Neuber (eds), *Spirits Unseen: The Representation of Subtle Bodies in Early Modern European Culture* (Leiden, 2008), p.219. A painting, *The Garden of Eden with the Fall of Man* (c.1615) by Jan Brueghel and Peter Paul Rubens, in the Mauritshuis, The Hague (inv. 253), is here discussed and includes amongst other animals, birds of paradise.

10 The father of McQueen's close collaborator, Simon Ungless, was a gamekeeper. Ungless, who sometimes shot with his father, would often upon his return to London bring with him pheasants and other birds that McQueen would incorporate into his designs. McQueen himself never joined any of the shoots. Instead, McQueen flew hunting falcons and hawks with Isabella Blow at her home – Hilles Castle, in Gloucestershire; see BBC documentary *The Works*, series 3, episode 9: Alexander McQueen 'Cutting up Rough', July 1997.

11 It has also been suggested by Caroline Evans, in *Fashion at the Edge. Spectacle, Modernity and Deathliness* (New Haven CT and London, 2003), pp.151–3, that the antlers express the terror of predators, but historically it is more about the princely hunt and display.

12 Angela Carter, *The Sadeian Woman: An Exercise in Cultural History* (London, 1979), p.26, cited in Evans (see note 11), p.154. Carter discusses McQueen's interest in a 'Museum of Woman-Monsters', in connection with McQueen's show *Elect Dissect* (Spring/Summer 1997). Simon Costin, acting as art director, described the 'story' of the collection, his collages inspired by anatomical sixteenth-century prints by Vesalius and nineteenth-century fashion plates. McQueen's inspiration came from the return of dead women.

13 McQueen's use of bone and antlers is also apparent in jewellery, such as the necklace 'Memento Mori' by Simon Costin (The Metropolitan Museum of Art, New York, inv.no. 2006.354a–c), which was used in his MA collection.

14 Jay Massacret, 'I know it looks extreme to other people. I don't find it extreme' in *Art Review*, vol. 54, September 2003, p.69.

15 Alexander McQueen interview, *Fashion in Motion*, Victoria and Albert Museum, London, 2000: 'The V&A never fails to intrigue and inspire me'; https://www.youtube.com/watch?v=buPyMyog8Jo and http://www.vam.ac.uk/content/articles/f/fashion-in-motion-alexander-mcqueen/; accessed August 2014.

16 For example, McQueen commissioned Robert Bruce Muir's giant male anatomical steel sculpture for the Alexander McQueen flagship store in Los Angeles.

Modelling McQueen: Hard Grace
Caroline Evans

1 Alexander McQueen, quoted in *The Guardian Weekend*, 6 July 1996; cited in *Alexander McQueen: Savage Beauty*, exh. cat., The Metropolitan Museum of Art (New York, 2011), p.53.

2 Alexander McQueen, quoted in *Domus*, December 2003; cited in *Alexander McQueen: Savage Beauty*, exh. cat., The Metropolitan Museum of Art (New York, 2011), p.36.

3 Rebecca Lowthorpe, telephone interview with Caroline Evans, 10 August 2014.

4 Etymologically the Italian word *torso* derives from *tursus*, the Vulgar Latin form of the Latin word *thyrsus*, meaning stalk, or stem. *Chambers Dictionary of Etymology* (Edinburgh, 1988; reprinted 2008).

5 Polina Kasina, interview with Caroline Evans, London, 28 July 2014. All subsequent Kasina quotations are from this interview. A fit model is a model employed in-house by a designer, and who models for him or her throughout every stage of the design process, including trying on the samples when they come back from the factory. Fit models thus have a unique perspective on the design process, and are likely to have tried on many of the looks in each collection. McQueen's fit models also routinely modelled one or two looks in his fashion shows.

6 Claire Wilcox, telephone interview with Caroline Evans, 12 August 2014.

7 Wet-moulding is a method of forming leather into three-dimensional shapes. It requires undyed veg-tan, a type of leather tanned using vegetable products that becomes pliant when wet. Once thoroughly saturated, the leather is soft and stretchy; it can then be formed by pushing and pulling it over a mould and leaving to dry for 24 hours. The mould is then removed, leaving a rigid leather form in the same shape. The thicker the original leather, the more rigid the final form.

8 Kees van der Graaf, email interview with Louise Rytter, 21 July 2014.

9 Laura Morgan, interview with Caroline Evans, London/New York, 25 July 2014. All subsequent Morgan quotations are from this interview.

10 Kees van der Graaf, email interview with Louise Rytter, 23 July 2014.

11 Vac-forming, or vacuum-forming, is a technique that is used to shape a variety of plastics. Like wet-moulding leather, the plastic is formed over a mould, which can be a life cast of a torso. For the clear plastic butterfly bodice, van der Graaf used PET-G because it is both strong and thermo-formable; also known as polyethylene terephthalate, it is used for bottled-water bottles. Forms can also be vac-metallized to produce a shiny metallic finish in gold or silver, as they were for van der Graaf's mirror bodice in *The Overlook* and the gold breastplate on the gold bodysuit in *Salem*.

12 Shaun Leane, V&A filmed interview, 2001.

13 Kees van der Graaf, telephone interview with Caroline Evans, 5 August 2014.

14 Shaun Leane, V&A film interview, 2001.

15 Naomi Filmer, email interview with Caroline Evans, 1 August 2014.

16 Kees van der Graaf, email interview with Louise Rytter, 1 August 2014.

17 Erin O'Connor, interview with Caroline Evans, London, 6 August 2014. All subsequent Erin O'Connor quotations are from the same interview.

18 Bruno Latour, *Reassembling the Social* (Oxford, 2005). See 'Third Source of Uncertainty: objects too have agency', pp.63–86.

19 Latour (cited note 18), p.79.

20 Latour (cited note 18), p.82.

21 Aimee Mullins, quoted on http://blog.metmuseum.org/alexandermcqueen/tag/no-13/; accessed 2 September 2014.

22 Georges Vigarello, *Le Corps redressé: histoire d'un pouvoir pédagogique* (Paris, 1978).

23 Catherine Brickhill, interview with Louise Rytter, Paris, 10 May 2014.

24 Lily Cole in conversation at SHOWstudio. See http://showstudio.com/collection/alexander_mcqueen_paris_womenswear_s_s_2013/alexander_mcqueen; accessed 4 September 2014. Cole described the first show in which she modelled for McQueen, *Deliverance* (Spring/Summer 1994), which was themed on the dance marathons of the American Depression. Fashion models were partnered with professional dancers. Cole wore a diamante dress and was told to act as if she were 'falling apart'.

25 Naomi Campbell, telephone interview with Caroline Evans, 5 September 2014.

26 Richard Sennett, *The Craftsman* (London, 2009), p.8.

27 Martin Heidegger, 'The Question Concerning Technology' [1953], pp.311–41, *Basic Writings: Martin Heidegger*, ed. David Farrell Krell (London and New York, 1993), p.340. Heidegger also makes this point on the first page of his essay: 'Technology is not equivalent to the essence of technology … the essence of technology is by no means anything technological', p.311.

28 Heidegger (cited note 27), p.318. Heidegger examines the etymology of the word which stems from the Greek Technikon meaning that which belongs to technē, 'the name not only for the activities and skills of the craftsman but also for the arts of the mind and the fine arts. Technē belongs to bringing-forth, to poiēsis; it is something poetic'.

29 Sennett (cited note 26), p.11 and, on 'the craft of

experience', pp.288–9. Sennett's arguments follow those of Heidegger who links technē not only to poiēsis but also to epistēmē: 'both words are knowing in the widest sense. They mean to be entirely at home in something, to understand and be expert in it'. Heidegger (cited note 27), pp.318–19.

30 Maurice Merleau-Ponty, *The Phenomenology of Perception*, quoted in Sennett (cited note 26), p.174.

31 Sennett (cited note 26), p.178. Sennett circles around this idea throughout his book, using various terms: 'embodied knowledge', p.44; 'embedded' or 'tacit knowledge', pp.50–1 and 289; and 'the intelligent hand' pp.152, 174 and 238.

32 For an example of this kind of surrender on the runway, see the model Shalom Harlow's description of her abandonment to the moment in McQueen's *No.13* show, in this case in sexual terms, though sex would be only one example of abandonment. http://blog.metmuseum.org/alexandermcqueen/dress-no-13/; accessed 2 September 2014.

33 Sennett (cited note 26), pp.236–8.

Armouring the Body
Clare Phillips

1 *Alexander McQueen: Savage Beauty*, exh. cat., The Metropolitan Museum of Art (New York, 2011), p.201.

2 Tamsin Blanchard, 'Body jewellery: Silver stars', *Independent* (23 May 1998).

Crowning Glory
Oriole Cullen

1 Philip Treacy, interview with Oriole Cullen and Claire Wilcox, London, 30 July 2014.

2 British *Vogue* (November 1992), pp.186–91.

3 Philip Treacy (cited note 1).

4 Ibid.

5 Ibid.

6 A 'block' is a custom-made solid form, usually carved from wood, around which the millinery material is pressed and formed, or 'blocked'. In this instance, the original horns would have been too heavy to use, so material was blocked around them to create the headdress.

7 Philip Treacy (cited note 1).

8 Ibid.

9 Suzy Menkes, 'The Macabre and the Poetic', *New York Times* (5 March 1996).

10 Philip Treacy (cited note 1).

11 Ibid.

12 Ibid.

Show, and Tell
Alexander Fury

1 Colin McDowell, 'Shock treatment-style', *Sunday Times*, 17 March 1996.

2 Colin McDowell (cited note 1).

3 Sam Gainsbury, interview with Alexander Fury, London, 7 August 2014. All subsequent Sam Gainsbury quotations are from the same interview.

4 Lee Alexander McQueen, SHOWstudio, 'Plato's Atlantis', interview with Nick Knight, 2009; http://showstudio.com/project/platos_atlantis/interview, accessed 20 August 2014.

5 Lee Alexander McQueen interview, *The Frank Skinner Show*, Series 2, Episode 4, BBC One, 23 January 1997.

6 Melanie Rickey, 'England's Glory', *Independent*, 28 February 1997.

7 Lee Alexander McQueen, SHOWstudio, 'Plato's Atlantis' (cited note 4).

8 Ben Jonson, *The Complete Masques* (Newhaven CT and London, 1969), p.1.

9 The period was referenced frequently. Specific collections include *Highland Rape* (Autumn/Winter 1995), which was based on the Jacobean Highland clearances, while McQueen's Autumn/Winter 1999 haute couture collection for Givenchy was inspired by the brief reign as Queen of England of Lady Jane Grey and featured clothes elaborately slashed and worked in the Tudor style.

10 David Lindley (ed.), *The Court Masque* (Manchester, 1984), p.1.

11 Patty Huntington, 'On the wings of an eagle: Alexander McQueen's steel, LED and feather epitaph for Isabella Blow', Fully Chic blog, News.com.au, Saturday, 6 October 2007; http://blogs.news.com.au/fullychic/index.php/news/comments/on_the_wings_of_an_eagle_lee_mcqueens_steel_led_and_feather_epitah_for_isab; accessed 20 August 2014.

12 Patty Huntington (cited note 11).

13 *Voss* (Spring/Summer 2001) cost more than £70,000 to stage (Louise Davis, 'Frock Tactics', *Observer*, 18 February 2001).

14 Sarah Burton, interview by Alexander Fury, London, 3 September 2014. All subsequent Sarah Burton quotations are from the same interview.

15 Simon Costin, interview by Alexander Fury, London, 7 August 2014. All subsequent Simon Costin quotations are from the same interview.

16 Michael Howells created the set for the Spring/Summer 2000 Givenchy haute couture show. Michael Howells, interview by Alexander Fury, Devon, 24 October 2014.

17 Shaun Leane, interview with Alexander Fury, London, 28 July 2014.

18 Louise Davis (cited note 13).

19 Joseph Bennett, interview by Alexander Fury, London, 30 October 2014. All subsequent Joseph Bennett quotations are from the same interview.

20 The glass cube of *The Overlook* was intended to represent the malevolent hotel of Stanley Kubrick's *The Shining*. The staging was envisaged right from the start – Sam Gainsbury has a sketch faxed to her by McQueen mapping out the set of that show. (Sam Gainsbury, cited note 3.)

21 SHOWstudio, 'In Camera', live Q&A with Alexander McQueen, 2003; http://showstudio.com/project/in_camera/session/alexander_mcqueen, accessed 20 August 2014.

22 Jess Hallett, interview by Alexander Fury, London, 24 October 2014.

23 Lee Alexander McQueen, SHOWstudio, 'Plato's Atlantis' (cited note 4).

24 Katy England recalled that 'Lee looked to John as well, he was our hero. I remember when he got the job at Givenchy and John invited him for dinner and it was the most exciting thing: "We're going for dinner with John Galliano".' (Katy England, interview by Alexander Fury, London, 3 September 2014; all subsequent Katy England quotations are from the same interview.)

25 SHOWstudio, 'In Camera' (cited note 21).

26 Alexander McQueen Review, Sarah Mower, Style.com, 10 March 2009.
27 Guy Debord, *The Society of the Spectacle* (Detroit MI, 1984), p.23.
28 Christian Dior (trans. Antonia Fraser), *Christian Dior and I* (New York, 1957), pp.52–3.
29 SHOWstudio, 'In Camera' (cited note 21).

Making-up
Janice Miller

1 E. Moore, 'To Hell and Back', *The Sunday Times* (15 March 1998).
2 Alexander McQueen, interviewed by Nick Knight for the *In Fashion* series, SHOWstudio, 2010; http://showstudio.com/project/in_fashion/alexander_mcqueen; accessed 20 July 2014.
3 See Style.com, *Fashion Show – Alexander McQueen: Spring 2007 Ready to Wear*, 2013; https://www.youtube.com/watch?v=TMK_iuuuri0; accessed 2 August 2014.
4 Linda Rodriguez McRobbie, 'The history and psychology of clowns being scary', *Smithsonian Magazine* [online], 31 July 2013; http://www.smithsonianmag.com/arts-culture/the-history-and-psychology-of-clowns-being-scary-20394516/?no-ist; accessed 14 August 2014; see also Andrew McConnell Stott, *The Pantomime Life of Joseph Grimaldi: Laughter, Madness and the Story of Britain's Greatest Comedian* (Edinburgh, 2009).
5 Anon, 'Futuristic Faces', *Vogue* [online], 7 October 2009; http://www.vogue.co.uk/beauty/2009/10/07/peter-philips-alexander-mcqueen-backstage-beauty-paris-fashion-week-ss10; accessed 15 August 2014.
6 Sigmund Freud, 'Screen Memories', *The Standard Edition of the Complete Psychological Worlds of Sigmund Freud*, 3 (London, 1899).
7 Karl Abraham, *Selected Papers on Psychoanalysis* (London, 1988).
8 Anon, 'Alexander McQueen blows all the beauty rules', *Grazia* [online], 11 March 2009; http://www.graziadaily.co.uk/beauty/archive/2009/03/11/alexander-mcqueen-blows-all-the-beauty-rules.htm; accessed 19 July 2014.
9 Eric Wilson, 'McQueen leaves fashion in ruins', *New York Times* [online], 11 March 2009; http://www.nytimes.com/2009/03/12/fashion/12MCQUEEN.html?_r=0; accessed 23 July 2014.
10 Alan Dundes, *The Study of Folklore* (Upper Saddle River NJ, 1965).

Ghosts
Bill Sherman

1 Dick Straker (of video and projection collaborative Mesmer) created the effect for film-maker Baillie Walsh. Moss's performance was inspired in part by the Danse Serpentine developed by Loïe Fuller and filmed by the Lumière Brothers in 1896.
2 Helen Groth, 'Reading Victorian Illusions: Dickens's "Haunted Man" and Dr. Pepper's "Ghost"', *Victorian Studies*, 50:1 (Autumn 2007), pp.43–65. True holography emerged only after 1947, with the advent of laser technology: see Sean F. Johnston, 'A Cultural History of the Hologram', *Leonardo*, 41:3 (2003), pp.223–9.

3 The technology involved is described in X. Theodore Barber's 'Phantasmagorical Wonders: The Magic Lantern Ghost Show in Nineteenth-Century America', *Film History*, 3 (1989), pp.73–86. For the place of 'phantasmagoria' in the Romantic sensibility, see Terry Castle, 'Phantasmagoria: Spectral Technology and the Metaphorics of Modern Reverie', *Critical Inquiry*, 15:1 (Autumn 1988), pp.26–61; and for the phantasmagoric nature of the modern catwalk see Caroline Evans, *Fashion at the Edge: Spectacle, Modernity and Deathliness* (New Haven CT and London, 2003), esp. Chapter 4.
4 Professor Pepper, *The True History of the Ghost* (London, 1890), p.1.
5 See V&A: E.3706–2007.
6 Alexander McQueen, interviewed by by Nick Knight for SHOWstudio, 2009; http://showstudio.com/project/platos_atlantis/interview; accessed August 2014.

Coup de Théâtre
Keith Lodwick

1 David Bowie vs. Alexander McQueen, *Dazed & Confused*, Issue 26, 1995.
2 Michael O'Connor, interview with Keith Lodwick, August 2014.
3 Harold Koda, *Extreme Beauty: The Body Transformed* (New Haven CT, 2004).
4 Ian Buruma, *Tell A Man by his Clothes, Anglomania: Tradition and Transgression in British Fashion* (New Haven CT, 2006).

Dance
Jane Pritchard

1 Oskar Schlemmer's *Triadisches Ballett* (1922) illustrated the Bauhaus view of the body as the new artistic medium, free of the historical baggage of theatre; a form of choreographed geometry, transformed by costume and expressed through stylized movement. Schlemmer's 'figurines' appeared at the V&A in *Modernism* (2006).
2 Eugène Lami designed the muslin dress of the spirit/heroine, an ethereal costume that became the new uniform of the classical dancer. *La Sylphide* was the first of the 'ballets blancs'.
3 Models included Lily Cole in her second show.
4 Robert Lepage, quoted in http://www.theguardian.com/stage/2009/feb/19/eonnagata-theatre-dance-sadlers-wells; accessed August 2014.
5 Judith Mackrell, quoted in http://www.theguardian.com/stage/2009/feb/19/eonnagata-theatre-dance-sadlers-wells; accessed August 2014.
6 Robert Lepage (cited note 4).
7 Russell Maliphant, quoted in http://www.theguardian.com/stage/2009/feb/19/eonnagata-theatre-dance-sadlers-wells; accessed August 2014.
8 Russell Maliphant (cited note 7).
9 Ibid.

The Shining and Chic
Alistair O'Neill

1 David Hayes, 'A Jekyll and Hyde Finale', *Evening Standard* (19 October 1993), p.4.
2 Fleet Bigwood, interview with Alistair O'Neill, 17 July 2014.

3 Lucinda Alford, 'In Pursuit of Excellence', *Observer Life Magazine* (27 February 1994), p.16.
4 *Time Out* (24 September – 1 October 1997).
5 'On one occasion, Lee called members of his studio to his house to work on a collection, but as soon as they arrived he changed his mind and sat them down to watch *The Wizard of Oz*.' Sarah Burton in conversation with Claire Wilcox and Kate Bethune, London, 19 September 2014
6 Laura Mulvey, *Death 24x a Second* (London, 2006), p.181.
7 Louise Davis, 'Frock Tactics', *Observer* Magazine (18 February 2001), p.36.
8 Mimi Spencer, 'The Snow McQueen', *ES [Evening Standard]* Magazine (24 February 1999), p.3.
9 John Gosling, interview with Alistair O'Neill, 2 July 2014.
10 'On Style: an interview with Cinema', *Hitchcock on Hitchcock: selected writings and interviews*, edited by Sidney Gottlieb (California, 1997), p.288.
11 Lyn Barber, 'Emperor of Bare Bottoms', *Observer Life* Magazine (16 December 1996), p.4.
12 'The prints came from *The Birds*. A flock surrounding and engulfing the wearer. Lee and I picked the birds from my birdwatchers' identification book. At the first attempt we picked the wrong type and the print of overweight robins flying around wasn't very sinister. [Designer] Andrew Groves reworked it on a computer using swallows, which were much sharper.' Simon Ungless, interview with Louise Rytter, 10 September 2014.
13 Tania Modleski, *The Women Who Knew Too Much: Hitchcock and Feminist Theory* (London, 2005), p.41.
14 Gary James McQueen, interview with Alistair O'Neill, 5 August 2014.
15 Ludmilla Jordanova, *The Look of the Past: Visual and Material Evidence in Historical Practice* (Cambridge, 2012), p.107.
16 Roland Barthes, 'Leaving the Movie Theatre' in *The Rustle of Language*, trans. Richard Howard (New York, 1986), p.421.
17 Christian Metz, *The Imaginary Signifier: Psychoanalysis and Cinema* (Indiana, 1982), p.76.

Nightmares and Dreams
Susanna Brown

1 Alexander McQueen, interviewed by by Nick Knight for SHOWstudio, 2009; http://showstudio.com/project/platos_atlantis/interview; accessed August 2014.
2 Fashion in Motion: Interview with Alexander McQueen at the V&A, 2000, http://www.youtube.com/watch?v=buPyMyog8Jo; accessed August 2014.
3 BBC documentary *The Works*, series 3, episode 9: Alexander McQueen, 'Cutting up Rough', July 1997.
4 In the past decade, single photographs by Andrea Gursky, Cindy Sherman, Jeff Wall, Edward Steichen, Alfred Steiglitz, Richard Prince, Richard Avedon and Edward Weston have all sold for in excess of one million US dollars at auction.
5 Alexander McQueen (cited note 1).
6 Herbert List, quoted in Magnum Photos photographers' profiles, www.magnumphotos.com
7 Tate website, http://www.tate.org.uk/art/artworks/bellmer-the-doll-t11781.

8 I am grateful to Louise Rytter at the V&A for drawing my attention to this connection. André Durst's surreal photograph was published in American *Vogue*, 15 January 1936, pp.42–3. The *Vogue* caption reads: 'Rope, hurtling out of oblivion, surrealist-fashion; spring-coiling over Schiaparelli's purple satin dress: incredibly straight and clenched with a metal slide. Schiaparelli's friar cape of hunter-green ottoman, corded at neck and throat.'

9 Simon Ungless produced the prints.

10 Terry Jones: 'Creatively, when he did something, it was always beautiful' (*Independent*, 12 February 2010). Another McQueen scarf, made in 2004, used a purple print based on a 1940s photograph of singer Billie Holiday.

11 Andrew Bolton, Metropolitan Museum blog, http://blog.metmuseum.org/alexandermcqueen/about/; accessed August 2014.

12 Diary entry by Michelle Olley on Appearing in VOSS, Wednesday 22 September 2000, http://blog.metmuseum.org/alexandermcqueen/michelle-olley-voss-diary/; accessed August 2014.

13 Alexander McQueen, interview with Marcus Field, *ArtReview* (September 2003), p.70.

14 Alexander McQueen (cited note 13), p.67.

15 Ibid.

16 SHOWstudio, 'In Camera', live Q&A with Alexander McQueen, 2003, http://showstudio.com/project/in_camera/session/alexander_mcqueen.

17 *Financial Times*, 22 April 2011.

18 Tim Blake, senior design consultant at John Jones, interview with Susanna Brown, London, 17 September 2014.

19 Alexander McQueen (cited note 13), p.70.

20 McQueen's personal collection also included photographs by Patty Chang, Nick Knight, Don McCullin and Wolfgang Tillmans, an Andy Warhol diamond dust print of shoes, a painting by Cecily Brown and an edition of Allen Jones's *Table*, comprising a fibreglass dominatrix kneeling on all fours, her flat back supporting a glass table-top.

21 'Men of Vision', *Harper's Bazaar*, September 2008, p.292.

22 Anne Deniau, Claire Wilcox and Susanna Brown, in conversation at the V&A, 2014.

23 Terry Jones (cited note 10).

24 'Men of Vision' (cited note 21), p.292.

25 Ibid.

26 Deniau et al (cited note 22); this relates to all quotations in this paragraph.

27 Lauren Milligan, 'Beginning To End: The Real McQueen', *Vogue* website, 10 September 2013, http://www.vogue.co.uk/news/2013/09/05/alexander-mcqueen-book-photographs-nick-waplington; accessed August 2014.

28 Nick Waplington, interview with Rachel Newsome, *Ponystep*, January 2012.

29 Milligan (cited note 27).

30 Susannah Frankel, 'Alexander McQueen', SHOWstudio, 21 July 2003, http://showstudio.com.

31 Alexander McQueen, 'Paris Modes', Paris Première TV channel, January 2004, http://www.youtube.com/watch?v=hOA-osK6aHo.

32 Nick Knight conveyed his interest in trying to see the world through McQueen's eyes in an interview with Claire Wilcox in London in September 2014. He explained: 'Clothes are full of narrative and full of stories, once you start to see them, the image that they propose. It's like reading books, seeing a film, hearing a song – you see the mind of the person who created that garment. And Lee's was an exciting mind. It proposed visions to me that I didn't previously have. He had a real love of the difficult and the dark. And he was gay and I'm not gay. But I love the idea of finding things that I don't know about because I think that makes life more exciting. He could introduce me to a whole bunch of stuff, and I could do my version of it. So I had to understand what made him tick. I guess the pleasure of working is getting excited about someone else's mind, and seeing life through their eyes.'

33 Alexander McQueen, interviewed by Nick Knight for SHOWstudio, 2009, http://showstudio.com/project/platos_atlantis/interview; accessed August 2014.

34 Alexander McQueen (cited note 33).

35 One of Toni Frissell's images from Weeki Wachee Springs was later used as the cover image for several albums, including *Undercurrent* by Bill Evans and Jim Hall, *Tears in Rain* by This Ascension and *Whispering Sin* by the Beauvilles.

36 Alexander McQueen, quoted in *International Herald Tribune*, 8 October 2009.

Alexander McQueen, 1997
Photograph by Marc Hom

SELECT BIBLIOGRAPHY

Publications on Alexander McQueen

Alexander McQueen: Savage Beauty, exh. cat., The Metropolitan Museum of Art, New York, 2011 (ed. Andrew Bolton)

Deniau, Anne, *Love Looks Not with the Eyes: Thirteen Years with Lee Alexander McQueen* (Harry N. Abrams, New York, 2012)

Fox, Chloe, *Vogue On: Alexander McQueen* (Quadrille Publishing, London, 2012)

Gleason, Katherine, *Alexander McQueen: Evolution* (Race Point Publishing, New York, 2012)

Wallis, Gary, *Archive: McQueen backstage - the early shows* (big smile publishing, London, 2015)

Waplington, Nick, *Alexander McQueen: Working Process* (Damiani, Bologna, 2013)

Watt, Judith, *Alexander McQueen: Fashion Visionary* (Goodman Books, London, 2012)

Books and Journals

Arnold, Janet, *Patterns of Fashion*, vol. 1, 1660–1860 (Pan Macmillan, London, 1972)

Arnold, Rebecca, *Fashion, Desire and Anxiety: Image and Morality in the Twentieth Century* (Rutgers University Press, New Brunswick NJ, 2001)

Attenborough, Sir David and Errol Fuller, *Drawn From Paradise: The Discovery, Art and Natural History of the Birds of Paradise* (Collins, London, 2012)

Audubon, John James, *The Art of Audubon. The Complete Birds and Mammals* (Times Books, New York, 1979)

Breward, Christopher, Edwina Ehrman and Caroline Evans, *The London Look: Fashion from Street to Catwalk* (Yale University Press, London, 2004)

Brown, Susanna (ed.), *Horst: Photographer of Style* (V&A Publishing, London, 2014)

Clark, Judith, *Washed Up*, http://judithclarkcostume.com/wp-content/uploads/2013/01/16ppwashedup.pdf, 2011

Clarke, Sarah, E. Braddock and Jane Harris, *Digital Visions for Fashion + Textiles: Made in Code* (Thames & Hudson, London, 2012)

Corner, Frances, *Why Fashion Matters* (Thames & Hudson, London, 2014)

Darwin, Charles, *On the Origin of Species: 150th Anniversary Edition* (Bridge-Logos Foundation, 2009)

Davies, Kevin, *Philip Treacy* (Phaidon, London, 2013)

De Alcega, J., *Tailor's Pattern Book: 1589*, facsimile with translation by J. Pain, and C. Bainton, introduction by J.L. Nevinson, (Costume & Fashion Press, New York, 1999)

De La Haye, Amy (ed.), *The Cutting Edge: 50 Years of British Fashion, 1947–1997* (V&A Publishing, London, 1997)

Denis, Valentin, *All the Paintings of Jan Van Eyck* (Oldbourne Press, London, 1961)

Dickens, Charles, *Great Expectations from The Complete Works of Charles Dickens, 30 vols* (Cosimo Classics, London & New York, 2009)

Dollimore, Jonathan, *Death, Desire and Loss in Western Culture* (Routledge, New York, 2001)

Dürer, Albrecht, *Complete Engravings, Etchings and Drypoints of Albrecht Dürer* (Dover Publications, New York, 1972)

Escher, M.C. and J.L. Locher, *The Magic of M.C. Escher* (Harry N. Abrams, New York, 2006)

Evans, Caroline, *Fashion At The Edge: Spectacle, Modernity and Deathliness* (Yale University Press, New Haven CT & London, 2003)

Faccioli, Davide, *Joel-Peter Witkin* (Photology, Milan, 2007)

Faiers, Jonathan, *Tartan* (Textiles That Changed the World) (Berg Publishers, Oxford, 2008)

Flügel, J.C., *The Psychology of Clothes* (Hogarth Press, London, 1930)

Frankel, Susannah, *Visionaries: Interviews with Fashion Designers* (V&A Publishing, London, 2001)

Frizot, Michel, *The New History of Photography* (Könemann, Cologne, 1998)

Gallagher, Ann (ed.), *Damien Hirst* (Tate Publishing, London, 2012)

Gillette, Paul J., *The Complete Marquis de Sade* (Holloway House Classics, New York, 2008)

Grimm, Jacob and Wilhelm Grimm, *The Complete Fairy Tales of the Brothers Grimm* (Wordsworth Editions Limited, Ware, Herts), 2009

Haeckel, Ernst, Olaf Breidbach, Richard Hartmann and Irenaeus Eibl-Eibesfeldt, *Art Forms in Nature: The Prints of Ernst Haeckel* (Prestel, Munich, 2008)

Hogarth, William, *The Analysis of Beauty* (Yale University Press, New Haven CT & London, 1997)

Jackson, Anna, *Victoria and Albert Museum: Japanese Textiles* (V&A Publishing, London, 2007)

Knight, Nick, *Nick Knight* (HarperCollins, New York, 2009)

––––– *Flora* (Harry N. Abrams, New York, 2001)

Lange, Susanne, *August Sander: People of the 20th Century* (Schirmer/Mosel, Munich, 2013)

Leopardi, Giacomo, *Dialogue Between Fashion and Death* (Penguin Books, London, 2010)

Marks, Richard and Paul Williamson (eds), *Gothic: Art for England 1400–1547* (V&A Publishing, London, 2003)

Mauriès, Patrick, *Cabinets of Curiosities* (Thames & Hudson, London, 2002)

McCullin, Don, *Don McCullin* (Jonathan Cape, London, 2001)

McDowell, Colin, *The Anatomy of Fashion: Why We Dress the Way We Do* (Phaidon, London, 2013)

Muybridge, Eadweard, *Muybridge's Complete Human and Animal Locomotion, vols I, II, III* (Dover Publications, New York, 1979)

National Geographic Society, *The Complete National Geographic*, DVD edition, 2009

O'Byrne, Robert, *Style City: How London Became a Fashion Capital* (Frances Lincoln, London, 2009)

O'Neill, Alistair, *London: After a Fashion* (Reaktion Books, London, 2007)

O'Neill, Alistair, Caroline Evans, Shonagh Marshall and Alexander Fury, *Isabella Blow: Fashion Galore* (Rizzoli, New York, 2014)

Pacht, Otto, *Early Netherlandish Painting: From Rogier Van Der Weyden to Gerard David* (Harvey Miller Publishers, London, 1997)

Parry, Linda, *William Morris Textiles* (V&A Publishing, London, 2013)

Patterson, Angus, *Fashion and Armour in Renaissance Europe: Proud Looks and Brave Attire* (V&A Publishing, London, 2009)

Phillips, Clare, *Jewels and Jewellery* (V&A Publishing, London, 2008)

Plato, *The Atlantis Dialogue: Plato's Original Story of the Lost City and Continent* (Shepard Publications, Los Angeles, 2001)

Poe, Edgar Allan, *The Complete Tales and Poems* (Fall River Press, New York, 2012)

Ribeiro, Aileen, *Dress and Morality* (Berg Publishers, Oxford, 1986; new edn 2003)

Scott, Sir Walter, *Waverley* (Random House, London, 2014)

Shakespeare, William, *William Shakespeare Complete Works* (Modern Library, New York, 2007)

Sherwood, James B., *Savile Row: The Master Tailors of British Bespoke* (Thames & Hudson, London, 2010)

Spooner, Catherine, *Fashioning Gothic Bodies* (Manchester University Press, Manchester, 2004)

Steele, Valerie, *Gothic: Dark Glamour* (Yale University Press, New Haven CT & London, 2008)

Townsend, Eleanor, *Death and Art. Europe 1200–1530* (V&A Publishing, London, 2009)

Von Sacher-Masoch, Leopold, *Venus in Furs* (NuVision Publications, Sioux Falls SD, 2008)

Waugh, Norah, *The Cut of Men's Clothes: 1600–1900* (Faber and Faber, London, 1994)

Webster, John, *The Duchess of Malfi* (Methuen Drama, London, 2001)

Wilcox, Claire (ed.), *Radical Fashion* (V&A Publishing, London, 2001)

––––– *The Golden Age of Couture* (V&A Publishing, London, 2007)

––––– *Fashion in Detail: 1700–2000* (V&A Publishing, London, 2014)

––––– *The V&A Gallery of Fashion* (V&A Publishing, London, 2014)

Wood, Ghislaine, *Surreal Things: Surrealism and Design* (V&A Publishing, London, 2007)

ACKNOWLEDGEMENTS

This exhibition and book would not have been possible without the invaluable support of a great number of individuals and institutions; the Victoria and Albert Museum is indebted to them all. Swarovski and American Express have generously supported the exhibition and we would like to thank both companies for embracing the project so enthusiastically from an early stage. We would also like to extend grateful thanks to M•A•C Cosmetics and Samsung.

We are extremely grateful to Alexander McQueen, in particular to chief executive officer Jonathan Akeroyd and creative director Sarah Burton for their generous support and unfailing encouragement throughout this project.

Sincere thanks are due to Sam Gainsbury who has shown extraordinary dedication to the project as creative director of the exhibition. For helping to realise the scenography we owe a huge debt of gratitude to consultant producer Anna Whiting, production designer Joseph Bennett, director of scenography Simon Kenny, music director John Gosling, lighting designer Daniel Landin, head treatment and mask designer Guido and graphic designers Anthony Michael and Stephanie Nash. Very special thanks are extended to Katy England, Alexandra Granville, Ruth Hogben, Nick Knight, John Maybury, Baillie Walsh and Desi Santiago.

The Victoria and Albert Museum is especially grateful to the director of The Metropolitan Museum of Art, New York, Thomas P. Campbell, for granting permission to restage *Alexander McQueen: Savage Beauty*. The original 2011 exhibition was curated by Andrew Bolton, with the support of Harold Koda, curator in charge, both of The Costume Institute. We are immensely proud to inherit such an insightful and inspiring show and thank Andrew Bolton for assuming the role of consultant curator for the V&A's manifestation of the exhibition, and for contributing to this book. Further thanks are due to Jennifer Russell, Bethany Matia, Joyce Fung, Amanda Garfinkel and Nina Maruca for ably assisting the V&A in this ambitious project.

Enormous thanks are due to all the institutions and private lenders who have so generously permitted the loan of their objects to the exhibition: the Alexander McQueen Archive, Catherine Brickhill, Ruti Danan, Anne Deniau, Katy England, the Fashion Museum, Bath, Janet Fischgrund, Sam Gainsbury, Givenchy, the Honourable Daphne Guinness, Mira Chai Hyde, Tiina Laakkonen, Shaun Leane, Basya Lowinger, Alister Mackie, The Metropolitan Museum of Art, Annabelle Neilson, Dai Rees, Swarovski, Philip Treacy, Debonnaire von Bismarck and Amie Witton-Wallace. Additional thanks are due to Trino Verkade for lending from her personal collection and helping to facilitate loans from the charitable organization that Alexander McQueen founded, Sarabande.

We extend our sincerest thanks to Alexander McQueen's family: Janet McQueen, Tony McQueen, Michael McQueen, Tracy Chapman and Jacqueline McQueen for sharing their memories, helping us to ensure factual accuracy and lending their precious show invitations for the book.

At Alexander McQueen Andrew Leahy and Hongyi Huang have been instrumental in facilitating the exhibition, and Kevin Allan has provided much welcome advice and support for this book. We have also been greatly assisted by the following: Sidonie Barton, Nicola Borras, Carolina Daher, Judy Halil, Sarah Leech, Karen Mengers, Hanalei Perez-Lopez and Olivier Van de Velde. Rachael J. Vick has kindly helped us navigate our way through the McQueen Archive, assisted by Katie-Anne Reddington. In the design studio, we thank Carolina Antinori, Cristina Astolfi, Klaus Bierbrauer, Lorenzo Brasca, Alessandro Canu, Cristiane Chaves, Loredana Dituccio, Camilla Giotta, Johannes Heim, Andrea Lattuada, Deborah Milner, Chiara Monteleone, Gaetano Perrone, Maria Claudia Pieri, Ambrita Shahani, Francesca Tratto and Malin Troll. Additional thanks are extended to Clare Adams.

We wish to extend particular thanks to American Express and Kering for their support of the Victoria and Albert Museum's Fashion Gala. Special thanks are due to the event's co-chairs Suzy Menkes OBE, François-Henri Pinault, Naomi Campbell and Kate Moss. We are also grateful to Nicholas Coleridge and to Alexandra Shulman.

The authors of the essays in this book have been far more than contributors and we owe a huge debt of gratitude to them for sharing their expertise and insights into Alexander McQueen. Their work provides a lodestone for future research into this most talented of British designers. They are: Kate Bethune, Andrew Bolton, Christopher Breward, Susanna Brown, Oriole Cullen, Edwina Ehrman, Caroline Evans, Jonathan Faiers, Susannah Frankel, Alexander Fury, Jefferson Hack, Anna Jackson, Kirstin Kennedy, Keith Lodwick, Janice Miller, Alistair O'Neill, Helen Persson, Clare Phillips, Jane Pritchard, Louise Rytter, Bill Sherman, Lisa Skogh, Catherine Spooner, Eleanor Townsend, Abraham Thomas, Zoe Whitley and Ghislaine Wood. We also extend special thanks to our readers for their firm commitment to this project: Caroline Evans, Susannah Frankel, Bill Sherman and Sonnet Stanfill.

We are indebted to the many talented photographers who have provided such an array of spectacular images for this book. We are especially grateful to Nick and Charlotte Knight and Anne Deniau. Grateful thanks are also due to all the designers, makers and models who shared their professional insights and their memories of Alexander McQueen: Naomi Campbell, Lily Cole, Simon Costin, Karen Elson, Naomi Filmer, Honor Fraser, Kees van der Graaf, Jess Hallett, Shalom Harlow, Michael Howells, Polina Kasina, Rebecca Lowthorpe, Keir Malem, Laura Morgan, Polly Morgan, Kate Moss, Aimee Mullins, Erin O' Connor, Michael O'Connor, Michelle Olley, Laura de Palmer, Mr Pearl, Sebastian Pons, Stella Tennant, Simon Ungless, Gemma Ward, Patrick Whitaker and Raquel Zimmermann. Thanks in particular to Shaun Leane and Philip Treacy.

The skill and expertise of many colleagues at the V&A have helped to realise this project: director Martin Roth's passion helped to bring *Savage Beauty* to the V&A; deputy director and chief operating officer Tim Reeve has offered support and encouragement, as have deputy director and director of collections Beth McKillop and director of design, exhibitions & FuturePlan Moira Gemmill; the Research Department, led by Bill Sherman, has provided a most collegiate atmosphere, while colleagues Jo Norman, Donatella Barbieri, Edwina Ehrman, Sonia Ashmore, Leanne Wierzba, Katherine Elliott, Linda Sandino and Lucia Savi have been a great support; in the Department of Furniture, Textiles and Fashion, particular thanks are extended to keeper Christopher Wilk and Oriole Cullen; also to Clare Browne, Cassie Davies-Strodder, Jenny Lister, Lesley Miller, Susan North, Suzanne Smith and Stephanie Wood.

Thanks are also due to our many wonderful colleagues across the Museum: Geoffrey Marsh and Victoria Broakes; Donna Stevens; Alan Derbyshire, Victoria Button; John Clarke; Richard Edgcumb; Allan Hill, Jo Dickie; Bronwen Colquhoun; Annabel Judd, Jane Scherbaum, Joanne Glover, Claude D'Avoine; Lucy Trench; Jane Lawson, Jo Ani, Laura Sears, Sophie Hargroves, Sarah Ward; Camilla Graham, Kate Brier, Stuart South, Catherine Sykes, Olivia Robinson, Bethan Garland; Clare Inglis, Kathryn Johnson, Alison Bennett; James Beardsworth, Janette Murphy; Kati Price, Elizabeth Bullock, Peter Kelleher; Jenny Allchorn, Linda McCalister; Alex Stitt, Matt Thomas, Sarah Sevier, Annabelle Dodds, Susan Mouncey, Anni Timms, Amelia Calver; Sarah Armond, Jane Rosier; Olivia Colling, Zoe Franklin, Lily Booth, Lucy Hawes; Emmajane Avery, Jo Banham, Leanne Manfredi, Matty Pye; Sally Williams; Victor Batalha and his team in Visitor Services. With additional thanks to the following interns and volunteers: Liz Tregenza, Leigh Mitnick, Emilia Muller, Vanessa Jones, Antonis Daikos, Sophie Woods, Nadia Saccardi, Sandra Capt, Clementine Fiell, Alice Negrini, Marley Healy, Paula Alaszkiewicz, Ellen McIntyre and Susanna Cordner.

We are grateful for the support of colleagues at the University of the Arts London, in particular Nigel Carrington and Oriana Baddeley. At London College of Fashion special thanks are extended to Frances Corner; also Jane Harris, Charlotte Hodes, Amy de la Haye, Judith Clark, Ligaya Salazar, Naomi Richmond-Swift, Jane Holt, Polona Dolzan, Ben Whyman, Bre Stitt, Carolyn Mair and the Centre for Fashion Curation. At Central Saint Martins, we thank Anne Smith, Fabio Piras, Willie Walters, Debbie Lotmore, Judith Watt, Natalie Gibson, Fleet Bigwood and Hywel Davies. At the Central Saint Martins Museum Study Collection and Library, thanks are due to Judy Willcocks, Anna Buruma and Alexandra Duncan. Special thanks are due to Bobby Hillson.

Countless other individuals have generously given their time, expertise and support: Laure Aillagon, Jane Audas, Ashley Backhouse, Kent Baker, Stefan Bartlett, Paul Bhari, Chris Bird, Björk, Tim Blake, Tim Blanks, Conor Breen, John Bright, Tim Burton, Charlotte Bush, Jonathan Carmichael, Cameron Mackintosh Ltd, Andrew Carter, Fritz Catlin, Dinos and Jake Chapman, Michael Clark, Myriam Cordoux, Peter Costen, Simon Costin, Antonia D'Marco, Caroline Deroch-Pasquier, Primrose Dixon, David Dorrell, Rachel Duncan, Guillemette Duzan, Harry Evans, Robert Fairer, Vanessa Fairer, Richard Flack, Jutta Freedlander, Genevieve Frosch, Pat Frost, Silvia Gaspardo Moro, Daniel Goddard, Isobel Gorst, Alessandra Greco, Lisa Gregg, Sylvie Guillem, Erik Halley, Rosemary Harden, Sarah Harmarnee, James Harvey, Jonathan Howard, Jeremy Hull, Mark Hurcombe, Anika Jamieson-Cook, David Jode, Olga Kenny, James King, Nicole Lepage, Robert Lepage, Tessa Lewis, Hector Macleod, Russell Maliphant, Penny Martin, Don McCullin, Colin McDowell, Niall McInerney, Gary James McQueen, Christine McSweeney, Chris Moore, Sofia Nebiolo, Camilla Nickerson, Mark C. O'Flaherty, Kerry Panaggio, Christine Park, Brian Peters, Kate Petty, Adam Phillips, Justine Picardie, Stephanie Power, Cressida Pye, Emre Ramazanoglu, Jane Randell, Melanie Rickey, Jane Roser, Rosy Runciman, Adam Sammut, Roxanne Shante, Felicity Shaw, Kiko Sih, Donna Simmonds, Anthea Simms, Alice Smith, Doug Smith, Imogen Snell, Lee Starling, Lou Stoppard, Dick Straker, Paul Sumner, Minje Sung, Chloe Sutton, Nadja Swarovski, Plum Sykes, Lee Tassie, Kerry Taylor, Sam Taylor-Johnson, Natalie Tilbury, Birgitta Toyoda, Michelle Wade, Tania Wade, Gary Wallis, Nick Waplington, Mark Ward, Charlotte Wheeler, Raymond Watts, Jim Whelan, Timothy Williams, Mary Wing, Joel-Peter and Barbara Witkin, Nancy Wong and Helly Worsdell.

For the production of this book grateful thanks are due to managing editor Anjali Bulley for her vision and utter commitment to this project. Extended thanks are also due to other colleagues in V&A Publishing: Mark Eastment, Clare Davis, Tom Windross, Liz Edmunds, Vicky Haverson, Kate Phillimore and Zara Anvari. We offer special thanks to Denny Hemming for her meticulous copy editing skills and Charlie Smith for her elegant design, along with Hannah Buswell and Lana Zoppi. In the V&A's Photographic Studio particular thanks go to Richard Davis and Jaron James.

Warm thanks are extended to the V&A's exhibitions department: Linda Lloyd-Jones, Diana McAndrews, Dana Andrews, Alice Lobb, Sadie Hough, Amy Higgitt, Rhian Alexander, Lucien Smith and especially Rebecca Lim, Stephanie Cripps and Rachel Murphy for their professionalism and calm navigation of this project. In Textile Conservation, thanks go to Sandra Smith and Marion Kite, and also to Lara Flecker, Frances Hartog, Sam Gatley, Roisin Morris, Keira Miller, Louise Egan, Sarah Glenn, Chantelle Lau, Lilia Tisdall and Gesa Werner for their inspiring work. In Technical Services thanks go to Robert Lambeth, Stephen Warrington and Phil Sofer.

I extend special and heartfelt thanks to senior research assistant Kate Bethune and research assistant Louise Rytter. Their selfless dedication to this project has made the impossible possible. Thanks also to Sonnet Stanfill for her support, expertise and encouragement.

Finally, I thank Mark Wilcox, Gail Sulkes, Mog Scott-Stewart and, especially, Julian, Rose and Hattie Stair.

Claire Wilcox Senior Curator, Department of Furniture, Textiles and Fashion, Victoria and Albert Museum, and Professor in Fashion Curation, London College of Fashion, University of the Arts London

PICTURE CREDITS

Nick Knight/Trunk Archive: pls 15, 156, 265, 290, 303, 310; p.308 (invitation below), p.318 (invitation above)

Nick Knight/Trunk Archive/Model Agency: VIVA London: pl.72

Sean Knox.com: p.304 (invitation below)

© Érick Labbé: pls 261, 262

David LaChapelle/Contour by Getty Images: pl.123

© Annie Leibovitz/Contact Press Images: pl.57

Library of Congress, Prints and Photographics Division, Toni Frissell Collection, LC-F9-02-4712-072-10: pl.308

© Herbert List/Magnum Photos: pl.302

Courtesy of John Maybury: pl.309

© Don McCullin/Contact Press Images: pl.291

© Craig McDean/Art + Commerce: pl.130

Niall McInerney/ © Bloomsbury Publishing plc: pl.44; p.304 (catwalk image above); p.305 (catwalk image below), p.308 (catwalk image below)

Courtesy of Nuno-Contemporary Antwerp: p.320 (invitation below)

© Donald Mcpherson: pl.119

Artwork by Gary James McQueen: p.320 (invitation above), p.321 (invitation above)

© Steven Meisel/Art + Commerce: pl.95

© 2015 Image copyright The Metropolitan Museum of Art, New York: pls 2, 3, 4, 5, 6, 7, 8

MGM/UA/Kobal: pl.272

Courtesy of Polly Morgan/Photograph by Tessa Angus: pl.166

Darylene A Murawski, National Geographic Creative: pl.117

Design by Michael Nash Associates: p.313 (invitations above and below), p.314 (invitation above), p.315 (invitation above), p.316 (invitations above and below), p.317 (invitations above and below), p.318 (invitation above)

Artwork by Michael Nash in collaboration with Spencer Wallace at Nirvana CPH: p.314 (invitation below)

National Museum of Ancient Art, Lisbon, Portugal/ Bridgeman Images: pl.148

National Museum, Gdansk, Poland/Bridgeman Images: pl.149

Photograph Michael le Poer Trench © Cameron Mackintosh Ltd: pl.255

© National Portrait Gallery, London: pl.23

Courtesy of Annabel Nicolson and LUX, London: pl.279

© Frank W. Ockenfels 3: pl.253

PA Images: pl.132

Palomar/ABC/Kobal: pl.281

Paramount/Kobal: pl.106

Philadelphia Museum of Art, Pennsylvania, USA/Gift of Mme Elsa Schiaparelli, 1969/Bridgeman Images: pl.107

© Pierre et Gilles: Diana, Naomi Campbell, 1997: pl.204

Photograph by Phil Poynter: p.309 (invitation below)

Private Collection/Prismatic Pictures/Bridgeman Images: pl.161

© Marc Quinn/Courtesy White Cube: pl.306

© Arnulf Rainer: pl.28

Photograph by Rankin: p.305 (invitation below)

REX: pl.110

REX: Brendan Beirne: p.305 (catwalk image above)

REX/Mark Large/*Daily Mail*: pl.197

REX/Alex Lentati/*Evening Standard*: pl.244

REX/Neville Marriner/Associated Newspapers: pl.56

REX/Ken Towner/*Evening Standard*: pls 88, 198

REX/Richard Young: pl.38

REX/Sipa Press: pl.223

Photo (c) RMN-Grand Palais (Musée d'Orsay/Michéle Bellot): pl.125

Courtesy Röntgen Museum, Germany: pl.305

Courtesy of Sarabande: pl.42

Ferdinando Scianna/Magnum Photos: p.312 (invitation below)

Photograph and artwork by Nicola Schwartz: pp.306, 307 (invitations below)

Photograph by Nicola Schwartz: p.306 (invitation below)

© Anthea Simms: pls 32, 64, 93, 100, 104, 109, 139, 164, 194, 195, 203, 205, 218, 234, 245, 246, 263, 264, 287, 298; p. 307 (catwalk image below), p.309 (catwalk images above and below), p.310 (catwalk images above and below), p.311 (catwalk image below), p.312 (catwalk image above), p.313 (catwalk image below), p.315 (catwalk image above and below), p.319 (catwalk

image below), p.320 (catwalk image above)

© Anthea Simms/Model Agency: VIVA London: pls 105, 214

With thanks to SK Film Archives, LLC, Warner Bros and University of Arts, London: pls 277, 278, 280

© Kurt Stüber und MP1Z 1999: pl.114

© Sølve Sundsbø/Art + Commerce: pl.9

© Sølve Sundsbø/Art + Commerce/Model Agency: Marilyn Agency: pl.82

Courtesy of Swarovski Archive: p.317 (catwalk image below)

© Sam Taylor-Johnson/Courtesy White Cube: pls 101, 134

Mario Testino/Art Partner: pl.154

Uffizi Gallery, Florence, Italy/Bridgeman Images: pl.91

United Artists/Photofest: pl.283

Courtesy of Universal Studios Licensing LLC: pl.286

Courtesy of Kees van der Graaf: pls 128, 200

Pierre Verdy/AFP/Getty Images: pls 260, 282

Pierre Verdy/AFP/Getty Images/Model Agency: Marilyn Agency: pl.11

Courtesy of Bill Viola and Blain|Southern/Photograph by Edward Woodman: pl.155

Victor Virgile/Gamma-Rapho via Getty Images: pl.98

Image © Victoria and Albert Museum: pp.4, 12, 34, 80, 138, 176, 186, 218, 258, 302; pls 12, 13, 21, 27, 35, 36, 90, 92, 99, 116, 133, 142, 144, 145, 168, 169–192, 207, 213, 228, 249, 258, 294

© Gary Wallis from *Archive: McQueen backstage - the early shows* (Gary Wallis/big smile publishing): pls 30, 31, 58, 59, 193, 266, p.326

© Nick Waplington from the series *Alexander McQueen: Working Process*: pl.307

© Warner Bros: pl.271

WireImage/Getty Images: pls 146, 252

Photograph by Joel-Peter Witkin: p.318 (invitation below)

© World History Archive/Alamy: pl.250

INDEX